INTELLIGENT INFLUENCE IN BASEBALL

Amazing Stories of Influence, Success and Failure

Thankyou for sharing
in my dream . . .

All the Best

Bob Hunt

"Intelligent Influence in Baseball *is a novel concept that goes beyond statistics and anecdotes and has something for everyone, from fans just learning about the game to the most diehard among us.*"

– Mike Lynch: Founder and President of Seamheads.com, he is the author of three books on baseball. He was the finalist (2009) for the prestigious "Larry Ritter Award," and was also nominated for the equally prestigious Seymour Medal.

"*I thoroughly enjoyed Chapter 8 as it brought back so many great memories from being drafted in the first round of the MLB draft to throwing a 15 inning no-hitter in AA baseball to seeing my son Neil get drafted in the first round of the MLB Draft and seeing him surpass 10 years of MLB service time. Thanks for putting a great book together.*"

– Tom Walker: Former Major League pitcher for parts of 6 years. Was a 1st round pick by the Baltimore Orioles in 1969, he is the father of Neil Walker, who was also a 1st round pick by the Pittsburgh Pirates in 2004

"Intelligent Influence in Baseball *illustrates the 'close knit' cohesiveness on the 1971 Pirates. The key was how every man on the roster picked each other up.*"

– Dave Giusti: Former Major League pitcher of fifteen years in Houston, St. Louis, Pittsburgh, Chicago and Oakland. He is a proud member of the 1971 World Series Champions Pittsburgh Pirates.

"*Bob Hurte came into our lives many years ago. I can remember my dad relaying the story of Bob's dad and grandfather's interaction with my dad at a Pirates game. Bob's love of the game and knowledge was appreciated by my dad. His biography of my father is one of the best that we've ever seen. He picked up on all of the details. Over the years a true friendship evolved. My dad looked forward to Bob's calls and letters. We thank Bob for his interest and friendship with our father.*"

– Cathleen Westlake Corr, on behalf of the Westlake Family.

Intelligent

i²

Influence ®

INTELLIGENT INFLUENCE IN BASEBALL

Amazing Stories of Influence, Success and Failure

Dr. Dale G. Caldwell
and Robert V. Hurte Jr.

MENTOR
BOOKS

Mentor Books
is a joint imprint of
Absolutely Amazing eBooks
and AdLab Media Communications, LLC

Library of Congress Cataloging-in-Publication Data

Caldwell, Dr. Dale G.
Hurte Jr, Robert V.
Intelligent Influence In Baseball
p. cm.

1. SPORTS & RECREATION / Baseball / Essays & Writings
2. SPORTS & RECREATION / Baseball / History
3. BIOGRAPHY & AUTOBIOGRAPHY / Sports

ISBN: 978-1-955036-31-3, Trade Paper
Copyright © 2021, Caldwell and Hurte
Electronic compilation/ paperback edition
copyright © 2021 By Absolutely Amazing eBooks

February 2022

For information contact:
Publisher@AbsolutelyAmazingEbooks.com

Dr. Dale G. Caldwell –

This book is dedicated to my daughter Ashley, my parents Gilbert and Grace and my brother Paul.

Robert V. Hurte Jr. –

This book is dedicated to my wife Barbara, my children Matthew (deceased), Tegan and Samuel. My mother Marjorie and father Robert Sr. (deceased) and of course Wally Westlake.

INTELLIGENT
INFLUENCE
IN
BASEBALL

Amazing Stories of Influence,
Success and Failure

Contents

Dale's Acknowledgments

I have been influenced in many positive ways by the wonderful family members, friends, teammates, co-workers and bosses that have enhanced my life over the last 50 years. I also learned a great deal from the people and events that have been negative influences in my life. I feel blessed that the combination of these influences has given me the insight to develop a new way to strategically use influence to achieve personal and professional success.

I am among a fortunate group of individuals who have held some very interesting senior leadership positions in both sports and the public, private and nonprofit/civic sectors. These positions, in combination with my passion for research, have given me unique insight into the patterns of both successful and failed athletes, teams and businesses leaders. *Intelligent Influence: The 4 Steps of Highly Successful Leaders and Organizations* describes, in a fascinating and unique way, the influence-based patterns of success of extraordinary businesses and their leaders. It is based both on my research and my successes and failures as a student, new employee, human resources executive, nonprofit leader, government official, financial planner, real estate executive, management consultant, board member and chief executive officer (CEO). In *Intelligent Influence in Baseball,* Bob Hurte and I use our understanding of influence to provide insight about some of the most fascinating stories in baseball history. We have included some fascinating stories of influence in this publication that we are confident readers will enjoy.

I will never be able to thank everyone who has taught me important life and career lessons over the years. However, it is important that I begin these acknowledgments by thanking my daughter Ashley for her support in the development of this book. Her love, patience and guidance helped to make this book possible. I thank my brother Paul who has been a successful engineer with several of the largest aerospace engineering companies in the world. He helped me develop a passion for all sports. In addition, as his older brother, I forced him to be the first victim of my many attempts to influence. I am grateful to him for putting up with a bothersome older brother and always being there to support me.

I am eternally grateful to my wonderful parents Reverend Gilbert Caldwell (a retired United Methodist Minister) and Grace Dungee Caldwell (a retired School Teacher). I cannot imagine having better parents. They were able to influence my brother Paul and I to believe that, if we worked hard enough, we could accomplish anything that we wanted to in life. This belief has been the foundation of my life and the reason why I truly believe that this book, which describes the amazing power of influence, will help to change some reader's lives.

Bob's Acknowledgments

I feel fortunate and thankful for all the wonderful people that influenced and molded my life. I am very thankful for my wonderful Mom and Dad. I will also be forever grateful to my grandfather for taking me to my first professional baseball game at Connie Mack Stadium in 1965. I consider myself lucky to have some amazing childhood coaches. The influential baseball coaches in my life include Barney Neesen, Jimmy Madison and Jigs Shepard. In the larger scheme of things, where would my love for baseball be without the words and deeds of Roberto Clemente and Jim Bouton? I truly appreciate my friendship with former players Nellie King, Frank Thomas, Wally Westlake and Tom Walker. Each of them became like family and shared great stories about their careers with me.

I am indebted to the following friends for opening the door and giving me the opportunity to write and be published. Thank you Mark Dau, Mark Amour and Jan Finkel. Special thanks to Jan for your patience with a novice writer like me. I learned more about writing from you than I ever did in school.

I was a sickly kid for most of my childhood. The illness started with pneumonia at age one and expanded to having every childhood disease in third grade, missing much of fifth grade and taking five summer school classes to advance to sixth grade. I, therefore, learned to read in unconventional ways. I owe special thanks to "Baseball Digest," "The Sporting News," and Topps baseball cards for teaching me how to read. The New Jersey school system taught me the basics, but I improved my ability to read because of my passion for baseball. Thank you Dad for bringing them home to me!

And if not for Strat-o-matic Inc., I might not have become enamored in the history of Major League Baseball. Because of this board game, I learned about Hank Aaron, Roberto Clemente, Willie Mays and Sandy Koufax. I played several games against myself and kept detailed players' statistics and team standings. Once again, the New Jersey school system provided the basics for mathematics. The board game gave mathematics a purpose.

When I was five years old, the first team I played for was Barney's Toy Center. We played on a field that Barney constructed in his backyard which paid homage to his beloved Ebbetts Field. It had a large, working scoreboard in centerfield, with ads for toys from his store painted on its fence. There were dugouts, an announcer's booth, with loud speakers to play the National Anthem, and announce the players.

I owe so much to Lee Stadele, who was one of the biggest influences in my life for so many reasons. Our conversations started my love of literature, history and politics. I developed my love for baseball because of him. In 1971, I ended up making my middle school baseball team, we went undefeated and won our conference championship. That summer my Babe Ruth team also won its championship. I was only the third-best pitcher on the team. But I pitched and won the championship game and we won 5-2, and I got a hit and scored a run.

I went on to play four years of high school baseball, some senior league and several years of men's softball. But, it was not until I was got married and in my mid-thirties that my interest in baseball and writing came together. In January 1993, my wife surprised me one Christmas by sending me to Pirates Dream Week Camp. Not only was I able to play baseball for a week in Florida, I met and got to know some of my favorite players. It was because of this week that I began a twenty-four-year correspondence with Frank Thomas. My first published bio for SABR was about Frank.

I read a quote about SABR from Ted Williams. He called the Society of American Baseball Research the best kept secret. Fortunately, I discovered that secret twenty years ago, and have been a member ever since! I received this note from Bob Broeg, a member of the writer's wing of the Hall of Fame in Cooperstown, N.Y.

12 – 11 – 98

Dear Bob,
Welcome to SABR and thanks
for the compliments, always appreciated.
I honestly don't know how
to help you. I've never used an agent.
My only suggestion, if you have the
spare time that doesn't neglect your
job or your family, is to write and
submit. For instance, to Baseball
Digest and other magazines.
I hope our paths cross come time
and that you do well. Very best.

SINCERELY
BOB BROEG

P.S. A good book publisher,
If you're that far along,
Is Sagamore Press, Champagne, Ill.

Foreword

Bruce Markusen

Baseball is a game played by teams, but it is the individual players, managers and coaches who eventually become the focal point of our attention. While we as fans each have a favorite team – leading some to callously say that we are rooting for laundry and logos – it is the players who provide the human quality with which we can truly identify. If we didn't know about the players, their strengths and weaknesses and their personality traits and quirks, we would likely lose interest rather quickly in watching the games. When all is said and done, it is the players, and our knowledge of them, that truly drive our interest in the sport.

The players whom we like have an impact on our lives. For better or worse, they become our heroes and our role models. If they have done their jobs well, and more importantly, led their lives well, we want to become like them. Of course, most of us don't have the talent to play the game as well as they do, but their words and actions in everyday life became a template that we tend to follow. I often find myself quoting players and managers, not just when watching or playing sports, but in trying to overcome challenges in the workplace and at home. Whether we are conscious of it or not, these players become influences – usually positive ones – on the way that we think and speak.

As rabid fans of the game, we also learn that the players themselves have been influenced by others, usually beginning with their childhood years. For some, it is their fathers and mothers, while for others it is an outside force, like a coach or even a political figure. For many, it is a combination of all of these influences, helping to shape the attitudes that each player takes into his adult life – and into his career as a professional ball player.

Growing up in the early 1970s, my favorite player was unquestionably Roberto Clemente. He died when I was only seven, so my firsthand memories of him are somewhat faint, but his death didn't stop me from trying to learn as much about him as I could fathom. I chose Clemente in part because of my own Puerto Rican heritage. My mother, Grace, was Puerto Rican, having been born in Santurce as Ana Graciela Rodriguez. By coincidence, Santurce was the first professional team with which Clemente played, prior to his signing with the Brooklyn Dodgers in the mid-1950s. On the one hand, I never lived in Puerto Rico and only visited there once as a young child. I looked nothing like Clemente – he was black, I am white – and I certainly didn't have any of his talent as a ball player. But we still shared something in common, that connection to the American territory of Puerto Rico, along with the ability to speak Spanish, and that was more than enough to spark my interest.

Of course, it helped that Clemente was one of the best ball players on the planet. He was a dynamic athlete who ran distinctively with his arms flailing side to side, made extraordinary throws from right field that no other player could match and never seemed to age in terms of his facial appearance or his physique. It certainly helped that Clemente almost singlehandedly carried his Pittsburgh Pirates to a world championship in 1971, putting on a one-man show of hitting, throwing, and base running that finally gained him the nationwide attention that had eluded him for much of his career. When you see a ball player perform in such a way, in a fashion that seems almost superhuman, it tends to garner the attention of even a six- or seven-year-old mind.

Other than his status as a phenomenal player, and our shared heritage of Puerto Rico, I knew little else of Clemente at the time that he was killed in that New Year's Eve 1972 plane crash. That knowledge would come much later, when I read biographies of him, studied his file in the Hall of Fame Library, and eventually wrote my own book about the player known as "The Great One." As I read and wrote about Clemente, I learned about his influences. I learned about his hard-working parents, Luisa and Melchor, who set in place the remarkable work ethic that marked Clemente's career. I learned about Roberto Marin, the Puerto Rican businessman who discovered Clemente playing softball and recruited him to his youth baseball team. Then there was Phil Dorsey, the local postal worker who helped Clemente acclimate to life in Pittsburgh, a culture and environment so different from that of his native Puerto Rico. And there was also Luis Munoz Marin, a political leader who would greatly spur Roberto's own interest in becoming an activist and advocate for the poor and underprivileged, children stricken with fatal illnesses and those suffering at the hands of natural disasters.

All of these influences shaped Clemente into the hero and humanitarian that he became. It is these influences that Bob Hurte and Dale Caldwell will explore in the pages of this book. Some of the influences involve superstars like Clemente, including the likes of Jackie Robinson, Mickey Mantle, and Derek Jeter. But there are also stories of lesser known journeymen, players like Wally Westlake, Jim Gosger, and Nellie King, whose influences were just as pivotal, if far less publicized. And there are also examinations of teams that proved influential – after all, baseball is a team sport – such as the racially integrated Pirates of 1971 and the "Miracle Mets" of 1969, teams that overcame enormous odds to defy the skeptics and naysayers.

There are so many of these stories to be explored in the pages ahead. It is a book about baseball, yes, but it is much more. It is a book about how the players came to be, who helped them along the way and the influence that they would come to have on the fans who have so passionately followed them.

Clearly, there is much to be learned here. Read on, and enjoy.

Bruce Markusen is the Manager of Digital and Outreach and serves as a museum teacher at the National Baseball Hall of Fame. Bruce is also the author of 7 baseball books, including the award-winning A Baseball Dynasty: Charlie Finley's Swinging A's. He is the recipient of the Seymour Medal from the Society of Baseball Research (SABR).

Section I
Introduction to Intelligent Influence

Chapter 1

Influence in Sports

Like many sports fans, I have spent my entire life attempting to figure out the secret of athletic achievement. I have always wondered why teams like UCLA basketball and the Green Bay Packers football team dominated their sports in the 1960s. I wondered why the New York Yankees remained so dominant in baseball for so many years. I wondered why Muhammad Ali was such a great fighter; and why Rod Laver and Roger Federer were successful tennis players; why Wayne Gretzky was an amazing hockey player; and, why Michael Jordan, Lebron James and Kareem Abdul-Jabbar were extraordinary basketball players.

In addition, I attempted to identify the common best practices that have enabled companies like Coca-Cola®, Disney®, Johnson & Johnson® and Nike® to achieve extraordinary success. Many books have attempted to be the first to uncover the secrets of the success of legendary athletes, businesses and their leaders. Some of the best non-fiction writers in history have developed excellent theories about athletic achievement, business management and corporate profitability. However, no one has identified one common trait to successful people and organizations in sports, business and life.

I have read many of the best sports and business books ever written. In reviewing these well-crafted publications, I was surprised to discover that none of these books provided an extensive analysis of the foundation of sustainable success in sports, business and life. They overlooked the powerful role of "influence" in human and organizational accomplishment. Some writers ignored the connection between influence and success. Other authors mention influence in passing without providing a well-thought-out strategy for maximizing influence. I wrote my first book on influence: *Intelligent Influence: The 4 Steps of Highly Successful Leaders and Organizations* to fill this void in business strategy. In that book, I outlined a unique four-step framework on influence in business. In this book, Robert Hurte and I share fascinating stories related to the connection between influence and baseball legends.

There are some amazing books about sports and baseball in particular. However, *Intelligent Influence in Baseball* is the first book to identify the role of influence in every one of these captivating stories. We are beginning the book by explaining the *Intelligent Influence* framework so that readers can connect, in a very personal way, with the baseball stories shared in this book. The framework presented in the pages that follow provides a road map on the strategic use of influence that promises to transform the way that readers look at both baseball stories, their careers and their own lives.

My fascination with the subject of sports, business and life success was inspired by one of my first classes at Princeton University. I remember sitting in the large lecture hall on the very first day of Economics 101 thinking how exciting it was that someone like me (who had grown up in poor urban communities in Boston and New York) had a chance to attend one of the best universities in the world. However, my excitement quickly turned to boredom when I discovered that the focus of this class was on the theory of economics, not the application of this discipline in the real world. I remember wishing that I could find a business course (i.e. Business Success 101) that would teach me the foundation of success in business (especially the sports business). Unfortunately, no course of this type existed at Princeton or any other university. I grew to appreciate the value of theoretical thinking and went on to major in economics. However, I always dreamed of developing a course that covered the secrets of success in life, business and sports in an entertaining and practical way.

In many ways, my research on influence for my book *Intelligent Influence* has been the course that I dreamed about. It took me 30 years (and executive positions in management consulting, finance, education, government, real estate and sports) to develop and write. I have had the wonderful opportunity to present the *Intelligent Influence* framework to thousands of people over the last few years. I continue to be amazed by the way that this concept has changed the manner in which many people in my audiences approach their business and life. Prior to the publication of this book, the Intelligent Influence™ framework has been successfully adopted by corporate entities including Viacom®, Marriott® International and Kelloggs®. In addition, the sports world has also embraced it, including the U.S. Tennis Association, Under Armor® and the American Tennis Association.

Bob and I wrote this book to build on these presentations and transform the way in which readers view baseball and other sports. Our hope is that readers will develop a deeper interest in understanding the influences that guided athletes, politicians and business leaders on their path to success or failure. We also want readers to use the stories in this book to give them ideas on ways that they can intelligently utilize influence to achieve their personal and professional goals.

Since this publication is presenting a radically different view of extraordinary accomplishments in sports, it is intended to be an interesting introduction to a very unique four-step process. I present a new language around the elusive concept of influence. Readers will find themselves thinking very differently about human interaction and accomplishments in baseball, other sports and life.

Hidden in Plain Sight
"Influence is the primary reason why all people *do what they do, think the way they think and accomplish what they accomplish*."

Amazingly, the word "influence" is "hidden in plain sight" in the language of today's complex world. The word is used by millions of business people on a daily basis without a comprehensive understanding of the vitally important role influence plays in their success or failure and the success or failure of their organization, their government and their favorite sports star or team. Virtually everyone uses the word. However, few people understand that influence is the primary reason why all people *do what they do, think the way they think and accomplish what they accomplish.*

Tragically, most people have no idea how to intentionally use influence to increase their personal success in relationships, at work or in life. The strategic use of influence is the foundation of individual and organizational success in any field at any time. Corporations seeking to exceed productivity and profitability goals must develop business strategies focused on maximizing their influence in the marketplace. Sports teams that want to win championships must develop influence-based strategies to win. Every athlete that wants to become the most valuable player must consciously bring the right influences into their training at the right time to be the best they can be.

Just as the success or failure of a product is proportionate to the influence it has on consumers, the success or failure of a sports team or individual competitor is based on the influence the coach or leader has on the athletes. The effectiveness of individuals at every level of a sports organization is directly related to the amount of influence they have on their teammates. The positive or negative influence of teammates can be the difference between success and failure. The use of influence in strategic ways is always the difference between winning a championship and having a horrible season.

Intelligent Influence

The influence of factors like the integration of sports and the focus on intensive training has made the world of sports more diverse and complex than ever before. Leaders and coaches are challenged with developing new approaches to creating extraordinary athletes and successful sports teams in the diverse and highly competitive world of sports. Things have changed quite a bit in every major sport in the world. However, many of the influence-based challenges that athletes face are the same. In this book, Bob and I share some amazing baseball stories. What makes our telling of these stories different is the connection we make between the influences in baseball fans, players, managers and owners' lives and their success or failure in the sport.

Successful sports administrators, coaches, athletes and trainers recognize that commanding people to do things limits their effectiveness, creativity and engagement with the athletes and staff. They utilize a leadership style based on the strategic use of influence that motivates others to achieve peak performance. The discovery of this common foundation of effective leadership in business and sports inspired me to develop a new approach to individual and organizational success that I call *"Intelligent Influence."*

This trademarked revolutionary new formula for human interaction provides a framework that explains how any individual or organization can enhance their effectiveness and success by managing how they are both influencing others and being influenced. I define *Intelligent Influence* as *"a learned competency that, without exertion of force or direct exercise of command, produces an effect that leads to extraordinary results driven by effective human interaction."* In short, in the context of competitive sports, *Intelligent Influence* provides a proven step-by-step approach to increasing an athlete's capabilities or a team's victories.

"A Good Coach Can Change a Game; A Great Coach Can Change a Life"
– John Wooden, Former UCLA Basketball Coach

Armed with knowledge about how people have been influenced and how they intelligently influence others, leaders, coaches, captains and teammates can approach problems and challenging situations more effectively. Insight into how these individuals have been influenced and how they influence others enables them to maximize their effectiveness as leaders within the world of sports. The *Intelligent Influence* process helps both athletes and individuals in business value the influence-based differences of their peers, subordinates and supervisors in a way that increases their engagement and effectiveness within the team or organization where they spend most of their time.

This unique approach to influence applies equally well to individual athletes and sports teams. Regardless of how they are formed, why they come together and for how long, all effective teams need to learn how to manage their internal influences and maximize their external influences to achieve their competitive goals. All successful teams understand how to manage their internal influences in a way that will enable them to have the external influence they need to win on a regular basis. The *Intelligent Influence process* provides a unique influence-based strategic approach that will increase the success of teams of any size in any sport.

Chapter 2

Influence Awareness

My introduction to the power of influence came more than 30 years ago in South Africa when, during Apartheid (a rule of law that prohibited citizens of different races from living in the same neighborhoods or attending the same schools), I stayed in the home of the former white South African Ambassador to Bolivia. I was the only African American on the trip. However, because I was an American I received a special approval from the government to stay in the homes of several white South Africans.

When I arrived at the Ambassador's house in the early evening I was dressed in jeans and a t-shirt because I wanted to be comfortable on the long trip from Zimbabwe. That night I had a chance to interact extensively with the Ambassador, his wife and their 7-year-old daughter. I had a lot of fun playing board games with the engaging young lady. I wore a suit the next morning because I had a business meeting in Johannesburg. At the breakfast table, their beautiful daughter looked me up and down, turned to her parents and surprised us all by saying *"You know, black Americans aren't any different than white South Africans!"*

In an instant, I saw the role of influence in the country's public policy. For decades, young white South Africans were influenced to think that blacks were inferior. Black residents of the country were not allowed to hold national leadership positions of any type (except in black-only areas). As a result, young whites were influenced to believe that black Africans were incapable of doing what whites could do. They were influenced to view most black people as intellectually inferior individuals who could clean an office but never manage it. This influence led to inhuman racial discrimination and the murder of thousands of black South Africans who had the audacity to believe that they deserved the same rights as white residents.

This insightful young girl taught me the power of positive influence. I discovered that the right kind of influence at the right time can change the views of one person, and potentially, the world. However, it took me more than 25 years of experience as a competitive athlete; senior executive in the public, private and civic/nonprofit sectors; and, extensive research on leadership to realize that influence is the foundation of athletic, business and individual success. Like most people in leadership roles, I was so fascinated with the concept of exceptional leadership that I overlooked the incredible power of influence. The primary reason that I wrote *Intelligent Influence: The 4 Steps of Highly Successful Leaders and Organizations*, was to show, through the proven success of executives and companies, that influence is the foundation of successful leadership. The four-step framework that I introduce in the book teaches readers how to develop the empathy they need to become extraordinary leaders in the 21st century.

Malcolm Gladwell

Prior to Jackie Robinson's entry into Major League Baseball, the owners, managers and teams were all comprised of people of the same race, gender and birth country. In that scenario, the old-fashioned "command and control" model works because when people have largely similar backgrounds, you can motivate them all in the same way. As the demographics of sports teams changed to include people of differing ethnic and racial backgrounds, the same motivational style did not work as well. This required a shift to use influence management. In today's sports world, teams are more likely than ever to have players, coaches and owners from multiple generations, different races and birth countries. The modern international, multi-generational and multi-racial sports world requires leaders and athletes to have the ability to understand the needs, wants, desires and struggles of people who are very different than they are. They need to develop the powerful skill of empathy. This unique insight and sensitivity that comes from the skill of empathy will enable owners, coaches and players to motivate every athlete on the team in a customized way that will establish them as extraordinary leaders.

Owners, coaches and athletes who cannot (or will not) empathize with the needs of the athletes on their team will fail because they will not be able to influence others to do what is necessary for team success. The foundation of successful leadership in sports today is the ability of leaders to empathize with a diverse group of athletes by understanding the varying influences in their lives.

Lead with empathy; develop sensitivity to the influences on people different from you.

This is easier said than done because, in many ways, developing the skill of empathy is like learning to read. You will never be able to learn to read if you don't practice on very basic books and progress to more complicated books gradually. Likewise, you will never learn to empathize and lead others effectively if you do not gradually develop deeper and deeper sensitivity to the unique influences in the lives of people that are very different than you are. It is important to note that learning to empathize with others requires both practice and self-reflection. You cannot develop the ability to empathize with others if you are not skilled at understanding the influences in society and in your life.

Most people are not aware that it is virtually impossible to effectively understand the influences in other people's lives if they do not understand key influences in their own life. For example, many young people ignore the fact that their political views are based on the positive or negative influences of their parents. For the most part, their peers do not care much about politics. They identify with conservatives, moderates or liberals primarily because they either adopted or rebelled against their parents' political beliefs. It's important to note that we are born with no influences. We enter the world as a blank slate, or "tabula rasa" as they say in Latin. However, far too often these same people mistakenly assume that their political preference is based purely on a critical analysis of party platforms. Consequently, these individuals have great difficulty understanding why someone would join a different political party. If they had taken time to understand (and accept) the power of influence on their personality and political preferences they would be better able to empathize with the perspective of a person who was likely influenced by circumstances beyond his or her control to join a different party.

The concept of *Influence Awareness*™ (the first step of the *Intelligent Influence* framework) is an essential component of individual and organizational leadership in both the sports and business world because it provides a framework through which anyone can develop the very difficult skill and learned competency of empathy. I have discovered that before some people can effectively explore influences in their personal life they need to be convinced of the impact of influence in society. The best way to convince people of this is to explore the writings of an author who has provided valuable insight on the important role influence plays in the world.

No recent writer has done more to help the world understand the power of influence than Malcolm Gladwell. His "New York Times" number one best-selling books *The Tipping Point*, *Blink* and *Outliers* transformed the way that people viewed influence in their lives. These books have changed parenting, coaching and everyday living for millions of people around the world. I developed and trademarked the *Intelligent Influence* process before I read his excellent books. However, after reading his books I realized that *Intelligent Influence: The 4 Steps of Highly Successful Leaders and Organizations* provides the framework for implementing much of what readers have learned from Gladwell's extraordinary insights.

The latest edition of *The Tipping Point* begins with a section called "Acclaim for Malcolm Gladwell's *The Tipping Point*." The very first quote in this section comes from the well-respected writer Deidre Donahue of "USA Today." She is quoted as saying "...One of the most interesting aspects of Gladwell's book is the way it reaffirms that human beings are profoundly social beings influenced by and influencing other human beings, no matter how much technology we introduce into our lives."

This extremely insightful statement is the reason why the concept of *Intelligent Influence* has the potential, over time, to reach a "tipping point" that will change the way that people around the world run their sports teams, businesses and live their lives. Influence is not only the foundation of athletic and business success, it is the primary reason that we all *do what we do, think the way we think and accomplish what we accomplish*. The strategic management of influence in our lives is the foundation of both happiness and the attainment of personal, organizational and team goals.

Influence Awareness

I have learned (through my research of hundreds of businesses, sports teams and individuals combined with my many years of management consulting experience) that every organization and individual that has achieved extraordinary success has consciously or unconsciously utilized each of the four *Intelligent Influence* framework competencies. These steps/competencies *Influence Awareness, Influence Impact, Influence Management* and *Influence Maximization* are the secrets to success in any endeavor requiring human interaction. In my book, *Intelligent Influence: The 4 Steps of Highly Successful Leaders and Organizations* I used case studies to demonstrate how the *Intelligent Influence Framework* is the secret to individual and organizational success. In this book, Bob Hurte and I use stories about baseball legends to inspire readers to reflect on the role of influence in the story and in their own lives. If readers take the time to think about each of these steps they will see that the central person in every story either succeeded because they used the four steps or failed because they did not use these steps effectively.

Each of the subsequent chapters in this book support the guiding premise that the baseball coaches, athletes and owners that understand how to implement each of these steps will be extraordinarily successful. Those who don't fail miserably. These enlightened individuals have a better sense of their strengths and weaknesses and those of the team they lead or play on. They have specific strategies for improving themselves and their teammates even in the most challenging economic times. They inspire other athletes in a way that influences them to get the most out of their skills and abilities.

This framework is initiated through exercises designed to create *Influence Awareness* in individuals, organizations and teams. This first foundational step of the *Intelligent Influence* process refers to the conscious effort by an individual, organization or team to understand how they have been influenced. I define *Influence Awareness* for an individual as *"the process of understanding the most significant ways in which you have been influenced in the past and how you are currently influenced."* Likewise, *Influence Awareness* for an organization or team is *"the process of understanding the most significant ways in which an organization/team has been influenced in the past and how the organization is currently influenced."*

Knowing the past is in many ways the secret of creating an extraordinary future. It is essential that individuals, sports teams and organizations take an inventory of both the ways that they have been influenced and the manner in which they influence others. Every executive and athlete has been influenced by family members, classmates, co-workers, teammates, previous experiences, bosses, coaches training manuals, what they have read and popular entertainment to *do what they do and think they way they think.*

Every company, organization and team has been influenced by their history, culture, other corporations or teams, customers, fans, governing bodies and the financial markets to operate their business or organization in a certain way. By assessing how their prior influences impact what they do and how they think, individuals and organizations can identify the areas of improvement that they need to achieve their objectives.

The myth of the self-made man or woman is just that – *a "myth."* We are all products of the influences in our lives. No one in history has become successful without significant help from one or more influential people. Whether we choose to admit it or not, each of us has been influenced in many different ways by many different people on many different subjects. It is essential that we come to terms with those influences and understand the way they impact how and what we do today.

Most of us can identify more than one teacher, coach who was a positive influence in our lives when we were in school. We remember the English teacher who inspired us to read (or write), the math teacher that made algebra fun or the coach that taught us self-discipline. We remember the history teacher that made the past come alive, the science teacher that created interesting educational experiments or the baseball manager that convinced us that games are won or lost based on the quality of practices.

Many of us occasionally think about the adults who taught us right from wrong and influenced us to follow the career path we are on today. We recall the boss or coach who inspired us to succeed and the co-workers or teammates that made our role fun. We reminisce about the amazing team that we worked with on a successful project/championship season and the fantastic promotion and raise that we got because we had a boss that recognized our value to the organization.

Each of these individuals influenced us to be the people we are today. However, surprisingly, most of us spend little time reflecting on the extensive influence that they had on our lives. These people did not know it at the time; however, each of them utilized some of the concepts of *Intelligent Influence* in one way or another to motivate and inspire us to succeed.

It is important to note that everyone has also had some very bad influencers in their life. These negative people (or experiences) also played a role in influencing how we live our life today. It is therefore equally important (even though it is sometimes painful) to reflect on the role of negative influences in our personal development.

What influences have shaped who you are today? What influences have contributed to making your organization or favorite team what it is today? The process of putting the *Intelligent Influence Framework* into action requires, first and foremost, a comprehensive *"awareness"* of influences, past and present – in your career, in your business and in the market overall.

We do what we do, think the way we think and like what we like largely because of significant influences in our lives. The same is true for organizations and sports teams. They achieve what they achieve, sell what they sell and operate the way they operate, in a large part due to both internal and external influences. It is important to note that *Influence Awareness* is a skill that can be enhanced by developing the important habit of regularly reflecting on the people and situations that have had the greatest influence on your life and the life of the organization you lead. We will discuss the three other Intelligent Influence steps later. We begin with the Influence Awareness step because it is the foundation that enables people to strategically use influence to accomplish their goals in life, at work or on a sports team.

Chapter 3

The Intelligent Influence Framework

I first developed a passion for studying leadership at a very young age. When I was a child, all of my heroes were famous athletes and celebrities who were leaders in their respective endeavors. I was mesmerized by iconic individuals like Arthur Ashe; Jackie Robinson, Lew Alcindor (who became Kareem Abdul Jabbar); Cassius Clay (who became Muhammad Ali); Thomas Edison; Henry Ford; Mahatma Gandhi; John F. Kennedy; Dr. Martin Luther King, Jr.; John D. Rockefeller; Franklin D. Roosevelt and others who used very different styles to lead very diverse groups of people toward extremely difficult goals. I was fascinated by their success. However, at that time in my life, I could not understand why some people holding leadership positions succeeded and others failed.

I learned a great deal more about leadership later in life because I had the honor of serving as the President and/or Chief Executive Officer (CEO) of 9 organizations (3 for-profit, 3 government and 3 not-for-profit). These positions convinced me that leadership is one of the most important and least understood subjects in the world. Leadership plays a vitally important role in every aspect of human society and life. Sports, health, education, the environment, religion, science, business, government, nonprofits, families and basic human interaction are all directly affected by leadership in one way or another.

Effective leaders can improve the quality of life for every human being on earth while ineffective or unethical leaders can create global chaos. Since the right leader can inspire followers to win a championship, cure disease, eradicate poverty, sustain the environment, increase employment, eliminate illiteracy, reduce crime and bring about global peace, it is essential, for the good of humanity, to understand the foundation of successful leadership.

"Leaders develop an intimate connection with a wide variety of people"

Several years ago, I began the process of learning as much as I could about leadership. I read many books and papers on the subject, observed leaders at all levels of society and immersed myself in the research of a great variety of organizations dedicated to the study of leadership or the training of leaders. My goal was to figure out what makes a leader successful. To my surprise, this analysis taught me much more about success in life than I ever imagined it could. In my research, I uncovered some amazing secrets about leadership and successful human interaction. I learned that effective leadership was not about command and control. I discovered that extraordinary leaders humble themselves more often than they show off their strength. Most importantly, I found that leaders had the unique ability to develop an intimate connection with an amazingly wide variety of people.

I have always been fascinated by word definitions. In my review of the definitions of common leadership terms, I was surprised to discover that one word connected many of the traditional definitions of leadership. Merriam-Webster's Dictionary defines a *"Leader"* as *"a person who has commanding authority or influence."* *"Authority"* is defined as *"power to influence or command thought, opinion or behavior."* *"Command"* is defined as *"exercising a dominating influence over."* Since a *leader's authority* and ability to *command* is driven by *influence* it is logical to conclude that the relative success of a leader is determined by the extent of their influence over others. In other words *"Leadership is driven by influence."*

Merriam-Webster's Dictionary defines the word *"Influence"* as *"The act or power of producing an effect without apparent exertion of force or direct exercise of command."* This definition forced me to examine whether influence was more than just the foundation of leadership. I was challenged to consider whether influence was the foundation of life. I, therefore, spent a great deal of time studying the role of influence both on the world and in my life.

In doing this research, I learned how important influence was to the lives of every person on earth. Influence "produced" many of the most important "effects" both in everyday activities and major human events. *We all do what we do, think the way we think and accomplish what we accomplish because of influence.* Our favorite foods, sports teams and recreational activities are guided by the unique influences in our lives. Our political views, the people we find attractive, our language and accent are all dictated by the influences in our lives. I was surprised to learn that the success or failure of sports teams, athletes, corporations and business leaders was also rooted in influence.

There is an amazing amount of research on leadership. However, I was extremely surprised to discover that, in spite of the incredible power of influence on every aspect of human life, there was little substantive targeted research on the specific role of influence on daily life and major historical events. I decided that I would become one of the first people to focus my research on "influence as the foundation of leadership" instead of "leadership as the foundation of influence" as others had done.

Influence in Sports

One of my favorite influence quotes is from Friedrich Nietzsche. This 19th century philosopher said, "*The future influences the present just as much as the past.*" Modern technology provides the historical data necessary for today's coaches to develop comprehensive plans for the future of the team they lead. As described by Nietzsche more than 200 years ago, these future plans not only have a direct influence on the current success of the team, they also impact how athletes need to leverage past athletic and personal influences for future success.

The strategic use of influence is the foundation of individual and team success. The productivity of members of a team is directly correlated with the influence they have on their peers, subordinates and supervisors.

Teams seeking to improve their record must develop game plans focused on maximizing their influence on their competition during the game, match or championship. I was amazed to discover that all successful teams and athletes intuitively utilize the four *Intelligent Influence* steps to achieve extraordinary success. They do not think about each of the four steps. They naturally followed each of these steps on their way to victory after victory.

The strategic use of influence as explained using the *Intelligent Influence* process provides the guidance coaches, teams and athletes need to enhance both the quality of their play and the success of their team in today's highly competitive sports world. This unique approach to team leadership transforms the way in which coaches and managers approach success and teams develop game plans.

One of the most fascinating things about this new framework is how it explains the reasons why legendary athletes succeed in their respective sports. In my book *Intelligent Influence,* I explored some of the most fascinating stories of business success in the context of the *Intelligent Influence* framework. In this book, Bob and I use the framework to explain why legends of baseball did what they did to make history.

The *Intelligent Influence* framework is identified by the following trademarked symbol:

Intelligent Influence Framework

If applied correctly in the world of sports, the strategic use of influence will not only help individual athletes succeed in competition, it will enable any team of any size in any sport to maximize its success. The foundation of this new approach to business and sports success is the *Intelligent Influence Framework*™ shown below:

Intelligent Influence Framework™

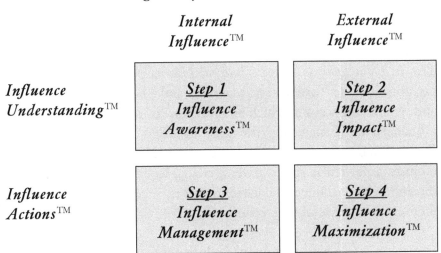

	Internal Influence™	*External Influence*™
Influence Understanding™	**Step 1** *Influence Awareness*™	**Step 2** *Influence Impact*™
Influence Actions™	**Step 3** *Influence Management*™	**Step 4** *Influence Maximization*™

Each of the four boxes depicts a step in the *Intelligent Influence* process that we consider to be an "*Influence Competence*™." These steps (or competences) are based on a learned capacity rooted in *Intelligent Influence* that, in combination, results in outstanding performance in any endeavor that requires significant human interaction. These four steps are the secret of success of extraordinary individuals and organizations. This comprehensive approach to organizational improvement in the world of sports is based on enhancing the internal and external influences of both athletes and teams in a way that will help them maximize their effectiveness in competition.

Intelligent Influence is more important than Intelligence Quotient (IQ) or Emotional Intelligence (EI) in determining performance in individuals because success or failure in sports and life is determined largely by the type of influence one has on the people they interact with on a regular basis. This framework is also the foundation of an organization and team success. If utilized effectively, *Intelligent*

Influence will help individuals and organizations identify important developmental needs that will enable them to make the adjustments necessary to increase their probability of success in any endeavor involving human interaction.

Internal Influence™

The steps in the *Intelligent Influence Framework* can be divided into two categories related to the internal or external impact of influence. The first category is called *"Internal Influence™."* The steps in this category include *"Influence Awareness™"* and *"Influence Management™"* and refer to the ways in which an individual or organization has been influenced or is managing the ways in which they are influenced. Extraordinary athletes are usually aware of the influences that drove them to a particular sport (parent, coach, legend, etc.) and seek out the influences (trainers, coaches, mentors, etc.) necessary to make them more successful than others.

External Influence™

The second category is called *"External Influence™."* The steps in this category include *"Influence Impact™"* and *"Influence Maximization™"* and refer to an individual or organization becoming aware of their current influence on others or the ways in which they can maximize the influence they have on others. This type of influence is focused on the external branding of a person, organization or product. It represents the way in which an athlete influences others or the manner in which a team influences athletes or the coaching staff. The most successful athletes and teams understand their strengths and weaknesses. They build on their strengths and compensate for their weaknesses in a way that enables them to have more influence on their competitors than their competitors have on them. This basic influence equation is the foundation of victory.

Influence Understanding™

The steps or competencies in the *Intelligent Influence Framework* can also be divided into two categories related to the development of an understanding of influence or taking action on influence. The first of these categories is called *"Influence Understanding*™*."* The steps in this category include *"Influence Awareness*™*"* and *"Influence Impact*™*"* and refer to the effort of individuals and organizations to understand how they have been influenced or how they influence others. It is essential for every athlete and team to assess the ways in which they have been influenced in their sport and the manner in which they are currently influencing each other and their competitors.

Influence Actions™

The second of these categories is called *"Influence Actions*™*."* The steps and competencies in this category include *"Influence Management*™*"* and *"Influence Maximization*™*"* and refer to actions taken by individuals or organizations to manage how they are influenced to achieve a particular goal or how they maximize their influence on others. Successful athletes and teams recognize their weaknesses and improve (or compensate for) these weaknesses by injecting the influences they need to achieve their specific performance goals.

These influences help them have the type of impact on their opponents that leads to victory. For example, a baseball team that loses the World Series primarily because of weak relief pitching will spend the off season trying to sign the quality relief pitchers they need to adequately strengthen their bullpen. These pitchers need both a good arm and the ability to be a positive influence in the locker room. If the team has managed their influences correctly, these pitchers will have the ability and chemistry to help the team maximize their influence on their opponents in a way that will enable them to win the World Series the next year.

The Secret of Success
or Failure in Baseball

Throughout *Intelligent Influence in Baseball,* we examine the extraordinary achievements of legendary baseball players and teams in the context of *Intelligent Influence.* Amazingly, the success or failure of these athletes and teams is directly related to the ways in which they adhered to this framework. We begin each chapter with a paragraph explaining the general relationship of the story to influence. Our hope is that readers will have fun thinking about the relationship between the story and each of the four *Intelligent Influence* steps. The readers that do this will begin to find that they will be able to use the *Intelligent Influence* competency in a way that will help them in their daily life. Whether you choose to do this or not we are convinced that you will enjoy reading the fascinating baseball stories on the pages that follow.

Section II
A Parent's Baseball Influence

Chapter 4

A Unique Father Son Relationship

*F*ar too often we celebrate the extraordinary accomplishments of great athletes without thinking about the people who influenced them to be great. Whether you are a baseball fan or not, you probably know that Willie Mays was one of the best baseball players in history. Very few baseball players can claim to be the best on both offense and defense. Willie was one of those rare baseball players who was the best in the league at the plate and in the outfield. However, even though he was born to a family of gifted athletes, he might not have turned out to be a legendary player if he had not benefitted from the positive influence of Leo Durocher. This chapter describes how their wonderful father-son type relationship helped him become the legend that we know today.*

In today's fast-paced, high-tech, multi-tasking world where every second counts, it is easy to wonder why a traditional sport that takes several hours to complete remains so popular. If the sport of baseball was introduced to the public for the first time this year, it might not survive.

Those who recognize the power of influence understand that baseball's popularity is rooted largely in the influence of a parent taking their children to their first baseball game. When I give presentations on *Intelligent Influence*, I like to make the statement "I know what the best music in the world is!"

When they hear this many people in the audience think to themselves or say to the person next to them, "How does he know what the best music in the world is?" I answer their question by saying that "The best music in the world is the music that you heard between the ages of 10 and 20." This does not mean that you don't like other music but the music that you heard during this point in your life connected with you because it was an emotional time when you were developing as a person and experienced your first love, kiss, heartbreak, deep sadness or wonderful success.

Baseball is popular today because, like music, the love for the sport is rooted in the positive memories that many fans have about their parents (or some other adult role model) taking them to a baseball game during a very formative time in their life. Bob Hurte was influenced to fall in love with baseball because of the influence of his father. In this chapter, he shares the story of various baseball influences by fathers.

The National League's 1951 regular baseball season culminated with an iconic third game of a three-game playoff between the Brooklyn Dodgers and New York Giants.

The deciding moment was arguably captured by one of the most famous home run calls in baseball history.

> **"Bobby Thomson up there swinging ... Brooklyn leads 4-2 ... Branca throws ... There's a long drive ... It's gonna be ... I believe ... THE GIANTS WIN THE PENNANT! (four times) BOBBY THOMSON HAS HIT INTO THE LOWER DECK OF THE LEFT FIELD STANDS AND THEY'RE GOING CRAZY!"**
> **– Russ Hodges, October 3, 1951**

Thomson's homer is considered one of the most dramatic in baseball history. It is commonly known as, "The Shot Heard Around the World." Unfortunately, that moment seemed to over-shadow a teenager from Alabama's outstanding season. The teenager was Willie Mays who went on to win the Rookie of the Year award. Genetically, he was destined to play the game of baseball. His father was William Howard Mays Sr., a legendary semi-pro baseball player who starred in the Tennessee Coal and Iron League. His grandfather was considered an outstanding pitcher in the area. Willie's mother, Anna Sattlewhite was equally athletic. She was a high school track star who also played basketball, leading her school's basketball team to three consecutive championships.

Willie was said to sleep with a baseball in his crib as an infant. There is also a popular family story about his father putting a baseball on top of a chair causing Willie to wobble toward it.[1] It is no wonder that Willie was attracted to the game of baseball.

Willie Mays played for the legendary Birmingham Black Barons of the Negro League as a sixteen-year-old. He was discovered by a New York Giants' scout who went to a Baron's game to watch the team's first baseman Alonzo Perry, but instead became enamored with their young centerfielder.[2] Eventually, the New York Giants would sign Willie Mays for $4,000. They started him at the "B" class level in Trenton, New Jersey. Mays played there for only the 1950 season.[3] His impressive statistics moved him up to "AAA" in Minneapolis for the 1951 season.

During the spring of 1951, the Giants set up an exhibition game between Ottawa and Minneapolis in Sanford, Florida, to showcase Mays. Giants' manager Leo Durocher was so impressed that he claimed to remember everything Willie did in that game. Willie hit two line drive singles, a 370-foot homer, made two great catches and threw someone out at the plate. The Giants' manager wanted him in New York immediately, but upper management felt that he was not ready.[4]

Willie tore up the American Association League with the Minneapolis Millers, the New York Giants' top minor league team.[5] Durocher finally got his wish on May 25, 1951; the Giants called him

---

1   James S. Hirsh, *Willie Mays: The Life, The Legend* (NY, NY: Scribner, 2010) 13

2   Ibid., Hirsch, 59

3   Willie Mays batted .353 with 20 doubles, 8 triples, and 4 homers in 306 at bats at Trenton

4   Ibid., 72

5   Willie Mays hit 18 doubles, 3 triples, 8 home runs while batting .477 in 35 games while playing at Minneapolis,.

up to New York and Willie began his Major League career against the Phillies in Philadelphia. The young center fielder left Philadelphia hitless in twelve at bats after three games.

Durocher sat in his office figuratively contemplating suicide after the game. A couple of his coaches interrupted him and recommended that he talk to his young centerfielder. Leo found Willie crying. Willie turned to his manager and told him that he could not hit up here and he should go back to Minneapolis.

Undeterred, Leo Durocher informed Mays that he was here to play centerfield for the New York Giants. Leo then told Willie that he was the best centerfielder he ever saw, and as long as he was the Giants' manager, Willie would play centerfield. With that, Leo told the youngster to get a good night's sleep and tomorrow was another day. [6] He was not only a major influence in Willie's life. He was his advocate, someone who got him to believe in himself. From that moment their relationship evolved into something bigger than simply a manager/player relationship; they became more like a father and a son.

Durocher's talk must have worked because the next game Mays broke out of his slump by hitting his first major league homer off of Warren Spahn on the third pitch he saw. The ball went clear over the lights in left field. This proved to be a turning point, because Mays took the Giants on his back, and carried them for the rest of the season. Willie won the "Rookie of the Year" award in 1951.[7] Leo Durocher bragged, "… He's got more talent in five minutes than the rest of us will have in a lifetime."

Leo never cared about the color of one's skin, as long as the player helped his teams win baseball games. When Leo was the manager of the New York Giants, he brought up the first four black players: Monte Irvin, Hank Thompson, Ray Noble and Willie Mays, because he felt they would help him win.

---

6   Ibid, 103
7   Mays batted .274, 22 doubles, 5 triples, and 20 homers for his Rookie of the Year honors.

Giants' announcer Russ Hodges said, "Mays was the only player I ever saw who could do no wrong in Durocher's eyes."[8]

Willie Mays would say this, "All the things that Leo says bout me make me feel like I want to go out there and do all those things he says I can do."[9]

Some people felt that Leo coddled Mays. Maybe, but the Giants' manage wanted to influence Willie in the most positive ways he could. Durocher even refrained from using four letter words when he was around Willie. Leo also made sure to pair Mays up with an older teammate, Monte Irvin, when he came to New York City. Monte Irvin was responsible for watching Willie, to keep an eye on the young outfielder – who he talked to and more importantly, who tried to talk to him. Durocher purposely placed Irvin and Mays' lockers next to each other in the clubhouse. If people considered Leo to be Willie's father, then Monte was his surrogate brother.

Leo also hired a boxing promoter named Frank Forbes, to watch Willie.[10] Forbes found Willie a suitable place to live. Thanks to Forbes, Mays lived with a black couple named David and Ann Goosby. Ever committed to Mays as a person as well as an athlete, Leo called Willie on the telephone almost every night while he lived with them. Their relationship became more than the normal player/ manager pairing. Leo gave Willie tips on everything from buying clothes to playing pool, to dealing with the press and negotiating with the owner. Durocher also advised him on dating. Ann Goosby was surprised by their closeness. She felt that Willie did not make a move before first hearing Durocher's word on it.

Willie Mays was very close to Durocher's family, as well. He became very partial to Chris, the adopted son of Larraine Day (Durocher). When Chris traveled with the team, he stayed with Willie. At first, Willie felt that he was babysitting Chris, but actually, Chris was babysitting Willie. Because of his relationship with Durocher's

---

8   Ibid, 105
9   Ibid, 105
10   Ibid, 114

son, Willie was limited to where he could go. Even so Mays did not abuse the nightlife; the strongest thing he drank was cherry coke. Chris and Willie enjoyed spending time together – whether reading comic books, watching cartoons or going to the movies together. Because of his skin color, even Willie could not eat at certain places. As a result, Chris Durocher became used to a steady diet of Southern cooking. When Leo found this out, he told Willie he wanted his son to eat steak. Willie replied that he needed "steak money." Durocher pulled out a bunch of twenties and handed them to him. It turned out that Chris actually enjoyed soul food, so Willie kept the extra money. Years later, Chris Durocher would say that he considered Willie like a brother.[11]

For that period in time, the relationship between a middle-aged Caucasian like Durocher and a young African American man like Mays was amazing. In Willie's own words, "Durocher was like a father to me. I don't think I could have made it without him."[12]

Willie Mays enjoyed a twenty-two-year career in the majors and in 1979 he was inducted into the Hall of Fame. When Mays retired, he had the third most career homers behind Babe Ruth and Hank Aaron. One can only wonder what would have happened if Leo Durocher was not Willie Mays' first major league manager.

---

11   Ibid., 237
12   Ibid., 281

Chapter 5

"A Baseball Prodigy"

Tragically, many people believe in the myth of the self-made man. They believe that there are extraordinary people who are successful because of their own efforts. These super human individuals "pull themselves up by their own bootstraps" and become successful simply because of their hard work. Research has proven that no one has ever done it alone. Someone at some point influenced and helped someone on their path to success. Mickey Mantle was one of the most iconic figures in baseball history. Many believe that he was a superior baseball player who succeed because simply of his talent and hard work. Bob Hurte provides interesting insight into the influences that helped Mickey Mantle become one of the most successful baseball players in history.

Back during the nineteen-sixties when I was playing youth baseball in central New Jersey, my teammates would constantly fight over who got the number seven uniform. It was a number that normally went to the best player or the biggest boy on the team. It was the number of Yankee legend Mickey Mantle; a name that was synonymous with baseball during my youth. The "Mick" was the gold standard and we all wanted to wear number seven, just like him

The definition of a "prodigy" is a young person endowed with exceptional qualities and abilities. Mickey Mantle was a baseball prodigy.

Mickey Charles Mantle was born on October 20, 1931, in Spavinaw, Oklahoma. Elvin "Mutt" Mantle might have been a little too early to ordain this baby boy as a baseball prodigy, but he was

33

determined that his son would become a professional baseball player. Mutt Mantle was a former semi-pro baseball player himself. He was also a baseball fanatic. Before his first child was born, he already decided that if it were a boy, its name would be Mickey. Mickey Cochrane was his favorite player. Cochrane's actual first name was Gordon; years later, Mickey joked how he was glad that his father did not know Cochrane's legal name.[13]

Parents were unable to learn the sex of their child before birth in nineteen thirty-one. Still, Mutt ordered a baseball cap for his child before he was born. He also placed a baseball in his crib. Family members said Mutt and his father would prop him up in a corner so that they could roll balls across the mattress to him. Mutt even went as far as to have a cobbler fasten spikes on his shoes like cleats.

When Mickey was three years old, it was in the Great Depression. Mutt Mantle became unemployed until finding work with the Eagle-Pitcher mining company. Although Mutt worked many long, hard hours, he always found time to throw batting practice to his son.

Neighbors heard the constant, rhythmic banging against the ramshackle shed each afternoon, from the Mantles' backyard during Mickey's batting lessons.[14] Mutt pitched right handed and Charles, his father, threw from the left. This made Mutt a visionary, because he taught his son to switch hit before it became popular. In 1938, the year Mickey began switch hitting, there were only eleven switch-hitters on MLB rosters. Mickey was the first great hitter to swing from either side of the plate. He no doubt influenced "switching hitting's" popularity. When Mickey retired in 1971, there were 41 switch-hitters in the major leagues, including Pete Rose, Maury Wills, Wes Parker, Reggie Smith and Roy White. Arguably, each player's career was greatly improved by hitting from either side of the plate.

Mickey was not as confident batting from the left side as he was batting from the right. If given a choice, he would rather bat

---

13 Jane Leavy, *The Last Boy: Mickey Mantle and the End of America's Childhood* (NY, NY, Harper Collins, 2010) 50

14 Ibid., Leavy, 57-58

right-handed. One day, when his father was at work, Mickey thought he could get away with batting right-handed against a right-handed pitcher. Unfortunately, Mutt was able to get out of work early to attend his son's game. When Mutt saw that Mickey was not batting from the left side against a righty, he went ballistic. Mickey's cousin Max remembered it well, relating, "Boy, the crap hit the fan over that. That was a no-no; Mickey quickly learned to never do that again!"[15]

Although Mutt Mantle drove his son like a nail, still Mickey admired his father. He realized that his father made sacrifices for him, such as spending twenty-two dollars of his thirty-five dollar weekly paycheck to buy a Marty Marion model baseball mitt for him. Mickey hated disappointing his dad. When he was younger, Mickey would wait for his dad to come home from the mines. Then they would walk back together talking baseball. Mickey remembers this with fondness, "That's all he (his father) lived for, was to see me make the major leagues."[16] Mickey remembers listening to a radio announcer talk about his dad after he died. The first thing that the announcer mentioned was how his father taught him to switch hit, and how he raised his son to be a professional baseball player. His father was his biggest fan. Mutt Mantle always showed patience. When Mickey was fifteen, they played on the same team. Mickey looked back fondly at those times.

Right Place, Right Time...

Tom Greenwade, a scout for the Yankees, was instrumental in starting Mickey's journey into the major leagues, and it all started accidentally the day he saw him play in Coffeyville, Kansas. Greenwade was there to scout a third baseman by the name of Billy Johnson. Johnson was a good player but never made it to the major leagues. That evening in Coffeyville, Mickey went 3 for 4 with two home runs, one from each side of the plate. The veteran scout admitted that he was unaware that Mantle was a switch hitter. After the game's last out,

15 Ibid.,58
16 Ibid., 147

the veteran scout quickly walked over to Mickey and Mutt Mantle, taking them to the back of the grandstands where, in Greenwade's car, they signed a contract to play baseball.[17] Finally, Mutt Mantle's hard work and influence paid off.

In 1949, Mickey made his professional debut at the age of 17 for the Independence Yankees of the Kansas-Oklahoma-Missouri Class D League. He responded by batting a more than respectable. The following year Mickey moved up to class C to play with the Joplin Miners of the Western Association.[18] *The Sporting News* called him the "Jewel From Mine Country." Following that season, Mickey was invited to Yankees spring training in 1951. Although the Yankees did not expect him to make the team, he was too impressive not to. Longtime clubhouse man Pete Sheehy gave Mantle number 6, placing him among the star Yankee lineage of Babe Ruth (#3), Lou Gehrig (#4) and Joe DiMaggio (#5).

Halfway through the 1951 season Mantle found himself in a slump. When the Yankees acquired pitcher Art Schallock from the Brooklyn Dodgers on July 14, 1951, the team demoted Mantle to Kansas City to make room for Schallock. While Mantle was the Yankee's leader in RBIs at the time, they sent him down to clear a spot for the new pitcher. Casey informed his budding star, "This is going to hurt me more than you."[19] Casey added that Mickey needed more seasoning and he would be back. The young Mickey did not understand and cried.[20]

Mickey called his father crying, telling him that he wanted to quit baseball. Mickey expected Mutt to come out to Kansas City and give him a pep talk like he always did. Mutt told Mickey to wait and he would come out to see him. Instead of encouragement, Mickey was shocked to hear what his father had to say!

---

17   Ibid., 66-67
18   Mantle hit 26 homers and batted .383
19   Ibid., 25
20   Ibid., 27

Mutt was so disgusted, he scolded his son, "If that's all the man you are, then get your clothes and let's go home."[21]

This was the last thing that Mickey expected to hear; his father had always been supportive. Instead, Mutt had stinging words for his son; "What's the matter? I thought I raised a man. You ain't anything but a goddamn coward."[22]

Mickey pleaded for his dad to stop. Mutt continued by telling him that he was taking him back to Oklahoma where they could work together in the mines. The words lit a fire under his son's behind, Mickey decided to keep trying. After 40 games,[23] the Yankees called him back up to New York where he played the final 27 games of the regular season.[24] He was the Yankees' starting right fielder for the 1951 World Series. Mutt came to New York City to watch him play.

His father became sick and ended up in the hospital, but Mutt left his sick bed to watch his son play in the World Series. Seeing his son play in the World Series was the proudest moment in Mutt Mantle's life. Unfortunately, Mickey ripped up his knee on a drainage cover in the second game, ending his World Series. When Mickey was admitted to the hospital, so was his father. He shared a room with his dad and they watched the last four games of the World Series together on a small black and white television set.[25] Sadly, Mutt Mantle was eventually diagnosed with Hodgkin's disease and died on May 7, 1952. Mickey was devastated and always regretted never telling his dad that he loved him.[26]

Cancer was rampant in the Mantle family, claiming his father, grandfather and two uncles. It was referred to it as the "Mantle curse." Throughout his career, Mickey believed that he would himself die

---

21 "Yanks see Mantle as 52' Dimag," Daniel, Dan, The Sporting News, July 25, 1951, 6

22 Ibid. Leavy, 27

23 Mantle batted .361, 11 homers and 50 runs batted in the minors for Kansas City Blues of the American Association

24 He finished the season by batting .287, 6 homers and 20 runs batted in.

25 Ibid, Leavy, 36

26 Ibid., 79

young, which might be responsible for his bad behavior. When Mutt Mantle died, Mickey's behavior became reckless, probably because his father nor anyone else was there to say no to him.

Even with his disruptive behavior, it never shortchanged his accomplishments. He won three MVP awards and appeared in 16 All Star games. Mickey Mantle was inducted into the Hall of Fame in 1974.[27] Then in 1999, he was elected to Major League Baseball's All-Century team.

A young fan once told Al Kaline of the Detroit Tigers, who was a big fan of Mantle, that he was not half the player Mickey Mantle was. Kaline simply responded, "Son, nobody's half as good as Mickey Mantle."[28]

Mantle's health began declining in 1965; coincidently the Yankees never went to another World Series again during his career. The Yankees' lack of success was surely due to Mantle's declining health, as well as his aging teammates. The team did not return to the heights of their prior success until George Steinbrenner bought the team and started adding star players on the Yankees' roster.

Mickey felt that he never had a good season after he became thirty-three years old. He averaged exactly 100 hits, never driving in more than 56 runs or hitting more than 23 homers over his last four seasons.

As he was dying, Mickey admitted he would be a better player if not for his drinking. Still, Mickey was arguably the best player during his era. He became a member of the Hall of Fame in 1974. Unfortunately, Mickey Mantle was also an alcoholic for forty years. He was fond of saying that if he knew he was going to live this long, he'd have taken better care of himself.

---

27 Mickey hit 536 home runs in his career, not including the eighteen he hit in twelve World Series. During his career, Mickey had 2,415 hits, 1,509 RBIs, and a lifetime batter average of .298.

28 Fritz Peterson, Mickey Mantle is Going to Heaven (Outskirts Press, Denver, Co., 2009) 7

"God gave me a great body and the ability to play baseball. God gave me everything, and I just…pfftt! I'd like to say to kids out there, if you're looking for a role model (pointing to himself) this is a role model, this is a role model. Don't be like me."[29]

When his career began, Mickey Mantle was the product of his father's influence. Arguably, his decline resulted from his father's death and lack of his influence.

---

29   Ibid. Leavy, 374

Chapter 6

The Influence of Cal Ripken Sr.

*N*o *one is born with the ability to persevere in all circumstances. The skill of perseverance is almost always developed because of the influence of other people. In this chapter, Bob Hurte shares the amazing story of how the influence of Cal Ripken, Sr. led to the development of the most resilient baseball player in history.*

Several years ago, I was responsible for assigning the baseball umpires in my community. Since the umpires were normally high school age, I made it a point to attend their games to evaluate while showing them support. One day, in particular, I was at a game involving nine/ten-year-olds. As I stood among the parents, I remarked how enjoyable it was to watch games at this age, because they were still playing for fun. Then I followed that up with how one or two might play on their high school team, possibly one might play at college, and maybe, just maybe a professional baseball career. All of the parents' eyes turned to me.

Let me say ... if looks could kill!

Too many parents dream, and actually believe that their child will be the exception. It is a nice dream to have, but it is a trap that parents allow themselves to fall into. Instead, parents should simply enjoy watching their children play instead of projecting their athletic future. The following pages are about a man who might have had that dream, one that actually became true, not once, but twice.

Calvin Edwin Ripken Sr. was born on December 17, 1935, in a tiny room above the general store that his parents Clara Amelia and

Arend Frederick Ripken owned in Aberdeen, Maryland. Calvin would become a baseball lifer with the Baltimore Orioles. Many considered him to be one of the greatest baseball instructors of the game, and Ripken is credited with being the architect of the "Oriole's Way."[30]

Cal Ripken Sr. played catcher in the minor leagues. Unfortunately, his career was derailed by a shoulder injury. Instead of making a comeback as a player, he went into coaching and then managing, which eventually led him to the major leagues.[31] While Cal always dreamed of playing in the majors, he never pressured his children to play baseball. Yet, two of his sons, Billy and Cal, made it to the major league level. In an unprecedented move, years later, their father would become their manager. The biggest lesson that Cal taught his sons was to approach anything they did in life with the best of their abilities.

Cal's baseball journey began in 1957. Although it did not start without inconvenience, the scout who signed Cal Sr. had to borrow a pen from a fan to sign the contract.[32] Cal started by playing catcher for the Phoenix Stars of the class C Arizona-Mexico League. Ripken's career consisted of stops at ten cities from Aberdeen S.D. to Rochester, N.Y., over seven seasons.[33] His best professional season was 1960 when he played for the Fox Cities Foxes of the class B Illinois-Indiana-Iowa League.[34] As fate would have it, this was also the year his oldest son Cal Jr. was born. The Fox City Foxes finished in first, and Cal was selected to the All-Star team as a catcher, where his manager was Earl Weaver.

During his career, he once volunteered to catch three consecutive double-headers, which would be unheard of nowadays. While in the minors, he had future Oriole's star, Boog Powell and longtime Major

---

30 "Cal Ripken Sr," by Keenan, Jimmy, Society of American Baseball Research-Bio Project

31 "Cal Ripken Sr., 63, Veteran baseball coach, Litsky, Frank, New York Times, March 26, 1999

32 "Cal Ripken Jr., *The Only Way I Know* (NY, NY, Penguin Books, 1997) 24

33 Cal Sr.'s career totals were playing in 583 games, hit 29 home runs while batting .253.

34 Cal Ripken Sr. batted .281 with 74 RBIs in 1960

League Baseball executive, Pat Gillick as teammates. Both believed that Cal had natural coaching ability. Although Powell and Ripken were teammates, Boog considered Ripken like a coach. Powell felt that Ripken had the consummate baseball mind, and Gillick admired how he never swayed away from his principles.

During a spring training game in 1961, Cal Sr. was hit twice on his right shoulder by foul tips. He attempted to play through it but lost too much strength in his throwing arm. His son Cal Jr. explained later, "If my father wanted to stay in baseball, he needed to go into coaching and managing."[35]

Cal Sr. never wanted to be quoted. All he wanted was to do was teach. He never criticized his players or took credit for their success. To be honest, people would not blame him if he did; there is a popular explanation in life that states: Everything happens for a reason. Those foul tips hitting his shoulder, for example.

He was considered a teacher, leader, friend and father to many of his young minor league players. Both Hall of Famer Eddie Murray and journeyman infielder Rick Dauer thought of him like a surrogate father. He coached three Hall Of Fame members: Jim Palmer, Eddie Murray and his son Cal Jr.

You could ask anyone who played for Ripken: it was an honor to be called *lunk-head* by him. Elrod Hendricks, a friend and fellow coach considered Cal Sr. a walking baseball encyclopedia. Pitching guru Ray Miller remembers that Cal Sr. taught him how to fill out his first pitching chart.

Cal Sr. began his managing career in 1961, the start of a fourteen-year ascension to the MLB.[36] During that period, he won three championships and over 1000 minor league games. He was headstrong and possessed a fierce work ethic and a passion for baseball. When he hit grounders during infield practice, Cal was fond of pointing out the weight of the ball. According to him, a ML ball weighs 5 ¼ ounces, so how bad could it hurt? He tutored many

---

35 Ibid., Keenan
36 Ibid., Keenan

young players about the *Oriole way*; it came easy to him because he exemplified it.

Ripken coached the Aberdeen Pheasants of the Northern League in 1964. They ran away with the pennant that year. Cal was named the manager of the year. It was no wonder; the team's roster had nine future MLB players on it like Jim Palmer, Lou Pinella, Andy Etchebarren, Eddie Watt, Mark Belanger, Tom Fisher, Mike Davidson, Dave Leonard and Mike Fiore. Six of his players represented Aberdeen at the league's All-Star game.

Cal Ripken Sr. always felt that if you did the small things right, there would not be big things to worry about. He was a great influence to many of his players. He convinced Hall of Famer Eddie Murray to become a switch hitter, and Jim Palmer, who is also a member of the Hall of Fame, also acknowledged Ripken's influence. Johnny Oates, one of his former players, and future manager, was also a protégé, feeling that Ripken Sr. taught him more about baseball and life than anyone else.[37]

Cal Sr. was not always serious; he also knew how to have fun with his team. Jim Palmer remembers an instance one time when Cal stopped the team bus at a wheat field. He took out his golf clubs, told the players to move back six hundred feet and began to tee off golf balls. The players chased them trying to catch them in their gloves.

No surprise, the press made a big deal about their father/son relationship when Cal Jr. became a member of the Baltimore Orioles. Cal Sr. shrugged his shoulders, replying that, "They're all my sons." In truth, he spent more time with his players than his own children during the baseball season. A father figure exhibiting extreme patience with young rookie players, his commitment and loyalty to the Baltimore organization made him a wonderful role model.

Ripken knew each aspect of the game, even pitching. One time, he and Ray Miller noticed a flaw in Steve Stone's delivery. Both of

---

37 "Cal Ripken Sr. cool after winter of his discontent," Steadman, John F., The Baltimore Sun, March 24, 2014

them noticed that Stone was not extending his arm properly, and after some tinkering by the two of them, Stone went out and pitched five good innings in his next start. Then the following season, Stone was named the 1980 Cy Young Award winner as the top pitcher in the American League.[38]

Cal Jr. felt that his dad was a great father and mentor. Cal Jr. recalled a conversation he had with his dad when he was 17 years old. It seems that Cal Jr. was staying out later than his father wanted. When he asked Junior why he was out late, his son explained that none of his friends needed to come in early. Senior nodded, and said "uh-huh." His father listened to what his son had to say, and then gave his perspective about the situation. Since they were outside pulling weeds, the discussion did not last long. Cal Jr. never felt like he was being chewed out. However, after their conversation; he began coming home earlier while out with his friends. Apparently, his father's point of view made an impact on him.

Most fans might think that Cal Sr. drilled, trained and force-fed baseball into his sons, which was furthest from the truth. Sure, two of them went on to play in the MLB, with Cal Jr. becoming a member of baseball's HOF in 2007. To be sure Cal Ripken Sr. did not force his sons to play the game, but he did expose them to his love of it. Both Billy and Cal saw their father's love for it every time he threw a ball, picked up a bat or made out a line-up card. That was the influence on them. Baseball was always fun for him. Cal Jr. felt he had a front row seat to his dad's passion. Because his father enjoyed baseball, he wanted to enjoy it along with him. His father played the role of the old sage, with his honest observations, like noting how too many people are working at jobs they absolutely hate. He told his son that the secret to happiness is not in the money you make. It's the quality of your work and how it makes you feel. So find out what you love to do and pour yourself into it.

---

38   With a record of 25-7

Influence Pays Off in a Big Way

Cal Jr. really displayed his love for baseball. Between May 30, 1982, and September 19, 1998, he played 2,632 games over sixteen years, breaking arguably one of the most hallowed baseball records that formally was held by Lou Gehrig, the "Iron Horse."

As much as Cal Jr. dedicated himself to baseball, his younger brother Fred did not. Fred Ripken did desire to be a baseball player, but he gave up on baseball once he reached high school. Like his brothers, he was influenced by his father, just not in baseball. Like his dad, he enjoyed tinkering with things. Fred Ripken loved working on motorcycles. He eventually opened up a motorcycle shop in Harford County, Maryland.

While Cal Jr.'s hero was Brooks Robinson, Fred's was Evil Knievel. During the 1980s Fred Ripken was drawn back to the baseball diamond when he began coaching his daughter Austyn's softball team. The girls on the softball team loved him. They called him Mr. Fred!

The youngest Ripken son, Billy, played twelve years in the MLB and is still involved with baseball. Cal and Billy are involved in several baseball ventures, such as *Ripken Baseball,* a youth baseball league. They own several minor league teams, such as the *Aberdeen Ironbirds, Augusta Greenjackets* and the *Charlotte Stonecrabs.* Billy also serves as an on-air studio personality for *MLB Network.*

Cal Sr. had a fierce work ethic mixed with a diehard passion for baseball. He tutored many young players in the Baltimore Orioles organization about the "right" way to play baseball. Doug Decinces, a former player of his, called Cal Sr. a dictator, but in a warm sense. Cal Ripken Sr.: "…Instructed us on everything, down to how to wear our socks. Take pride in your appearance and you'll take pride in your game." He also liked to say, "It's like a bank men. You can't take out more that you put in!"

In life, Cal Edwin Ripken Sr. was never overdrawn. Cal Edwin Ripken Sr. died at Johns Hopkins Hospital after a six-month battle with lung cancer. He was 63 years old and a heavy cigarette smoker. Cal Sr. will be remembered as a headstrong man with a passion for baseball who was stern and exacting.

Chapter 7

Derek Jeter: The End of an Era

In today's sports world an athlete's character is viewed as being significantly less important than one's achievements in their sport. Unfortunately, many sports fans would rather watch a good athlete with a bad attitude than an accomplished athlete who is a gentleman. In this Chapter, Bob shares a story about the important influences in the life of one of the most respected baseball players in history.

Many debate Derek Jeter's place in baseball history. His detractors feel his status has been inflated; they have made sport of tearing down his legacy. Still, statistically, he is a future member of the Baseball Hall of Fame; and was elected to enter Cooperstown on the first ballot. It does not hurt that he was very popular and played for an iconic team like the New York Yankees.

If someone was to ask me, "Is Derek Jeter the best player I have ever seen?" I would quickly answer, "No." There is no doubt that I admire how he played the game, and especially the way he carried himself both on and off the field.

I also had the good fortune of seeing players like Mays, Aaron, Clemente and Mantle play. Do I think that Derek is the greatest shortstop of all-time? "Nope!" While I never saw Honus Wagner play, the "Flying Dutchman" (Wagner's nickname) still owns that status. Was he the all-time best Yankee? "Nope!" Unfortunately, he had some hard acts to follow, considering that Derek played for the same franchise as Babe Ruth, Lou Gehrig, Joe DiMaggio and Mickey

Mantle! With that in mind, he might not even crack the top ten list of "great" Yankees.

But as someone who has coached youth baseball for over a decade, I have always held Derek Jeter as a role model for the players that I coached. Unlike other sports figures, Jeter has been able to avoid controversy. I have never heard anything negative said about him. Think about it. We live in a world where people have cameras on their phones; anything can be filmed or recorded – and often is. The second a mistake occurs, its sordid details are splattered all over the Internet in a matter of seconds. Life no longer has secrets. What makes it more impressive, he plays in New York City, which is the biggest stage for the best-known sports franchise in the world! Somehow, Derek Jeter's career has never been tainted by controversy. If that does not qualify him as a role model, then what does?

Several years ago, during his playing days, Charles Barkley infamously said, "I ain't NO role model!" He felt that athletes should not be viewed as role models.

While I feel that Derek is not the greatest Yankee player, I would never want Yankee greats like Babe Ruth, Joe DiMaggio or Mickey Mantle as my son's role model. Character counts. If you suggested Derek Jeter, my answer would be a resounding "Absolutely!"

Mike Lupica of the New York "Daily News" said, "No one has been the face of the Yankees more than Derek."

Rick Reilly, a writer for ESPN, felt that Derek was the best player in baseball for about a decade. Then, on the other hand, there is Keith Olberman, a former ESPN employee, ranted that Jeter's last season was a long love fest for Jeter. He was not alone; many like him in the media have difficulty understanding the Yankee captain's worth. Olberman even insinuated that Jeter was closer to mediocrity than superstardom.

The undeniable fact: Derek Jeter accumulated superb career statistics that qualify entrance into Baseball's Hall of Fame. There should be no doubt that his plaque should be placed among the other players of greatness.[39] In my opinion, those numbers and accomplishments over a twenty-year career qualify him entrance into Cooperstown. Without a shadow of a doubt, he is also a Hall of Famer because of his character.

For almost two decades, Derek Jeter was the Yankee player that the kids wanted to be. He acted like a Yankee. Derek spoke to the media every day. He dated some of the most beautiful women, yet you never saw him embroiled in controversy on TMZ, or on page six of the "New York Post" or "Extra." When he was out in public, he made fans feel important by making eye contact when signing autographs. His former teammate David Cone says, "It's good being Derek."

Of course, the Yankee captain also had imperfections; if someone crossed him, you were ostracized. He is also a bit of a germ freak, never using public bathrooms unless for an emergency.

The Making of a Captain

Even as a young player, Jeter realized the importance of giving back. In 1996, he began a foundation called the Turn 2 Foundation.[40] It was created to support programs that motivated young people to stay away from alcohol and drugs. His father, Dr. Sanderson Charles Jeter, is a substance abuse counselor and serves on its board of directors. Derek's mother, who is an accountant, serves as the foundation's treasurer.

Derek Jeter was born in Pequannock, New Jersey on June 26, 1974. His family moved to Kalamazoo Michigan when he was four years old. Both he and his sister Sharlee lived in Michigan during the school year but returned during the summer to live with their grandparents in New Jersey. The Yankees signed him out of

---

39   His 3,465 hits lifetime, a career batting average of .310, 260 homeruns, 544 doubles, 66 triples, 1,923 runs scored with 1,311 runs batted in, winning five of his seven World Series appearances, fifteen selections to the American League All-Star team, and being awarded the1996 Rookie of the Year in the American League; elected to the Hall of Fame on the first ballot.

40   "Derek Jeter's Path from Kalamazoo to Cooperstown," by Jim Baumbach, Newsday, September 29, 2012.

Kalamazoo Central High School in Michigan as their top draft choice in 1992. He was the overall sixth pick in baseball's amateur draft.[41] The level of competition in Michigan was pretty bad, certainly nothing compared to California or Florida. Still, the American Baseball Coaches Association voted Jeter the 1992 high school player of the year.[42]

Before signing with the Yankees, his parents asked them to promise to first pay for their son's college education no matter the outcome of his career.[43]

Derek moved quickly up the ladder, starting in Class A and finishing the season at AAA in 1994. He played a full year at AAA in 1995. The Yankees loved his defense and he also batted .317 in 123 games. The following year he became the Yankees' starting shortstop, replacing former four-time gold glove winner Tony Fernandez. They felt that if he batted .240 or .250 and fielded his position, the team would have been happy.[44]

Derek was voted the Rookie of the Year in 1996.[45] The Yankees would beat the Atlanta Braves in the World Series that year. Over the next twelve years, Derek never batted lower than .291 and appeared in ten All-Star games. He played in 150 or more games almost every year.

When Derek and his sister spent summers in New Jersey, they saw their grandfather Sonny Connor's work ethic firsthand. Sonny was a great influence on Derek's baseball career. For fifty years, Sonny Connor was the head of maintenance at Saint Michael's parish. Sonny began working at Saint Michael's in Jersey City during the 1940s.[46] He was responsible for both the high and grade schools. Derek felt that

---

41 Derek batted .557 as a junior, and .508 as a senior.

42 "Kid Gloves: This season, when it comes to shortstops, it's New York," Klapisch, Bob, The Sporting News, April 29, 1996, 22-23

43 Ibid.,23

44 Ibid.,23

45 He batted .314, with 183 hits, scoring 104 times, ten homers and 78 runs batted in.

46 "Priceless," by Adrian Wojnarski, The Sporting News, February 7, 2000, 4

his grandfather enjoyed what he did, although he never made millions of dollars.

"He was the type of person that never missed work. NEVER! Even on a bad day he always seemed to go there. That's the lesson I learned from him."[47]

Seeing his grandfather's work ethic helped make Derek into one of the most admired, respected stars in sports.

Derek's upbringing taught him how to have respect for others – whether you were a cook or a king. For instance, when Gene Monahan, a long time Yankees trainer was fighting throat and neck cancer, Jeter began texting him instead of calling him.[48]

Derek also had a sense of humor. Before President George W. Bush was to throw out the first pitch for the 2001 World Series, which was the first World Series game after September 11th, the President stood tensely on the mound. Derek walked up to him and said, "Throw from the mound or else they'll boo you." President George W. Bush smiled and delivered a strike.[49]

His parents taught him a valuable lesson; each year they made him sign a contract promising good behavior. The agreement addressed schoolwork, curfew times and abstaining from drugs and alcohol. One could only wonder if Derek signed that same contract every year while he played in professional baseball!

Jeter's respect for the game ran deeper than simply playing it, which elevated him into baseball royalty, such as a modern day DiMaggio, but with an "everyman's touch." Jeter admitted to visiting Monument Park often. "I'd be lying to you if I said I didn't want to be a part of (Yankee) history."[50]

While in the fourth grade at St. Augustine Cathedral School, he stood in front of his class and informed them that he planned to play shortstop for the New York Yankees. "When I grow up, I'm going to

47 "Priceless," Wojnarwski, Adrian, The Sporting News, February 7, 2000, 34
48 "Jeter State of Mind," Reilley, Rick, ESPN Magazine, May 28, 2014
49 Ibid
50 Ibid.

be a shortstop for the New York Yankees."[51] Although Derek was a young child when he made this prophecy, it demonstrates the power of self-influence.

Little did Derek realize how prolific his words were! As profound as it might have been, they were probably influenced by his grandmother Dorothy. She took her grandson to Yankee Stadium often, where they watched Winfield, Mattingly and Guidry play.[52] Derek claimed it was Winfield who inspired him to pursue a baseball career. Derek's ability to play shortstop was probably genetic. His dad played shortstop at Fisk College in Tennessee.

Jeter can thank several influences that helped shape his life, like his grandfather, his parents and the Yankee tradition. In return, Derek Sanderson Jeter influenced future generations by the way he carried himself.

No one was more the face of the Yankees than Derek Sanderson Jeter. "That is why on September 28, 2014, when Derek played his last ML game, it signaled the end of an era."

---

51   Ibid., Baumbach
52   Ibid.

Chapter 8

Living a Baseball Dream
With the Walkers

Neil and Tom Walker during travel baseball

In this chapter Bob shares a story about a father and son, who were both first round picks in the Major League Baseball draft. The father, Tom Walker, was a first round pick by the Baltimore Orioles in 1968, and his youngest son Neil Walker, became a first round pick by the Pittsburgh Pirates in 2004. This fascinating story describes the influences that helped and hurt their respective careers.

Many Little League baseball players wish to play in the "big" leagues someday. Many fathers have the same dream. This explains why I am envious of my friend Tom Walker, a veteran of six major league seasons. His youngest son Neil was a first round draft pick by and began playing for the Pirates. My dream of having a son play major league baseball became his reality!

Any time when the Pirates are playing at home, Tom can be found in a seat behind home plate at Pittsburgh's PNC Park. Until Neil was traded to the New York Mets in 2016, his son Neil was the starting second baseman for the Pirates. He went on to play for the Milwaukee Brewers, the New York Yankees and now the Miami Marlins (2019), and Philadelphia Phillies (2020), Neil retired from baseball in 2021.[53] There have been 193 father/son combinations in the history of Major League baseball. The first one was Henry Doscher (father/Brooklyn Athletics) and Jack Doscher (son/Brooklyn Superbas) in 1903.

Tom Walker admits, "It's a dream come true for our family and for me, getting to participate in Major League baseball again, as a father. It's very fun."[54]

Since the MLB amateur draft began in 1965, the Walkers are one of only ten father/son combinations to both be selected in the first round. The others are the Grieves, Swishers, Burroughs, Mayberrys, DeShields, Boxbergers, Witts and Soderstrom. Tom was selected in the first round by the Baltimore Orioles as the ninth pick overall out of Brevard Junior College. Before college, he pitched for the Florida championship team at Chamberlain High School in Tampa, Florida, where Steve Garvey was his teammate. His son Neil was the Pirates' first round pick, eleventh overall out of Pine-Richland High School in Gibsonia, Pa. in 2004. He was a member of the Western Pennsylvania Interscholastic Athletic League Championship team. Both Walkers also faced career roadblocks during their climb up the major league ladder.

---

53 Began the 2020 season with the Philadelphia Phillies
54 Interview, Tom Walker

Tom pitched for the Baltimore Orioles organization, which was loaded with pitching talent. The Orioles rotation had four 20-game winners that featured Dave McNally, Jim Palmer, Mike Cuellar and Pat Dobson. They became the second team to ever accomplish that. The 1920 Chicago White Sox was the first. Due to the rarity of 20-game winners and four man rotations, Baltimore will probably be the last to accomplish this feat.

Tom considered returning to college after the season. That was before fate intervened on August 4, 1971. He was pitching for the Dallas-Fort Worth Spurs of the Texas League against the Albuquerque Dodgers. That night, he won 1-0 by pitching a 15 inning no-hitter.[55]

Tom felt that this was the game that opened up many eyes around the Major Leagues. Following the season, the Montreal Expos selected him in the Rule 5 draft. He made his debut on April 23, 1972, at the age of 23, pitching an inning against the St. Louis Cardinals. He walked Joe Torre, the first batter he faced, but then got Ted Simmons and Jose Cruz to pop up before retiring Lou Brock on a grounder to third base.

His son Neil also faced roadblocks during this career. He was originally drafted as a catcher out of high school. At the time, the Pirates already had a couple of young catchers, Ryan Doumit and Ronnie Paulino, so he switched over to third base. Unfortunately, Jose Bautista and then Andy LaRoche were ahead of him. Then the Pirates drafted Pedro Alvarez with the second pick overall in the 2008 amateur draft.

Neil led the Indianapolis Indians (AAA) in batting and was rewarded by being brought up to Pittsburgh on September 1, 2009. Like his father, he made his MLB debut at age 23. Ironically his dad was in Indianapolis when his son was told the news. Neil remained in Pittsburgh for the remainder of the 2009 season. He started the 2010 season in Indianapolis.

During the 2009 off season, the Pirates acquired Akinori Iwamura for reliever Jesse Chavez. Iwamura began the 2010 season as

---

55 "Tom Walker," by Bob Hurte, SABR Bio Project

the Pirates' second baseman. Aki began the 2010 season in a horrific batting slump before becoming injured; the Pirates brought Neil Walker up from Indianapolis. He played his first game at second base on May 27, 2010. He would never relinquish his starting job. Although Aki was the highest-paid Pirate on the roster, he was released.

Tom did not mind driving the 22 miles from Gibsonia, a suburb of Pittsburgh, to PNC Park to watch his son Neil when he played for the Pirates, because he enjoyed reliving his major league career vicariously through his son. Tom admits that his son asks him about his own MLB experience and what it took to get there. Neil considers his dad's experience as a major influence on his career. They discuss the sacrifices that need to be made and how much time and effort is needed to be a MLB player. While Neil Walker has embarked upon a promising career, his father is living every father's dream![56]

---

56   Interview, Tom Walker

Chapter 9

The Griffeys: The First Father/Son MLB Teammates

The Griffey family is a baseball legend. If there were such a thing as a royal family in baseball, this family would qualify. It is amazing how different influences drove these legends to succeed in the sport. Bob tells this incredible story in this chapter.

Most fathers will attest that nothing is more magical than a simple game of catch in the backyard with your son. It is a rite of passage into fatherhood. The thrill of seeing your young son catch his first baseball is something that bubbles in your chest. It is at that moment that one entertains the dream of your son playing in the major leagues begins.

For this chapter, I have chosen to discuss the Griffeys, who are fine examples of both baseball and fatherhood. The Griffeys represent three generations of fatherly influence; of course, the family genetics does not hurt their baseball ability. In his book <u>Big Red: Baseball, Fatherhood, and My Life in the Big Red Machine</u>, Ken Griffey Sr. stated that relationships between a father and son are both unique and different, in a certain way.

George Kenneth Griffey was born in Donora, Pennsylvania, which is located twenty-three miles south of Pittsburgh, on April 10, 1950. It is a blue collar town nestled in a valley consisting of the towns of Monongahela, Monessen and Charleroi. This tiny industrial town consisted of 14,000 residents that worked in either its steel or zinc mills. The mills ran twenty-four hours a day and their men relied on working there to feed their families.[57]

On October 26, 1948, Donora was hit with a devastating calamity, known as the "Deadly Smog." While it was not unusual for smog to hang over the town of Donora, something seemed different that day; it was thicker than usual. Over four days, twenty-two people died and nearly half of the town's population became ill. Fifty more died later from related complications.

The smog even affected the attendees of a local football game; some reported that it was hard to see the players on the field.[58]

Birth of a Dynasty

Ken Griffey was born two years after the devastating smog. Robert Joseph "Buddy" Griffey was his father, and Naomi Bailey Griffey was his mother. Naomi went by Ruth, but preferred her nickname Ninky. His father was an outstanding athlete at Donora High School. He was so good that Kentucky State University gave him a football scholarship. His mother, Naomi Bailey Griffey, was quite an athlete in her own rite. She was the starting center on her high school basketball team in Kentucky. Blame it on heredity; Ken had no choice but to be athletic.

After college, Buddy returned to Donora, to work in the steel mill. Buddy and Ninky's children were Jim, Ron, Bill, Ruby, Ken and Freddy.[59]

The steel mill closed down, leaving his father unemployed, leaving him with a wife, and six hungry kids. Ken Sr. was only two years old. Buddy Griffey felt that his only option was to send his family off to Kentucky to live with his in-laws.

Buddy's plan was to drop his family off at a bus terminal in Pittsburgh. Unfortunately, he did not give his family enough money

---

57   Ken Griffey, and Phil Peppe, *Big Red: Baseball, Fatherhood, and My Life in the Big Red Machine* (Chicago, Il: Triumph Books, 2014) 20-21

58   Ibid., 20-22

59   Ibid., 21-22

to make the trip to Kentucky, so Ninky and the kids traveled back to Donora, only to find that Buddy was preparing to leave town.

Buddy had never informed Ninky of his intention. Surprisingly, no nasty confrontation ever occurred between them. Instead, Ninky told her husband to do whatever he felt he needed to do, and not to worry about her and the kids.[60]

Years later, Griffey admitted that he never resented his father leaving the family because his mom never held a grudge. When she was asked why their father had left, Ninky simply responded, 'That's your dad.'[61]

While growing up, Ken Griffey Sr. never knew much about his father. Yet, Buddy Griffey might have influenced him most about being a father. Obviously, Ken was very thankful for his father's athletic genetics, but strangely, it was Buddy Griffrey's abandonment that influenced him most on how to be a good father to his own children.

Ninky Griffey worked as a cosmetologist for a local funeral home. Ken considered his mom the biggest influence in both his career and life. She served both as a father and a mother. Since Ninky did not work a typical 9-5 job, she was able to adjust her work schedule to attend all of her son's sporting events. She never missed any of Ken's games.

It was not until years later Ken Sr. became aware of his father's athletic ability around Donora. It was not from his mother but from one of Buddy's old high school teammates.

After Ken had been a major league player for a couple of years, he ran into this teammate while playing against the Cardinals. From then on, Stan Musial always made a point to seek him out when he came to St. Louis. Musial and Griffey were both from Donora. Stan shared several stories about his father, Buddy. Musial shared that he (Musial) was a highly touted pitcher for Donora high school, and baseball scouts often came out to see him pitch. Soon they also took notice of Buddy Griffey, the team's left-handed third baseman. They were

---

60   Ibid., 22-24
61   Ibid., 24

impressed with his play.[62] There was no question of how good Buddy was, but the times were not right for the scouts to sign him, because Jackie Robinson had not yet broken the color barrier. The attention that Buddy received never amounted to much. He went to college in Kentucky, but came back to Donora to work in the steel mills.

Like the popular expression, the apple does not fall far from the tree, Buddy's son George Kenneth Griffey Sr. also starred at four high school sports. He played baseball, basketball, football and ran track. He was named Donora's Athlete of the year in 1969.[63]

He earned All-State honors playing half-back and wide receiver during his senior year. His gridiron play attracted several colleges. However, Ken chose to play professional baseball instead of going to college. He was drafted by the Reds as the 682nd player picked overall during the 29th round. Elmer Gray, an area baseball scout for the Reds was responsible for Griffey's baseball career. Gray coached basketball and football at Donora High School. He scouted Ken, eventually signing him to play for the Reds. Gray was impressed by both Griffey's speed and athleticism. So, he invited Ken to a couple of Reds tryout camps. There was one session in particular where Elmer invited a big time pitching prospect named Doc Medich from Hopewell H.S. in Aliquippa. Ken was able to hit a few balls off of him.[64]

"In 1969, Racism Reared Its Ugly Head in Florida"

After Griffey was drafted, he was assigned to Bradenton in the Gulf Coast League. This is where he faced racism for the first time. It was 1969; the Civil Rights bill was five years old, apparently, the news about the bill never made it to the Deep South, like in Bradenton, Florida. There were segregated drinking fountains, movie theaters and restaurants in that part of the country.

---

62   Ibid., 254
63   "Ken Griffey Sr., " by Charles Farber, SABR Bio Project
64   Ibid., Griffey and Pepe, 47

One particular night stood out. Ken was with two of his African American teammates, Clarence Cooper and Willis Ham. They were walking home from a local grocery store in Bradenton when a black Cadillac came up onto the sidewalk and almost hit them. First, they thought that the driver must have been drunk or sick until it returned for another try!

Bradenton was his first professional season of baseball. He played in 49 of the team's 54 games. His batting average was .281, good enough for 18th in the league. He had eleven doubles, a triple, a home run with eleven stolen bases.

After the 1969 season, he returned to Donora feeling pretty good about himself. Things began happening quickly in his life. First, he eloped with his girlfriend Birdie on September 4th; then on November 21st, she gave birth to their first son, George Kenneth Griffey Jr.

The following year, when "Uncle Sam" called Ken, Reds management stepped in by arranging for him to join the army reserves. Ken was able to fulfill his obligation by doing 6 months of active duty, thus allowing him to continue his baseball career uninterrupted. It also enabled him to play at Sioux Falls, South Dakota.

While living in Sioux Falls, the Griffeys faced other challenges. When Birdie and their new baby came up to live with him, housing became an issue; Ken could not afford to have them live in the hotel with him. The owner of the hotel, who had a nephew in real estate, found them an apartment for $60 a month. While this solved his housing issues, it did not help his performance on the field, with Ken finishing the season batting only .244. His low batting average caused him to stress about his playing future.[65]

After that season, the Reds sent him south. He played for the Tampa Tarpons of the Florida State League in 1971.[66] His average was the highest in the Florida State League, but he did not have enough at-bats to qualify for the league's batting title. The Reds moved him up in the final two weeks of the season to the Class AA Eastern League.

---

65   Ibid.,52-53
66   In 88 games, he batted .342, plus 25 stolen bases.

He played for the Trois-Rivieres Aigle or Three Rivers Eagles. They made the playoffs, only to lose to Elmira 3 games to 1.[67]

The 1972 season verified that Ken could play at the AA level.[68] His performance enabled him to move up in 1973 to play for Indianapolis of the AAA American Association League where he batted .327 in 107 games.

Ken was called up on September 27, 1973, after the Reds suspended Bobby Tolan. Griffey made the most for his twenty-five games that season; he batted .384. Ken also played in the National League Championship Series when the Reds lost to the New York Mets.[69]

The Reds returned him to Indianapolis in 1974, where he split time between the minors and Cincinnati. He batted an unimpressive .251.

When Griffey returned to Cincinnati to play full-time in 1975, Joe Morgan felt that he was the key to the team's improvement. Griffey became a significant cog in the "Big Red Machine." The team won 108 games that season. When they beat the Red Sox in the World Series it was the first time they won a World Series since 1940. They would repeat as champions in 1976; Griffey had a career season. He was in the NL batting race for the entire season, but lost by a single point on the last day. He ended with an average of .336, and was selected for the All Star game for the first time.

A baseball strike split the 1981 season. The Reds had the best overall record during the split season; since they did not finish in first for either half, the team was denied a post season berth. This was a disappointment for the franchise, and after the 1981 season, ownership decided to dismantle the team and traded Griffey to the New York Yankees. For the next six years, he played for both the Braves and the Yankees.

---

67   Ibid.,55

68   By the end of the season, he hit .318, 14 home runs and stole 31 bases.

69   Ibid., Farber

Griffey returned to the Reds in 1988. He attained the status of the respected elder statesman on the team. During the 1990 season, though the younger players took to calling him "Gramps," he served as a valuable reserve and mentor in the clubhouse. Because of the pennant race, roster demands resulted in his release that August. His young teammates were incensed; they still went on to win the NL pennant and the World Series without him, and they decided to award him a full World Series share.

"The Griffeys Became the Only Father and Son to Hit Back to Back Home Runs"

Ken was not inactive for long; the Seattle Mariners quickly picked him up, where he made history by becoming his son's teammate. They became the only father and son combination to hit back to back home runs.[70]

Retiring after the 1991 season, Ken Griffey Sr. enjoyed a stellar nineteen-year career.[71] Later, he returned to the Reds in 1997 as a coach before moving up to their front office in 2001.

In his Hall of Fame induction speech, Ken Griffey Jr. acknowledged that his father was his biggest influence. When Ken Jr. was young he wanted to be a major league player like his father. He also wanted to be a great father like him.[72]

George Kenneth Griffey Jr., who was born on November 21, 1969, shared his birthday with another famous Donora baseball player, Stan Musial.[73] Who would have thought that two Hall of Famers would come from the same small, western Pennsylvania town? By the time Junior was nine or ten years old his father recognized his baseball ability. It was obvious just from playing catch with him in the

---

70 Ibid.

71 His lifetime average of .296, with152 home runs, 859 runs batted in, 200 stolen bases, and 2143 hits.

72 Ken Griffey Jr.'s HOF speech (transcript), July 24, 2016

73 Ibid., Griffey and Pepe, 50

backyard. If a ball was thrown high to Junior, Ken Sr. could see how well his son handled the leather. Most kids his age were still awkward using their glove. When Junior began playing Little League, coaches would place his son at first base because, unlike his teammates, he could consistently catch the ball. At the age of twelve, Ken Sr. could tell his son was a talented hitter because of his swing, and how the ball jumped off his bat.

When Junior was thirteen years old, his father asked what he wanted to be.

"I want to be a major league baseball player."[74] His son replied.

Which made sense – with all of the time he spent in MLB clubhouses, he was not awed by big league surroundings.

Ken Griffey Sr. never cared if his sons watched him play in the majors; all he cared about was spending quality time with them. Back in the 1970s, the Reds clubhouse had Ken Jr. and his brother Craig, Pete Rose Jr., Eduardo and Victor Perez, Lee May Jr., and Brian McRae. They were affectionately known as the "Little Red Machine."

Ken Sr. was still playing in the MLB when Junior was playing in high school. So anytime that Ken Sr. got a chance, he went to watch his son's games. He did not get to see his son play often, but when he did, it seemed like Junior never got a hit.

It became so bad that coaches sent messages to his wife Birdie not to tell her husband when there was a game. They even dropped a "not-too-subtle" hint like sending binoculars if he insisted on watching his son's games. They hoped he would stand far enough away so Junior could not see me.[75]

While Ken Griffey Sr. did not see Junior play often enough to form an opinion of how well he played, others close to him did, like Bobby Cox. Cox would say years later that Ken Griffey Jr. was the best prospect that he had ever seen; nobody was even close.[76]

---

74 Ibid., 50
75 Ibid., 164
76 "Ken Griffey Jr.," by Emily Hawks, SABR Bio Project

There is a great story about a Seattle Mariner scout named Tom Mooney. He saw Jr. playing in high school and told the Mariners about him.

During the spring of 1987, Mooney invited Roger Jongewaard to watch Ken Griffey's high school team play at a new community park in Cincinnati. Jongewaard was higher up on the scouting 'food chain.' The park had a grove of trees located twenty feet behind the outfield fence. During Griffey's second at bat, he launched a high fly ball into the right field which traveled well over the fence. Jongewaard asked Mooney, "Which tree did it hit?" Mooney informed Roger that the ball actually went over the trees.[77]

At first, Seattle ownership was skeptical about using their number one draft pick on a high school player. They were burned the previous draft by Pat Lennon, their top pick, who was also a high school player. The Seattle Mariners finally decided to make Ken Griffey Jr. the number one overall pick on June 2, 1987, signing him for $160,000.

Hall of Fame manager, Dick Williams, who was at the time the Seattle Mariners manager, praised the teenager. Williams did not hand out compliments or accolades. After seeing Junior's workout, he told Seattle GM, Woody Woodward, "I'll take him on the team today, right now. I don't see a thing wrong with him."[78]

Junior began his climb in professional baseball at the Class A level in the Northwest League. His first minor league manager was Rick Sweet, the former catcher with the San Diego Padres and the New York Mets. Griffey played in 54 games for the Bellingham Mariners batting .313, with 14 home runs, and driving in 40 RBIs. He was not even eighteen years old yet!.

The next team he played for was the San Bernardino Spirit of the Class A California League. Junior became a fan favorite there. When he stepped into the batter's box, the Public Address announcer asked fans what time it was, and they responded that it was "Griffey time!" His numbers in the California State League were outstanding.

---

77   Ibid.
78   Ibid., Griffey and Pepe, 166

The Mariners saw fit to promote him to the Vermont Mariners of the AA Eastern League[79]. This was where he finished the season. He would not return the following year. Instead, he became the Mariners starting centerfielder in 1989 with an impressive spring training.

It was very important for Ken Griffey Jr. to make the Seattle Mariners roster since his dad's playing days were coming to an end, and it would be the first time that a father/son would play in the majors at the same time. He made the Mariners after spring training in 1989. Junior collected his first major league base hit, a double in his first at bat against Dave Stewart, on April 3, 1989. One week later, he hit his first home run off of White Sox pitcher Eric King. Then a month later, a candy bar was named after him, an example of true baseball stardom. It was called the "Ken Griffey Jr." and was put out by the Pacific Trading Card Company. Ironically Griffey could never enjoy one; he was allergic to chocolate.[80]

By late in July 1989, he was a leading candidate for Rookie of the Year,[81] until on July 25th, when he fractured his hand making a defensive play. After the injury, he slipped to third place in the voting.

The following year (1990),[82] he also made his first All Star game, won his first Gold Glove, and he also made baseball history on August 31, 1990, when he, along with his dad, they became the first father/son combination to play on the same team at the same time in the MLB. When the two Griffeys were teammates in Seattle, the elder Griffey reflected seeing his son standing next to him in the outfield. It brought back many memories from the father/son games when his son was just a boy. Being his son's teammate was the pinnacle of his playing career. Ken Griffrey Sr. and Jr. influenced each other mutually by causing each other to perform better. Up to that point, Ken Griffey Sr. felt his career highlight was the 1976 batting race.

---

79   where he batted .279, 2 home runs, and 10 RBIs.

80   "Griffey Jr. Allergic to his own candy bar," Baltimore Sun (on line), May 8, 1989

81   batting .287, 13 home runs, and 45 RBIs

82   Ken Jr. batted .300, 22 home runs and 80 RBIs

Both of them went 1-4 the first game they played together. Ken Sr. hit a single in his first at bat, winning the bet he had with his son about who would get a hit first. Then Griffey Sr. demonstrated his ability on the field by throwing out Bo Jackson at second base. The Seattle manager Jim Lefebvre raved about it and stated that the team did not get Griffey Sr. as a babysitter for his son.

Ken Griffey Jr. played with his father during his formative years. Having his dad around was like having a personal coach. But, like a baby bird leaving the nest, it was time to fly on his own. 1992, the year after his father retired, Junior increased his home run output to 27, his RBIs to 103, and hit .308. It became his third season in a row to bat over .300. After the 1992 season, he married Melissa Gay; they went on to have three children: Trey, Taryn, and Tevin, who they adopted in 2002.

On June 15, 1993, Ken Jr. clubbed his 100th home run, making him the sixth youngest to do so. He improved his power numbers again by hitting 45 home runs, driving in 109 runs, with a batting average of .309. He appeared in another All Star game while winning his fourth Gold Glove. Married life did not hinder his performance on the playing field; instead, his supportive relationship with his wife probably influenced his success in baseball.

Arguably Ken Griffey Jr.'s best year in the MLB was 1997. He won the American League Most Valuable Player award. He hit 56 home runs and 147 RBIs to lead the league; he made the All Star team and added yet another Gold Glove.

1999 was the last year that Ken Jr. played in Seattle[83]. After the season, Ken became disenfranchised with the Seattle Mariners and demanded a trade. He was a ten and five player, giving him the right to veto any trade. He vetoed trades to the Mets and to the Atlanta Braves. He ended up in Cincinnati. The trade took place on February 10, 2000. An indicator of his value, Griffey Jr. was traded for four players – Jake Meyer, Mike Cameron, Antonio Perez and Brett Tomko.

---

83   putting up his typical numbers 48 home runs, 134 RBIs, and a .285 batting average

Not only was Junior an outstanding player, he respected the history that African Americans made in the game of baseball. He asked baseball commissioner Bud Selig to request permission for him to wear #42 on April 15, 2007, which was the sixtieth anniversary of Jackie Robinson's MLB debut.

Junior felt, "It's just my way of giving that man his due respect." Robinson's number 42 has since been retired from the game of baseball. Now, on April 15th each year, every MLB player wears the #42 as a tribute to Jackie Robinson. It is no surprise that this tradition originated with the help of Ken Griffey Jr.[84]

It's Not Just a Game, It's a Personal Growth Medium

When Ken Griffey Jr. was enshrined into the National Baseball Hall of Fame, he paid tribute to the many people who molded him along the way, from teammates, to coaches, and opponents. His father of course received the bulk of credit.

"To my dad, who taught me to play the game, but more important he taught me how to be a man…"[85]

Several of Junior's teammates have attested that the way he was a father was instilled by his father's influence. "The apple did not fall far from the tree." It was his friend and former teammate, Harold Reynolds who really summed up what was important in Ken Griffey Jr.'s life:

"I have always believed that Junior's goal in life was to be a dad. That's what he wanted to do, more than hitting all the home runs, and more than be enshrined into the Baseball Hall of Fame. Junior loves his kids."[86]

---

84   "Mariners at forefront of establishing Jackie Robinson," Greg Johns, MLB. com

85   Ken Griffey Jr.'s HOF speech- transcript

86   Ibid., Griffey and Pepe, 212

Ken Griffey Jr. or "Junior" always wanted to be a major league baseball player, like his dad, but more than that; he also wanted to be a father like him. Although he ended up playing twenty-two seasons, and he entered the National Baseball Hall of Fame, it was being a father that made him most proud.

Each of his children went on to pursue their own sports careers. His two oldest attended and played sports at Arizona State University. His oldest Trey played football and went on to an NFL career. His daughter Taryn also attended Arizona, and played on the woman's basketball team. The youngest, Tevin, was recruited by Florida A&M this year (2020) to play football. Junior has always been supportive in anything that they chose to do. Because of their involvement in sports, he has become an avid amateur photographer.[87]

Ken Griffrey Jr. accomplished the two things that he always wanted to do in life, and was good at it! He passed along the influence he took from his dad to his own children.

---

87 "Ken Griffey Jr. is a proud Dad of Three Grown-up Kids," Pedro Marrero, Amo Mama, June 24, 2020

Section III
Personal Baseball Influences

Chapter 10

How I Became Friends
With Wally Westlake

*M*any *of us think that we were born to like certain things. However, if we take the time to reflect on our true influences, we often discover some fascinating reasons why we like what we like. In this chapter, Bob describes how his friendship with his father's favorite baseball player took his interest in the sport to a whole new level.*

To be honest, I cannot remember <u>not</u> being a baseball fan. And, I have my father to blame (or thank) for that. He was the major influence on me becoming a baseball fan. Dad was born in Pittsburgh, Pa. and he became a baseball fan because my grandfather was one. The game of baseball became a special connection between them, quite possibly the only one. That is because my grandfather, Elmer was not what you called a role model father.

April 18, 1947, will always be a special day in my life. The Pittsburgh Pirates played the Cincinnati Reds in their home opener at Forbes Field on that day.[88] The day began with my dad and grandfather packing a sack of chip-chopped ham sandwiches, and a jug of iced tea before catching a north side streetcar to the Oakland section of Pittsburgh. The round trip only cost twelve cents, while a seat in the Forbes Field bleachers cost sixty-five.

It was also the Pittsburgh Pirate debut of future Hall of Fame slugger Hank Greenberg. For years Greenberg played with the Detroit Tigers. Then he enlisted in World War II to fight the Nazis. Hank Greenberg returned as a war hero at the end of the 1945 season, just in time to join the Tigers World Series victory over the Chicago Cubs. The next season (1946) Hank led the American League with 44 homers and 127 RBIs. Unfortunately, he became embroiled in a nasty salary dispute with Tigers' management during the off-season. Instead of playing for less money, Hank announced his retirement. The Tigers decided to sell his contract to the Pirates. He was adamant about retiring, but Pittsburgh persuaded the prolific home run hitter not to retire. Greenberg became the first player to be paid over $80,000 for a season. They also accommodated Greenberg's pull-hitting style by reducing Forbes Field's cavernous left field by moving it in by thirty feet, so it would be 335 feet. The new fenced-in section became known as "Greenberg Gardens; it later became "Kiner's Korner" when Hank retired.

When Elmer and his son stood at the corner of Sennett and Bouquet Streets that Friday afternoon, they witnessed a crowd that rivaled a Hollywood premiere! The ballpark was packed with 38,216 fans, setting a Pirates' attendance record at the time. The crowd

---

88   https://www.baseball-reference.com/boxes/PIT/PIT194704180.shtml

included several baseball and political dignitaries. Among them was Pennsylvania Governor James D. Duff, Tom Herbert, the governor of Ohio and Pittsburgh's popular mayor D. L. Lawrence, along with Happy Chandler, the Commissioner of Baseball, Ford Frick, the President of the National League and movie star Bing Crosby, who was also a part owner of the Pirates. In order to handle the immense crowd management decided to rope off part of the outfield to accommodate the overflow.

Since I grew up in the New York Mets viewing area where Ralph Kiner, the former Pittsburgh Pirate, announced their games, I asked my dad if he ever saw Kiner play, and whether Kiner was his favorite player. Dad saw him play, he added that while Ralph hit a lot of homers, his favorite player was a guy named Wally Westlake. I soon learned why.

On April 18, 1947, my father and grandfather bought tickets for the roped off area at Forbes Field; because of that game, my father officially became a Wally Westlake fan. While the two of them stood there with hopes of seeing the "great" Hank Greenberg up close, unfortunately on that day Elbie Fletcher, the Pirates' first baseman got hurt, causing Greenberg to be moved to first base. So instead, a stocky rookie from northern California took Greenberg's place in the outfield. His name was Waldon Thomas Westlake. Wally went on to please the Pirates' faithful by slugging two homers into Greenberg's Garden as the Pirates beat the Reds 12-11.

But it was a long fly ball that made my dad a Wally Westlake fan. Someone drove a ball to deep right field. Wally gave chase and leaped over the rope to snag it. In the process, he also knocked my grandfather to the ground. After tossing the ball in, Wally helped Elmer to his feet and asked if he was okay. From that day on, my dad became a Wally Westlake fan!

For the longest time, on my dad's birthday, it had been a tradition for me to give my father a brand new Steelers' cap along with a six-pack of his favorite beer. My dad would proudly wear his new cap, and then the two of us would disappear into the basement to talk sports while drinking the beer.

For his seventieth birthday, I wanted to do something special. Since I am an avid collector of baseball autographs, I decided to give my father a ball autographed by Wally Westlake. So, I found my copy of *The Baseball Autograph Collector's Handbook* by Jack Smalling, and looked for Wally's address. Upon finding it, I wrote him a letter asking if he could sign a baseball wishing my dad a happy birthday. Later that week, I received an envelope from Sacramento, California. Inside was a note that simply read, "Send me the ball." It was signed W.W., so I sent a ball immediately. A week later the autographed ball arrived with the inscription "Happy Birthday Bob Sr., Wally Westlake!"

I bought a plastic cube to put the ball in. I was pretty excited and could not wait to give my father his present. When we arrived at my parents' house, I placed my gift on the coffee table. When it came time to hand out presents, I quickly grabbed mine to hand to my father. Needless to say, after opening it, my dad became speechless. His eyes filled up with tears. It was the first time I ever saw that. The baseball meant as much to him as it did to me. The game was an important bond between my father and me. I am forever grateful to Wally Westlake for the part he played in my relationship with my father.

Needless to say, I also became a big fan.

A couple of years later, my dad's health took a turn for the worse. Since I wrote biographies for the Society of American Baseball Research (SABR), I decided to write one on Wally. I did it mainly for my father but I also wanted to learn more about my father's childhood hero, the man who quietly became a part of my life.

I poured through the archives of several newspapers to learn about Westlake's career, I also wanted to learn more about him personally. So, I wrote Wally a letter asking if we could talk. A week went by before an envelope from Sacramento, California arrived in the mailbox. Wally agreed to speak but added the following, "Just remember there is a time difference. Call after twelve-noon my time, I need to feed the chickens." He included his telephone number, so I called him up. He seemed to get a kick out of talking with me. We spoke for close to an hour. When our conversation came to an end, he said to me, "Hurte, I really like talking with you. If you feel like shooting the bull about baseball again, give me a call!"

When my dad became seventy-five, I decided to do something special for his birthday again. I asked Wally if he could wish my father a happy birthday. He was more than happy to do that! So I called Wally up from my parents' home so he could wish my father a happy birthday. That afternoon when I informed my dad that someone was on the phone for him, at first he seemed annoyed. But after a few magical moments, I began to see a fifteen-year-old boy sitting in my father's chair as he talked to his childhood hero. Dad and Wally spoke for nearly half an hour, a lot longer than the day they met on April 18, 1947.

My father passed away in 2011. I miss talking about baseball with him. "Unfortunately, I no longer have his childhood hero to speak with. Wally died in 2019."

My dad's birthday present on his 70th birthday

Chapter 11

T-Ball: Children's Initiation to Baseball

S ociety often overlooks the importance of early influences in a person's life. The positive or negative influences on a young child during their formative years can have a profound effect on their whole life. When I give keynote presentations I often make the bold statement "I know what the best music in the world is!" I am convinced that when people hear this statement they quietly ask themselves "What does this old guy know about the best music?" However, when I tell the audience that "The best music in the world is the music that you heard when you were between the ages of 10 and 20!" they suddenly realize that I know what I am talking about. The music that you heard when you had your first successes and disappointments in life, your first romantic crush, your first kiss, your first heartbreak, etc. stays with you for the rest of your life. The same can be said about a person's introduction to playing the game of baseball. The early introduction of children to baseball is one of the main reasons that baseball has remained such a popular sport in many homes around the world. In this chapter, Bob talks about the importance of T-ball as an introduction of the sport to millions of young people.

I grew up in Central New Jersey during the nineteen sixties, and I played T-ball. Forty years later, I ended up coaching my son's T-ball team. When I played, it was considered a new alteration to the game of baseball. Some parents have likened T-ball to watching paint dry! But if you were to ask a child who plays the game, he would consider it one of the happiest experiences in his life. No one can place a price tag on seeing your young child play this game, because they have yet to be tainted by the world that surrounds us. If a child never plays another sport after T-ball, he or she will be supplied with memories that will be cherished for a lifetime! This might be the only time that a game is played strictly for fun. Sure, skill sets begin forming, but it's the social skills that are important.

Everybody wants to take credit for a good thing. The invention of T-ball is no exception. There is a lot of controversy about who actually invented it.

For instance, in 1960, John Zarea claimed to have invented the game of "Tee ball" on the Seymour Johnson Air Force Base in North Carolina. He considered the game's invention to be one of his greatest accomplishments. Forty years ago, John was a youth activities leader with the Air Force; he developed the simple game involving a batting tee. Initially, its purpose was to give kids between the ages of 5-7 an opportunity to bat without being intimidated by a thrown ball. Instead, children learned to swing level at a ball perched on top of a batting tee. (Professional batters still use tees to correct their swing.)

With the aid of his personal computer Zareas recently learned that others have made similar claims about inventing the game. In fact, there was a physician that claimed that he invented T-ball. This really bothered John. "I don't want to be made out to feel I'm a liar."

The 1965 publication of his copyrighted tee-ball rule book help support his claim as the game's true inventor. It cost him a whopping $20.00 to publish it. A copy of this rule book resides somewhere at the National Baseball Hall of Fame in Cooperstown, N.Y. His invention of the game is also mentioned in his military service records.[89]

To add more credence, the administration of George H.W. Bush, nominated him for a "Presidential Point of Light" for the creation of the game. Zareas is proud to claim, "I never took a dime from the sport."[90]

---

89   "Obituary: John Zareas," Dailey Sun, November 29, 2001
90   Ibid.

Dr. Dayton Hobbs also claimed to have invented the game. Hobbs was a thirty-eight-year-old elementary school principal in Baghdad, Florida. His game was geared for 14 and 15-year-old boys that played a game that involved them hitting a ball off of a tee. Hobbs felt that it would be the perfect game for players that had the desire to play but lacked the physical development or ability to play "real baseball."

In 1970, decades after his rules were published; Dr. Hobbs was given a patent on the name of Tee ball. His application met all the stringent requirements for approval and won him recognition as the originator of the game. He also won the patent on the four-ounce bright orange official tee-ball baseball. In Hobbs' Official Tee Ball Rule Book, he reminds us that it is "Nothing more than a game of children's baseball." Hobbs admonishes managers and coaches not to put pressure on children, but instead attempts to teach them to play the game to the best of their ability while enjoying it.

Hobbs demonstrated his diplomacy concerning the argument over who invented the game, "I've never made any claim. I don't argue with them. I know when we did it. If someone did it before, it doesn't matter."[91]

A third person also claimed to be the game's inventor; Jerry Sacharski, who was located up north in Albion, Michigan. Records claim that he invented it in 1956. The purpose was to teach the basics: throwing, catching, swinging the bat and running the bases. Mr. Sacharski's game was not called Tee ball but instead, "Pee Wee Baseball." The dimensions of his playing field were bases 60 feet apart. Fielders had to step within circles that were drawn around the bases to make an out. His game did not include a catcher or a pitcher, just an adjustable batting tee.[92]

The one thing that they all tend to agree on – it was about children playing and having fun doing it!

---

91 Ibid.

92 T-ball has an inventor that reluctantly owns up to it," by Tom Hoffarth, LA News, March 7, 2009

While we might never know for sure who created the game, what we do know is that a former Little Leaguer and a President of our country, supported the game of Tee-ball. Former President Georg W. Bush (#43) has chosen Little League International Baseball as the administrator for the South Lawn Tee Ball games held at the White House each year. As a youngster, President Bush played Little League baseball while growing up in Midland Texas during the 1950s. President Bush claimed that those days are among the fondest of his childhood. He is the first Little Leaguer to graduate to rise to our nation's presidency! Each year an estimated 2.2 million youngsters play Tee-ball

All I know is that when I coached T-ball I was always surrounded by a lot of smiling, happy children.

Chapter 12

Connie Mack Stadium:
My First Baseball Game

Many people remember their first baseball game. Their love for the sport can be traced to their very first experience in a ball park with one or more people that they respected. For many people, this experience is special because they remember the size of the stadium, the excitement of the crowd, the players in their fancy uniforms, the tasty hot dogs or something else. In this chapter, Bob describes his first baseball game.

Like most of us, there have been several firsts in my life, such as my first kiss, first bicycle, or the first time I drove a car, etc. ...

I can remember the first time I ever fell in love. It was on July 31, 1965; the place, Connie Mack Stadium in Philadelphia, Pa. It still feels like yesterday. Everything, I mean everything, opened up in front of my eyes as I walked down the steep stairs of the Connie Mack Stadium bleacher seats. Slipping out of the shadows, a glorious sight appeared before my very own eyes. There laid a manicured blanket of emerald green grass, which was punctuated by the smell of popcorn and hot dogs permeating the air, the sound of baseballs careening off of wooden bats, the echo of vendors hawking peanuts and Cracker Jacks. Like Ray Liotta, the actor who played Shoeless Joe Jackson in *A Field of Dreams*, I asked myself, "Is this Heaven?"

I was eight years old and my grandfather took me to my first baseball game as we rode to Philadelphia in an old yellow school bus.

Now that I think of it, I don't believe my Pop Pop was a big baseball fan; but no question that he was a big fan of his grandson.

This day could not have happened without a man named Barney Neesen, who is also a special person in my life. Barney owned the local toy store in Bridgewater, New Jersey where I grew up. Barney's Toy Center was more than just a toy store; its shelves were not just packed with toys but with dreams. When I see someone wearing the t-shirt, "Life is Baseball," I see Barney Neesen. Barney's involvement with youth baseball occurred after he learned about a lack of fields for the kids to play on; so he cleared out the woodlot from his backyard and built a baseball field. It was just like in the movie *Field of Dreams* before there was such a movie. But this was not an ordinary ball field. Barney built a miniature version of his beloved Ebbetts Field. It had a large, hand-operated scoreboard in center field, dugouts made of cinder blocks along the baselines, a tin outfield fence painted with advertisements and a clubhouse. On each foul pole were speakers that played a scratchy version of the "Star Spangled Banner" before the start of every game. Many of us claim to love baseball; instead, Barney Neesen showed how much he did!

Each year Barney arranged a bus trip for young baseball players to watch a major league baseball game. He invited all of the kids that played for him to go, at his treat. Barney was not rich but money did not seem to matter to Barney. He was unselfish that way. I think that he enjoyed seeing our happiness.

At the time I was trying to understand the game of baseball. I had just started playing the game. It was also a time that I began collecting baseball cards. Since my Dad was from Pittsburgh, I automatically became a Pirates fan. But since we lived between New York and Philadelphia, I knew more about the Mets and the Phillies.

Baseball cards were my dear friends. So, when I saw the players in person, it was like seeing life size baseball cards. I had cards for some of the players I saw that day; players like Jack Fisher, Ron Swoboda, Roy McMillan, Johnny Lewis, Jerry Grote from the Mets and Chris Short, Cookie Rojas, Richie Allen and Clay Darymple of the Phils.

In fact, I can still remember who was pitching that day. It was Jack Fisher,[93] the Mets ace versus Chris Short of the Phils. I also saw rookie sensation Richie Allen play third base and Tony Taylor, who hit a home run. There were two of my favorites, Ron Swoboda and Jim Hickman. The Mets won that day, and Jack Fisher was the winning pitcher.

Flash-forward to twenty years later, I was playing in a men's softball league in Palmer, Pennsylvania. After our games, the team went to "Fat Jack's" a local drinking establishment. One night, my team was sitting around a table drinking pitchers of beer. The topic of the first baseball game that we went to came up.

When it became my turn, I reminisced about seeing the Mets and Phillies at Ol' Connie Mack Stadium and how Jack Fisher beat Chris Short.

Then one of my teammates said, "Why don't you go tell him?"

I looked at him like he was half crazy, "Tell who?"

"Jack Fisher; who do you think owns this place? That's him over at the bar."

I was shocked. Sure enough, there was a man standing at the bar, who looked like he could be an older version of Jack Fisher. So, I grabbed my beer and sauntered over to this man. I tapped him on the shoulder to inform him, "You pitched against Chris Short in the first baseball game that I ever went to."

Jack Fisher turned around.

"Oh yeah, did I win?"

I nodded.

He smiled, "Well that was a rarity."

Wow! I met Jack Fisher. The man who won the first game that I ever attended. How many people get such an opportunity?

So, you are probably thinking that the story ends here, right? I am now the proud owner of a ball personally signed from Jack Fisher. And when people come to my house I like to show it to them. Then

---

93   https://www.baseball-reference.com/players/f/fisheja01.shtml

follow up by proudly telling them that Jack Fisher won the first game that I ever saw played. Everyone thinks that it is pretty cool.

So you might think this is the end of the story, and it might have been, if I did not decide to write an article about this experience. When I researched it on the Internet, I made an alarming discovery – not everything was exactly the way I remembered it. First off, the game was played in 1965, not 1964, although I was right about Jack Fisher facing Chris Short, and I did see Richie Allen…but there other facts that were different.

After locating some newspapers with the box score, I learned that the game played on July 31, 1965: Chris Short gave up three runs to the Mets, three runs in the first on a Charlie Smith three run blast. Smith would hit 16 that year after hitting 20 in 1964, but then Short pitched shutout ball the rest of the game until being lifted for a pinch hitter in the ninth. Jack Fisher would also pitch nine innings. He gave up a run in the first, another in the second and a third one in the fourth inning, which was a solo home run by Dick Stuart. That night, I also discovered that Jack Fisher was not the game's winner.

Actually, the winner was Gary Kroll,[94] who pitched a scoreless tenth inning. Then the Mets scored a run in the top of the eleventh. Pinch hitter Johnny Stephenson doubled home Johnny Lewis from second with two out. Stephenson would come to bat only 126 times that year, accumulating twenty-six hits, five of them being doubles. His game winning hit was off of Jack Baldschum; ironically, he hit another game winning single off of Baldschum a week earlier.[95] Reliever Gordie Richardson got Cookie Rojas to ground out to third for the save.

Although Jack Fisher did not get the win at the first game I went to, his ball still belongs in my display case. He has two other distinctions; he was the pitcher who gave up Ted Williams' last hit, a homerun in 1960. He also surrendered Roger Maris' 60th homerun in 1961 to tie Babe Ruth.

---

94   https://www.baseball-reference.com/players/k/krollga01.shtml

95   https://www.baseball-reference.com/boxes/PHI/PHI196507310.shtml

So, Gary Kroll won the first game I went to; it was also the last game that he won in the major leagues. He would finish 1965 with a 6-6 record.

Gary now lives in Tulsa, Oklahoma. Since that Jack Fisher did not win the first game I ever went to, I needed to get an autographed ball from the man who did. I wrote a letter to Gary Kroll to explain my dilemma and asked if he'd autograph a ball from me?

He sent me back a note on a postcard with a picture of him from his playing days. It read:

"Bob,

Thanks for writing to me. It's always great to hear from a baseball lifer. It sounds like we were like the same person at age eight. Connie Mack Stadium, the crack of the ball hitting the bat, the fans, I remember.

I go out to watch a few innings of the Tulsa "AA" team once in a while. The things I remember now are when I see a player throw a ball. I remember the feel of the ball rolling off my fingers. When I see a player running, I remember the feel of my spikes digging into the earth. I remember the feel of the bat hitting the ball … wonderful memories.

Send the Ball."

The story does not end here. I sent Gary a Little League ball. About a week later, a package arrived from Tulsa, Oklahoma. I opened it up to find the ball signed by Gary:

"Connie Mack Stadium, Mets vs. Phillies, July 31ˢᵗ, 1965, Gary Kroll."

What a nice surprise! Once again, I was able to display a ball signed by the person who won the first baseball game I attended.

Then I noticed something odd about the ball. Gary did not sign the ball that I sent; he must have purchased a National League one and sent it instead of the Little League one I had sent him.

I guess that Gary realized how special it was to me (and to him).

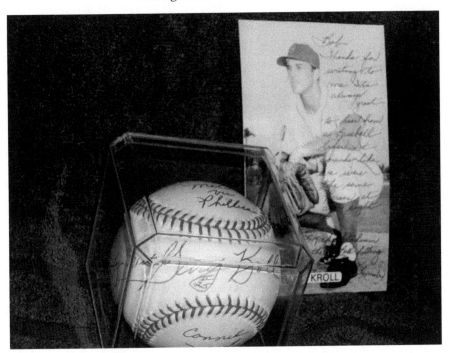

**Autographed ball and picture that I
received from Gary Kroll**

Chapter 13

Monte Irvin and the Lost Baseball

*M*ost people do not remember their first exposure to some form of racial *discrimination. Virtually everyone has seen prejudice because of a person's race in action. However, this experience is usually not remembered unless you are the victim of the discrimination. In this chapter, Bob discusses his introduction to racial discrimination.*

"Baseball is a Special Place Where Fathers and Sons Come to Meet"

I can still remember a car ride with my father when I was nine years old. It was a night that introduced me to my lifelong passion for baseball. We attended a baseball banquet at Rutgers University that featured Al Downing, Jeff Torborg, Tom Gorman, and Monte Irvin, all of them from New Jersey[96]. Everything aside from baseball seemed irrelevant. More importantly, it was a special "one on one" time with my father, the type of bonding between a nine-year-old and his father. To me, baseball is not just a game, but an attitude, or a way of life. Baseball is a special place where fathers and sons come to meet!

Back in the nineteen sixties, my dad moonlighted as a bartender at the Plainfield Country Club. Well, one of the country club members gave him his tickets for the banquet. Honestly, I think that my dad was

---

96 "Monte Irvin," by Larry Hogan, SABR Bio Project.

more excited about going to this event than I was. When I became a father, I can remember similar times that I got more excited than my kids about something. I can remember dragging them somewhere under the pretense that it was for them, when in actuality it was for me. I think that describes that night at the Rutgers University banquet.

There were four speakers at the event: The first guy to speak was Al Downing, a native of Trenton, New Jersey, and a left-handed pitcher for the Yankees. He appeared in three games during the 1964 World Series. He pitched well but lost his only start. Actually, Al was a decent pitcher in 1964. He was 13-8 with an earned run average of 3.47 during his rookie season. He won 123 games by the end of his career. Although, he is most remembered for the homerun he allowed to Hank Aaron., it was Aaron's 715th, passing Babe Ruth, at the time, making Aaron the all-time homerun leader.

The next speaker was Jeff Torborg, who originally grew up in Westfield, New Jersey, and played catcher for Rutgers University. He was an All-American there in 1963. He went on to play for the Los Angeles Dodgers, spending most of his career as a backup to Johnny Roseboro. Torborg was known as a very good handler of pitchers during his career. He caught three no-hitters in his career, including Sandy Koufax's perfect game, Bill Singer's only no-hitter and one of the seven thrown by Nolan Ryan. When his career was over, he went on to become the manager for the Cleveland Indians, Chicago the White Sox and the New York Mets.

The third person on the panel was Tom Gorman. He was an umpire well-known for his sense of humor. His barbs with Leo "The Lip" Durocher were legendary. Many of his stories would later be documented in his hilarious memoir entitled *Three and Two*, which was written in 1979. Gorman was probably the most entertaining speaker on the dais that evening.

The last speaker was a distinguished-looking African American gentleman. I whispered to my father, "Who is that guy?" My dad responded, "That's Monte Irvin; he played for the New York Giants baseball team, but his best years were when he played in the old Negro League."

This, of course, did not make any sense to me. "What do you mean, Negro League?"

My father explained that there was a time when players of color could not play in the major leagues.

"So you mean to tell me that there were separate leagues based on color?"

Dad nodded, adding that there was a league just for blacks even after Jackie Robinson broke the "color barrier" in 1947. Negro League baseball would eventually end in 1960.

As a nine-year-old kid, I found this difficult to understand, I mean, there were black people on the baseball cards I collected. So why would anyone want to play in a league that did not have baseball cards?

My father explained that there was a time when people of color did not have a choice.

Anyway, it was an eventful night. I was especially proud when my dad got up from his seat and asked Jeff Torborg a question. My father asked Torborg if he thought Clemente or Koufax should get the MVP award in 1966, especially since there was the "Cy Young Award" for pitchers. Torborg answered that Koufax was also the most valuable player for the Dodgers in 1966, although Clemente had an incredible year. Clemente won the "Most Valuable Player" award in 1966.

Monte Irvin chimed in by sharing that he remembered Clemente as a youngster when he (Irvin) played in Puerto Rico. I would later learn that Irvin was Clemente's favorite player. (Ironically, Roberto and Monte were inducted in the Hall of Fame the same year.) But the highlight of the evening was when my number was called as a winner for one of the door prizes. I won an autographed ball with signatures from all four men! I had to go up on stage to collect it and shook hands with each of the speakers. When I got home, I proudly displayed it on top of the family's television! In those days that was a place of honor in our household.

Shortly after attending the banquet, I was out playing with my buddies at Barney's Field and we eventually lost the ball we were playing with in the woods. When you are nine years old, nothing could be worse than losing a baseball. For one thing, they were hard to replace. During the nineteen sixties, there was not a sporting goods store on every corner like there is today. You were lucky if your town had just one. So a lot of work went into getting a baseball. Most of the time when you lost your ball, the game was essentially over. That day I wanted to impress the bigger kids, you know, be a hero. I proudly informed them that I had a ball at home. Like Scotty Smalls from *Sandlot*, I got on my bicycle and peddled home as fast as I could! I grabbed the ball from on top of the TV and rushed back to the field.

The fate of my autographed baseball shared similarities to the one Scotty Smalls lost in the 1993 film, except my ball did not fall in the hands or mouth of a large junkyard dog. Instead, I lost my baseball in the woods at Barney's Field before the movie ever came out. Not only did I lose my autographed ball but the game ended!

While my experience did not inspire that movie, it is fun to think that it could have.

That evening when my father found out what had happened to the ball, he looked really disappointed. To him, that ball was more than just an autographed ball. It was a memory between a father and a son. I will always have that memory, but unfortunately, it is not the same as having the ball …

Years later, a friend of mine at AT&T asked if I knew who Monte Irvin was. I told him my story. He asked if I wanted something autographed by him. My friend worked with Irvin's daughter. So now, there is a copy of *The Biographical Encyclopedia of the Negro Leagues* on my bookshelf with a forward written by Monte Irvin, and you probably guessed, it now has Monte Irvin's autograph!

Section IV
The Influence of
Segregation in Baseball

Chapter 14

A League That They Called Their Own
(The Creation of the Negro Leagues)

It is interesting that there is a great deal of discussion about inducting admitted or suspected steroid users into the Baseball Hall of Fame. Many people believe that it is not fair to validate the statistics of players who had an unfair advantage over those players that did not use performance enhancing drugs. Others suggest that these players be inducted into the Hall of Fame with an asterisk. It is interesting that there is little discussion about including an asterisk next to every Hall of Famer who played when Black players were not allowed to play in the major leagues. These players did not have to face all of the best baseball players in the world because a certain group of extraordinary players were excluded from the game. We are not suggesting that an asterisk be placed next to these players' names. However, we want true baseball purists to understand that a level playing field was an illusion for many years. It is important to recognize all of the influences when examining baseball history. In this chapter, Bob discusses the amazing influence of Negro League Baseball on the sport and on society.

I was confused when my father told me about the Negro Leagues. I became aware of racism at a young age. Americans began playing baseball around the late eighteen-hundreds, but racism is much older. They played the sport while in the military, at college or on their employer's teams. Before you knew it, professional teams were formed. At first, some of them were integrated, although blacks often did not play on them. Maybe one or two, like Moses Fleetwood Walker, his brother Weldy or Bud Fowler.

When the Movie *42* came out about Jackie Robinson in April 2012; it caused many movie viewers to believe that Jackie was the first black to play baseball. He was actually the fourth.

The first black to play in the majors was Moses Fleetwood Walker. He was born in Mt. Pleasant, Ohio, a village a few miles across the Ohio River from Wheeling, West Virginia. When he was born, Mt. Pleasant was a stop on the Underground Railroad. Ironically, Walker became the first Negro player in the major leagues. He played for Toledo of the American Association (AA) in 1884.[97] The American Association was considered a major league.

One afternoon in Baltimore, more than 3,000 curious people turned out to view the spectacle of a Negro playing with whites. A local newspaper was pleased to report how, "Every good play by him (Walker) was loudly applauded."[98]

While there were many positive feelings, negative feelings also existed. Integration had not yet been accepted in our country yet.

It was more common to read something similar to a letter sent from a local resident to the Toledo manager Charlie Morton, which read:

"We the undersigned do hereby warn you not put in Walker, the Negro catcher, the evenings you play Richmond as we could mention the names of 75+ determined men who have sworn to mob Walker if he comes on the grounds in a baseball suite. We hope you will listen to our word of warning, so alone can prevent. That there will be no trouble but if you do not, there will certainly be. We only write this to prevent much bloodshed."

Moses Fleetwood Walker would be released after the season; but not because of his skin color. Instead, the reason – Walker was prone to injury. The Toledo baseball club released the following statement:

---

97   'Fleet Walker," John R. Husnam, SABR Bio Project

98   *Only the Ball was White* (Peterson, Robert, Oxford University Press, NY, NY, 1970) 23

"To his (Walker) fine work last year, much of the success of the Toledo Club was due, as none will deny. This year, however, he has been extremely unfortunate having met several accidents which kept him disabled... by his fine, gentlemanly deportment, he made hosts of friends who will regret to learn that he is no long a member of the club."[99]

While Fleetwood Moses Walker endured racism from fans and the teams that he played against, it was actually his own team members that ultimately drove him out.

In many circles, it is popular to blame Judge Kenesaw Mountain Landis for baseball's segregation. While he obviously played a significant role, it was the game's first star that set the tone.

Cap Anson, a MLB first baseman, was regarded as baseball's greatest players at the time. He played in a record 27 consecutive baseball seasons. There was no debate about his playing ability or his bigotry! Anson's popularity was able to singlehandedly force Negroes out of organized baseball. Anson was fond of referring to people of color as "niggers."

Anson's attitude was prevalent among the National Association of Base Ball Players (NABBP), which was formed in 1871.[100] The association never had a written rule forbidding Negroes from playing in the "white" major leagues, but due to racism, there was no need to. The white owners' "gentleman's agreement" existed among major league owners. This agreement greatly helped to form the professional Negro baseball league.

"White Major League Baseball League Owners' 'Gentlemen's Agreement' Excluded Black Players"

There can be no denying that Cap Anson prompted the exclusion of blacks from playing professional baseball with whites. Historically, we cannot properly discuss the existence of Negro

---

99   Ibid., 23
100   *"Cap Anson," Fleitz, David, Society of American Baseball Research- BioProject*

League baseball without mentioning Sol White. Sol was actually playing second base as a nineteen-year-old when he witnessed Cap Anson stomping off the field rather than playing against a Negro, in effect, slamming the door shut on integrated baseball!

Thus, many baseball historians consider Sol White the GRANDFATHER of the Negro Leagues![101]

White began his professional baseball career in 1886 after barnstorming with the Bellaire Globes before playing on the integrated Wheeling Green Stockings of the Ohio State League. Sol was also a theology major at Wilberforce University in Xenia, Ohio. The school was founded in 1856, named after an abolitionist and was supported by the African Methodist Episcopal Church.

Sol White was also known as "King" Solomon. Noted Negro League historian John Holway felt that Sol White was the most influential figure in black baseball during the first decade of black baseball. Not only was he a sensational player from 1887-1902, he was also a very successful manager during the period of 1902-12. Sol even played in the white minor leagues for five years. During those integrated years he batted .356 while playing in 159 games, scoring 174 runs while swiping 54 bases.

During the years from 1902-07, White and his Philadelphia Giants were extremely successful. The Philadelphia Giants won several black championships, while also posting many of those wins over white teams. In 1902, many considered the Philadelphia Giants to be the most powerful black team of all time. Records showed that Philadelphia played 680 games between 1902-06 and won 507 of them. In 1903, they played in the first ever colored World Series against the Cuban X-Giants; Rube Foster won 4 games for the X-Giants. In 1904, Foster pitched for Sol White and the Philadelphia Giants won.

The Giants won an unheard of 134 and only lost 21 for the 1905 season. Since there was no league championship format, they

---

101 "Our Game," (Alexander, Charles C.Henry Holt + Company, NY, NY, 1991) 22-27, 32

challenged a team with the second best record to play a World Series, but the team failed to show up. The following year they finished with a 108-31 record, making the same challenge and receiving the same response.[102]

In his book, *The History of Colored Baseball*, White advised Negro players not to "showboat" or "clown around." He looked forward to the day when black and white players would play together. Sol White was 79, when he saw his dream come true as Jackie Robinson debuted with the Brooklyn Dodgers. Eight years later, Sol White died penniless in Harlem, New York. Posthumously, years later, Sol was elected to baseball's Hall of Fame in 2006 by the special Negro League Committee.[103]

Then there was Rube Foster who was known as the "FATHER" of Negro League baseball. He was born in Calvert, Texas on September 17, 1879. Calvert was a small hamlet located somewhere between Dallas and Houston. Andrew Foster quit school during the eighth grade and ran off to play baseball in Fort Worth, Texas, devoting his life to the game.

During his playing career, Foster pitched for the Cuban X-Giants, Philadelphia Giants, Leland Giants, and the Chicago American Giants.[104] For the era, he was a large man, 6'2" and 200 pounds. Rube pitched well against several white major league pitchers who became enshrined in the Hall of Fame (HOF), like his namesake Rube Waddell, Cy Young, and "Three Fingers" Brown.

During 1905, Foster was credited with an incredible 51-4 season. He was complimented by two HOF notables. They were Frank Chance of the famous "Tinker to Evers to Chance" fame, who said, "He (Foster) is the most finished product I've ever seen in the pitcher's box." Pittsburgh Pirates legend Honus Wagner, an original

---

102 Ibid.

103 *"Blackball Stars: Negro League Pioneers,"* (Holway, John B.Carroll & Graf Publishers, NY,NY, 1988) 1

104 "Rube Foster," by Timothy Odzer, SABR Bio Project

inductee to the HOF also said, "One of the smoothest pitchers of all time."[105]

Rube Foster formed the Chicago American Giants that included Negro League stars such as John Henry Lloyd, and Homerun Johnson. Their 1910 team played to an astounding 128-6 record. It has been rumored that legendary Giants manager John McGraw told Foster that he would gladly take nine of his players if they were white. McGraw purportedly asked Foster to teach Christy Mathewson how to throw his screw ball. Foster retired from active play after 1917, and concentrated on being a baseball executive and Negro League pioneer.

In 1919, Rube Foster set his sights on challenging the "color" line. He even put together a strong, well-financed plan for breaking the racial line. Rube met with Judge Kenesaw Mountain Landis to present his proposal. His plan was to put one all-black team in each of the American and National Leagues. Since whites would not need to play next to blacks, Foster felt that it enhanced desirability, and would hopefully increase Landis' acceptance of the plan. In addition, Negro teams would also stay at black hotels.

Foster's idea was rejected, which ushered in the concept of an all-black league.

Foster made his revolutionary decision during the winter of 1919. He called together the owners of the best black baseball clubs in the Midwest, and representatives of the African American press, including a young lawyer named Elisha Scott to propose the Negro National League.[106]

Elisha Scott is an interesting participant in the formation of the new league. His legal background was necessary in drafting the league's constitution and bylaws. From Topeka, Kansas, Scott would later be known for the landmark case of Brown vs. the Board of Education.

---

105 *Ibid., Holway, 12*
106 Ibid., Holway, 21

So it was on February 13, 1920, at a YMCA in Kansas City, that Andrew "Rube" Foster's vision of a Negro Baseball League came to fruition. Its charter members were: the Chicago American Giants, Cincinnati Stars, Indianapolis ABC's, Kansas City Monarchs, Saint Louis Giants, along with the Atlantic City Bacharachs and the Hillsdale team from Philadelphia. Foster became president and treasurer of the league. The other owners were upset because Foster refused to stop managing the Chicago American Giants while presiding over the league. The other owners felt it gave Chicago an unfair advantage. While it is hard to say whether it did, the American Giants won 5 NNL titles and two Negro League World Series championships during the 1920s.[107]

In 1926, Foster suffered a stroke, which some people blamed on the stress of running the league. The Father of Negro League Baseball was confined to an asylum for the remainder of his life and died on December 9, 1930. Because of his death, and the loss of his leadership, the league folded in 1931.

Gus Greenlee, a Pittsburgh bar owner, picked up the NNL's masthead in 1933. He became a dominant force behind the league. Greenlee made his money from bootlegging, running numbers, owning the Crawford Grill and Pittsburgh Crawfords baseball team. Many thought that the Crawfords were the best team in Negro League baseball. It featured legends like: Satchel Paige, Josh Gibson, Cool Papa Bell, Judy Johnson, Oscar Charleston and Buck Leonard. All of them are now enshrined in baseball's Hall of Fame. Greenlee organized another version of the Negro National League in 1933, which operated from 1933 until 1949.[108] Gus Greenlee suffered a heart attack in 1946 at the age of fifty and spent six months at the Veterans Hospital in Aspinwall, Pennsylvania in 1950. Greenlee died on July 7, 1952, while at home.

---

107 Ibid, Peterson, 84
108 Bankes, James, *The Pittsburgh Crawfords: The Lives and Times of Black Baseball's Most Exciting team* (Dubuque, Ia,William C. Brown Publishers, 1991) 28

Most historians feel that the Negro Leagues died in 1950 or 1951 because it could no longer offer quality baseball, although its actual last season was in 1960.[109]

In Monte Irvin's forward for *The Biographical Encyclopedia of The Negro Baseball Leagues*, he stated, "If it were not for the Negro Leagues, there would not have been a place for black Americans to develop their baseball skills properly."[110]

---

109 Ibid., Alexander, 21

110 Riley, James A., *The Biographical Encyclopedia of the Negro Leagues* (NY, NY, Carroll & Graf Publishers, 1994) xiii

Chapter 15

Jackie Robinson and the Great Experiment

People do not give enough credit to those owners, managers and players who had the courage and fortitude to break through barriers of racism and hatred. Most of us do not have any sense of the pain and suffering that Jackie Robinson had to endure as the first Black major league baseball player. Somehow he was able to become one of the best players in baseball in spite of these obstacles. It is extremely important to celebrate Jackie Robinson's accomplishments. However, it is also essential that we recognize those White people who risked their reputation and livelihood by using their influence to do the right thing. If we take the time to recognize these people perhaps others will be inspired to risk their livelihood to fight racism wherever it raises its ugly head. In this chapter, Bob provides an overview of the introduction of the first Black player into major league baseball.

When the movie *42: The Jackie Robinson Story* came out, a new audience was exposed to an important Civil Rights story. Next to Lincoln's Emancipation Proclamation, Jackie Robinson's debut with the Brooklyn Dodgers helped tear down society's racial barriers.

Integration was long overdue by 1947. Before Jackie's signing, the last player of color was Weldy Walker who played for Toledo sixty-three years before in 1884. Weldy's brother Fleetwood was the first African American to ever play professional baseball.

Up to that time, the absence of African Americans playing baseball had been greatly ignored. In fact, Commissioner Kenesaw Mountain Landis enjoyed bragging that there was no written rule preventing them from playing. What Landis conveniently failed to acknowledge is the secret agreement among the baseball owners that excluded non-Caucasians from playing.[111]

Baseball's first commissioner Landis died on November 25, 1944. Shortly afterward on April 24, 1945, when the baseball owners elected U.S. Senator Albert Benjamin "Happy" Chandler as Landis' successor, he became the new commissioner by a unanimous vote. The color of baseball was about to change; a four-man commission was formed to investigate the possibilities of racial integration.

Branch Rickey sensed the growing equal rights movement in the United States. Rickey knew that A. Philip Randolph, the President of the Brotherhood of Railway Porters union had threatened a march on Washington in June of 1941 if President Franklin Roosevelt did sign Executive Order 8802, which banned discrimination in government hiring.[112] He was also aware of the concerns of race riots in New York City, Philadelphia, and Detroit. The New York state legislature passed the Quinn-Ives act, which banned discrimination in hiring. Then a committee was formed by New York City's Mayor Fiorillo LaGuardia to investigate hiring practices in baseball. It established a committee to push the Yankees, Giants, and Dodgers to sign black players. It was called "End Jim Crow in Baseball Committee." It consisted of Larry MacPhail, Branch Rickey and the African American sports writer Sam Lacy, along with Joseph Rainey, an African American magistrate from Philadelphia. Rainey also had experience as an administrator in the Negro Leagues.

Unfortunately, the committee found it hard to schedule meetings due to Lee MacPhail's disinterest concerning the committee's meetings. His attitude made it impossible for all members to get together.[113] Rickey grew impatient with his former friend, eventually announcing that he was going to let nature takes its own course. At first, Sam Lacy

111 Rampersad, Arnolo, *Jackie Robinson: A Biography* (NY,NY, Alfred P. Knopf, 1997) 120

112 Lowenfish, Lee, *Branch Rickey: Baseball's Ferocious Gentleman* (Lincoln, Ne, University of Nebraska Press, 2007) 350

113 Ibid, Lowenfish, 377-78

was not sure what Rickey meant, but it quickly became obvious that the Brooklyn boss's intention was to integrate baseball.

Over the past three to four years, Branch Rickey had been secretively scouting minorities, which gave him a jump on the other teams. He kept his advanced scouting program quiet. At first, Rickey considered the Latin American countries a prime source of talent. He was very interested in Silvio Garcia, a shortstop he saw playing for the New York Cubans in the American Negro league. So, Rickey sent Tom Greenwade, one of his top professional scouts to Mexico to evaluate him. When Greenwade asked him what he would do if an opponent made racial slurs to him, Garcia replied, "I'd kill him!" This ended Greenwade's evaluation of the Cuban shortstop.[114]

Another player considered for breaking the color line was Monte Irvin of the Newark Eagles. Irvin possessed many of the qualifications that Rickey was looking for. Unfortunately, Monte suffered an injury during the war, one that did not involve bombs or bullets. Irvin's injury was not physical, but a personal struggle to maintain his dignity.

On May 7, 1945, Rickey announced that his Brooklyn organization was forming the Brooklyn Brown Dodgers to become a part of a new six-team Negro League. The League was to be called the USL and they would play a one hundred game schedule with teams in Chicago, Detroit, Pittsburgh, Philadelphia and Toledo. This allowed Rickey to openly evaluate black talent. Rickey sent his key scouts to watch Jackie Robinson.[115]

Rickey's scouts spoke glowingly about Robinson, especially George Sisler, who was impressed with Jackie's speed, along with his passion for the game and athletic intelligence. However, Sisler did not feel Robinson had the arm strength to play shortstop. Wid Matthews, another top evaluator considered Robinson a "hotdog," although noting that Jackie was superb at protecting the plate with two strikes

---

114 "Silvio Garcia," by Joseph Gerard, SABR Bio Project
115 Ibid., Lowenfish, 365

on him. Tom Greenwade, who highly recommended him, felt that he was the best bunter that he ever saw![116]

All of the facts added up to the "Great Experiment!"

The American Heritage Dictionary defines an experiment as a test made to demonstrate a known truth, examine the validity of a hypothesis, or determine the nature of something not yet known.

Branch Rickey's "Great Experiment" could have been hatched in 1903 when Branch Rickey was the student-coach for the baseball team at Ohio Wesleyan University. This was Rickey's often-repeated story about integration, concerning a college player named Charles "Cha" Thomas, his college team's first baseman and best player. When the team played Notre Dame in South Bend, Indiana, the hotel clerk informed Thomas that he could not stay at the same hotel as his team, because he was a Negro. When Rickey informed the clerk that he would share his room with Thomas, the clerk relented begrudgingly. After he finished checking the team in, Branch found Thomas crying and desperately scratching at his arms as if he was trying to scratch off the color of his skin. Rickey always regretted that he had not done more to correct the unfairness.[117]

"Although Acquitted, a Military Tribunal Court Martialled Jackie Robinson for Refusing to Sit in the Back of the Bus."

Mr. Rickey felt that the perfect candidate for integration needed to have both skill and character. Judging from the reports, Jackie had the talent, but Branch needed to be sure about his demeanor. He then asked the notable African American sports writer Wendell Smith of the "Pittsburgh Courier" about Robinson. Smith had followed Robinson's career when he played for the Kansas City Monarchs in the Negro leagues. The sports writer reported that Jackie was a clean living individual. Robinson did not chase women or drink. Rickey

---

116 Ibid., 368
117 Ibid., 355

was also aware of Jackie's military court martial in 1944. The court martial was due to Robinson's refusal to sit in the back of the bus. Mr. Rickey was also aware that Robinson was acquitted. The Dodger owner considered that Jackie's compassion for his race made him the best candidate to break the racial barrier. So in August 1945, Branch moved ahead with his scouting project.[118]

Branch also dispatched Clyde Sukeforth, one of his loyal, top scouts, the only member of Rickey's brain trust who had not seen Jackie play. Sukeforth went to Chicago to see the Monarchs play the Chicago Lincoln Giants. Branch asked him to carefully observe Robinson's arm. Clyde found out that Robinson had an injured arm. Still, Clyde brought Robinson back to Brooklyn, sharing a sleeper car with Jackie. He invited Robinson for breakfast but Jackie preferred to eat with the Pullman porters.[119]

When he dispatched him, Rickey's advice to Clyde was as follows:

"If you like what you see, Clyde, bring him back with you to Brooklyn. If he can't get away from his team, well, maybe I will come out and see him," suggested Rickey.[120]

When Sukeforth introduced Robinson to Branch Rickey he said, "Mr. Rickey, I think he (Jackie) is a Brooklyn kind of player."[121]

Branch shook Jackie's hand and proceeded to learn more about him. He asked Robinson if he had a girlfriend. Which Jackie did, her name was Rachel. He asked if Jackie planned on marrying her, which he was. Mr. Rickey learned that Robinson was a "God Fearing Protestant." He was also happy to learn that Jackie did not drink. Branch asked if Robinson was under contract with the Monarchs, which he was not. The Negro Leagues on the whole did not have formal contracts with players, so they were able to jump from team to team. Then, Mr. Rickey asked Jackie if he knew why Sukeforth

---

118 Ibid., 369
119 "Clyde Sukeforth: The Dodger's Yankee and Branch Rickey's Mine man," by Karl Lindholm, The Baseball Research Journal, Spring, 2014, 33
120 Lowenfish, 371
121 Ibid., 373

brought him back to Brooklyn. Jackie felt the reason was to play for the Brooklyn Brown Dodgers?[122]

"No, that isn't it. I want you to play for the Brooklyn Dodgers organization, possibly starting in Montreal."[123]

Branch continued with his vetting of the Dodgers' first black player. Branch quoted "Life of Christ" by Giovanni Papini.

"But whosoever shall smitten thee on thy right cheek, turn to him the other also."[124]

Jackie informed Branch that he was not afraid of anybody or anything. He asked if Mr. Rickey wanted someone who would not fight back.

To which the Dodger owner replied; "I'm looking for a ball player with guts enough not to fight back!"[125]

On April 15, 1947, Jack Roosevelt Robinson became the first black major league baseball player since Weldy Walker.

Jackie was faced with several challenges during his first season; many of them appeared to be insurmountable, like his Brooklyn Dodger teammates Dixie Walker and Kirby Higbe's Southern, racist heritage. Dixie believed that business at his hardware store in Leeds, Alabama, would be adversely affected if he played with a black man.[126]

Higbe was simply racist; in the past, Higbe bragged openly that he developed his fastball by throwing stones at blacks like he was hunting "small game." Jackie also faced unfair perceptions about a Negro's ability and toughness to play the game at a higher level.

Joe Williams, a popular New York City sports writer wrote that the reason was that, "Blacks have been kept out of big-league ball because as a race, they are very poor players."[127] Unfortunately, Mr. Williams

---

122 Ibid., Rampersad, 126
123 Ibid., 126
124 Ibid., 127
125 Ibid., 375
126 Ibid., Rampersad, 164-65
127 Higbe, Kirby and Quigley, Martin, The High Hard One (Lincoln, Ne., University of Nebraska Press, 1967) 11

expressed the opinion of many pro-segregationist whites, but luckily his opinion was not the prevailing attitude among baseball fans.

Just as the famous poet William Blake wrote "Great things happen when man and mountains meet." Jackie was being sent to meet his mountain.

Jackie Robinson began his trailblazing baseball career with an impressive season by playing with the Montreal Royals of the International League. He hit .349 and stole 48 bases while playing spectacular defense at second base. He was the unanimous choice for the MVP of the International League. Rickey decided that Jackie was ready for Brooklyn. The following year the Dodgers' spring training headquarters was moved to Havana, Cuba. The Dodger boss scheduled a series of exhibitions between Brooklyn and Montreal, hoping to showcase Robinson's talents. Rickey thought that if Jackie's future Dodger teammates could see him play, they would support his promotion.

Dixie Walker was considered the most popular and best player on the Brooklyn club and was known as the "People's cherce." He played a profound role in the "Great Experiment" of 1947. Leo Durocher counted on Walker as a ball player; Rickey also counted on Walker to ease Jackie Robinson's debut into the major league. However, this was a miscalculation by both men. Although Dixie was a Southerner, Branch felt that Walker could judge Robinson on his playing ability and not the color of his skin. Unfortunately, Walker's Southern upbringing did not allow him to see past Robinson's race.

For many Southern players, the connection with their Southern way of life superseded the team they played for. Rickey fully expected animosity from Howie Schultz and Ed Stevens because they would lose their jobs if Robinson was successful. So Rickey was most surprised that Walker was the one most upset about playing with Robinson.

Branch Rickey planned on breaking the color line in 1947, hell or high water, and he methodically laid out his plan. First, he moved Dodger's spring training to Havana, Cuba, feeling that the media exposure would be less than in America. He brought Jackie and the Montreal Royal team down to work out with the Dodgers.

Branch had them travel to Bermuda to play exhibitions with the hope of conditioning the Dodgers to play in front of predominately non-white crowds. While his preparations seemed to go as planned, it was interrupted with an infamous petition by some Dodger players, allegedly led by Dixie Walker that protested playing with Jackie Robinson. This protest was joined by most of the Southerners on the team, such as Bragan, Casey and Higbe, who were joined by Carl Furillo, an impressonable young player from the North. Years later Pee Wee Reese, who became Robinson's closest teammate, said that he saw the petition but did not sign it.

The incident that occurred at the Dodgers' spring training camp in Havana, Cuba, in 1947 was significant on so many levels. The movie (42) did an accurate job depicting the scene. It involved a petition plus a late-night meeting between Leo Durocher and the players. Leo Durocher was a hard-nosed shortstop who enjoyed his best playing years as a member of the "Gas House Gang" with the St. Louis Cardinals during the mid-nineteen thirties. So he did not back down from a confrontation.

"I hear that some of you fellows don't want to play with Robinson and that you have a petition drawn up which many of you are planning to sign. Well boys, you know what you can do with that petition? You can wipe your ass with it!"[128]

Durocher informed them that if Robinson was good enough to play, if he could help them win games, which meant putting money in his pocket, he did not care what color he was. He told them that Robinson might be the first, but not the last. There are many that would follow. They (black players) have talent and will come to play. He warned them that if they did not wake up, they could be out of a job.[129]

While Dixie Walker did not back away from his Deep South roots, he slowly learned to appreciate Robinson as a teammate. In fact,

---

128 Durocher, Leo, and Linn, Ed, *Nice Guys Finish Last* (NY, NY, Simon and Shuster, 1975) 205
129 Ibid.

most of the other Dodgers gained appreciation. Jackie's performance on the field was the first thing that helped change the attitude of his teammates. Then Eddie Stanky, who was born near Philadelphia, Pennsylvania, but had connections below the Mason-Dixon Line, let Jackie know his true feelings; "I want you to know something. You're on this ball club and as far as I'm concerned that makes you one of the twenty-five players on my team. But before I play with you, I want you to know I don't like you."[130]

Robinson's response was "All right. That's the way I'd rather have it. Right out in the open."[131]

At first, Jackie's Southern teammates were most concerned about how a black man would fit into society; they soon realized that not only could he (Robinson) play baseball but also put money in their pockets. Their attitude was slowly beginning to change toward their negro teammate.

Next, Jackie also needed to win over Red Barber, the "Voice of the Dodgers." Barber was born in Mississippi and grew up in Florida. When Branch Rickey told his announcer about making Jackie Robinson the first black major leaguer, Barber was unsure that he could do his job by broadcasting a black man. In fact, when he went home after his lunch with Rickey, he told his wife that he would need to quit. Her advice was to have a martini and go to bed, essentially recommending that her husband sleeps on it.[132]

Barber's dilemma was whether he could broadcast a black player. He remembered an analogy that Hall of Fame umpire Bill Klem gave about umpiring. Klem felt that the purpose of umpiring was to umpire the ball. Red re-worked Klem's advice, and decided s to broadcast the ball. As a broadcaster, his concern should be who was standing at the plate, the score, the excitement of the crowd and the drama of the moment.

---

130 Ibid., 206
131 Ibid., 206
132 Ibid., Lowenfish, 360-61

Barber critiqued how he broadcasted in 1947. He did not broadcast Jackie Robinson; he simply broadcasted what Robinson did. Sometimes it was quite interesting. All Red needed to do was broadcast; that was his job.

Years later, Barber related that the Robinson situation was simply accepting him for what he was; a man, a ball player. Barber did not resent him, nor did he crusade for him; he simply broadcasted the ball. Years after Robinson's career was over, Jackie told Barber how much he appreciated what he did in the booth. Barber admitted that Jackie Robinson did far more for me than I ever did for him.

Rickey's ability to change one's man's attitude like Red Barber was much easier than changing that of his opponents and his teammates.

For example, it was very true that opposing pitchers threw the ball at Robinson all season; some did it maliciously, and Robinson was hit nine times. Jackie did a lot of ducking; he also faced protest, hatred and bigotry. The movie *42* depicted several incidents, some exaggerated but mostly accurate.

Opening Day, April 15th, 1947, for the Brooklyn Dodgers ushered in the integration of major league baseball. Jackie did not receive a cold reception, but rather one of indifference from his new teammates in the Dodger clubhouse. The majority of them did not speak to him but instead nodded. The exceptions were Ralph Branca and Gene Hermanski; they shook his hand and welcomed him, telling Jackie how happy they were to have him on the team.

Opening day was a perfect one for playing baseball, which included blue skies and a soft breeze mixed with a slight chill in the air. Dodger Fans often called Ebbetts Field an intimate experience, one that brought people together. In her memoirs, Doris Kearns Goodwin referred to Ebbetts Field as a melting pot of ethnicities. Normally the Italians, Irish and Jews always came out in strong numbers with a few blacks spread lightly among the crowd.

This would change; when the Dodgers prepared to play the Boston Braves, three-fifths of the crowd was made up of blacks. 27,000 people came through the gates; 2,000 less than opening day in 1946 and 5,000 less than the park's capacity. It was confusing why the attendance was as low. The Dodgers had a good team and the weather was nice that day; the fans at Ebbetts Field witnessed history that day.

When Robinson stepped up to the plate for his first at bat, he was waving his thirty-three ounces, thirty-five-inch Louisville Slugger waiting for Johnny Sain's first pitch. Sain's first two pitches were curveballs; he followed them by whistling a fastball that Jackie grounded out to third base. The Dodgers were down 3-2 at the bottom of the seventh. Eddie Stanky walked. Jackie pushed a bunt up the first baseline; the throw glanced off of Robinson as he ran to first. Stanky continued to third. The Dodgers now had runners on second and third. Pee Wee hit a double to bring both runners in, putting the Dodgers up 4-3. Gene Hermanski drove in another run as the Dodgers went on to win 5-3.

Jackie Robinson's rookie year was filled with several challenges, such as the racial slurs hurled by the Phillies' Ben Chapman. Jackie admitted that the April 22nd game was a huge test. "For one wild and rage-crazed minute, I thought to hell with Mr. Rickey's noble experiment." Robinson entertained the thought of dropping his batting helmet, then going over to the Phillies dugout, grabbing a Philadelphia player to smash his teeth in. Fortunately, he did not need to, because this game was the first sign of acceptance by his teammates. His Dodger teammates stood up for him because they knew of his agreement with Mr. Rickey. The Dodgers' fiery second baseman, Eddie Stanky, challenged Chapman, telling him that he should pick on someone who could fight back. Dixie Walker informed Chapman that he went too far. This was significant because both Stanky and Walker were against Jackie being on the team.[133]

Before the Dodgers played the Phillies their record was 2-2 but they swept all three games they played with them. Next, they moved into first place after beating the New York Giants in their next game.

After the series between Brooklyn and Philadelphia several fans wrote to baseball commissioner Happy Chandler to complain about Chapman. Walter Winchell, the most popular journalist in the

---

133 Ibid., Rampersad, 172-73

country, used his influence on his Sunday night radio broadcast to attack Chapman's behavior. Rickey's great experiment began gaining support. The public's reaction makes you wonder why integration took so long.

The St. Louis Cardinals allegedly drew up a petition to protest playing against Robinson[134]. Owner Sam Breadon spoke to his players; it seemed that there were only two players that had any complaints. Red Schoendienst denied that a vote was taken to boycott. When the Dodgers traveled to St. Louis in June, there was no incident. In fact, the Cardinals seemed to go out of their way to be cordial.

On August 20th, Enos Slaughter, possibly one of the Cardinals that wanted the boycott, spiked Robinson during the 11th inning of the game. Many felt it was racially influenced, but Slaughter and several of his teammates denied that it was intentional. Slaughter argued that if he had done it on purpose, there were plenty of opportunities to do it earlier.

Once again Stanky stood up for Robinson, challenging Slaughter. Jackie's teammates' support became stronger for him each day. Their feelings for him went through a metamorphosis. Many did not want him as a teammate during spring training because he was black, but most of the team now supported him because he was their teammate without considering his skin color.

Even with all of the distractions of Jackie Robinson's first season, the Brooklyn Dodgers won the National League pennant. Unfortunately, the Dodgers lost to the New York Yankees in the World Series four games to three. Jackie Robinson batted .297, hit 12 homeruns, stole 29 bases and scored 125 runs. "The Sporting News" selected him as Rookie of the Year, but Jackie's biggest accomplishment was "winning over" this teammates and opponents in 1947.

Jackie Robinson went on to play ten years in the MLB and was voted into baseball's National Hall of Fame in 1962.

---

134 Ibid., Lowenfish, 430

The following are the feelings of those who played with and against him, or shared the same era, and were influenced by Robinson's courage and bravery.

"The three greatest men I ever met in my life were Jackie Robinson, Branch Rickey and Billy Graham."
— Bobby Bragan

"He was the greatest competitor I have ever seen."
— Duke Snider

"A lot of people are pulling for you to make good. Don't ever forget it."
— Hank Greenberg (HOF 1956) to Jackie the first time they met.

"To be perfectly frank, I think baseball is a greatly improved game because of the blacks. There is no question in my mind that they are outstanding athletes, and they have contributed much to the game."
— Dixie Walker

"He's a major leaguer in every respect. He can run, he can hit, he is fast and he is quick with the ball. And his fine base running keeps the other teams in an uproar."
— Ben Chapman

Arguably, Jackie Robinson was the most influential ball player to grace the baseball diamond. He showed that talent meant more than skin color; his determination opened the doors to integration in our nation. Jackie inspired both common and not so common people, like, for instance, Gil Jones.

Gil was in the stands as a young man and heard Robinson being taunted with racial slurs. So when he graduated, he went to Stanford University to be as far away from Brooklyn as he could. Jones was surprised to learn that Stanford had not been integrated. So he wrote to Roy Wilkins of the NAACP. Gil got involved with politics and was instrumental in integrating Stanford. Following college, he went to work for the NAACP and became one of the organization's leading fundraisers. Jackie became a member of its board of directors, and in 1960 they met. Jones would meet and have the opportunity to tell his hero how he was an inspiration to him as a young boy and how he changed his life.

Another person that Jackie influenced was Hank Aaron. Hank saw him during the spring of 1948 when he was fourteen years old. It was the year after Jackie broke baseball's color line. The Brooklyn Dodgers stopped in Hank's hometown of Mobile, Alabama. Jackie spoke to a large crowd. He spoke about segregation. Aaron did not hear a word that his hero said, because he was too busy gawking at him.

"They say certain people are bigger than life, but Jackie Robinson is the only man I've known who truly was. In 1947, there were separate schools for blacks and whites, separate restaurants, separate motels, separate drinking fountains and separate baseball leagues. Life was unkind to black people who tried to bring those worlds together, it could be hateful. But Jackie Robinson, God bless him, was bigger than all of that."

Then the former three-time heavyweight boxing champion and Olympic gold medal winner, Muhammad Ali, put the importance of Jackie Robinson into perspective; "Jackie Robinson was a hero. And he wasn't just special to black people. He was special to all people."

Dr. Martin Luther King Jr., Civil Rights activist and humanitarian, said to Dodger pitching great Don Newcombe; "Don, you'll never know how easy Jackie, you and Campy made it for me to do my job."

Every year on April 15th, baseball venues around the league honor Jackie Robinson by wearing uniforms with the number 42.

"So blessed and thankful for Jackie Robinson and what he did for baseball players and people everywhere. I am very proud to wear #42 tonight." – Curtis Granderson.

"Would not be where I am today if it wasn't for Jackie Robinson...a true hero." – David Ortiz.

"Thank you MLB for honoring Jackie Robinson's legacy with Jackie Robinson Day, and having all of the teams wear #42." – Magic Johnson.

"Number 42. He hit it out of the park." – President Barack Obama.

If Jackie Robinson had not turned the other cheek in 1947, if he did not show physical restraint after the racial slurs of Ben Chapman, do you think the following would have occurred?

- Would Babe Ruth's career homerun record be safe?
- Would Eric Gregg umpire in the MLB?
- Would Bill White or Leonard Cohen become league presidents?
- Would there have been a black manager, or general manager?

Probably not, Robert Ruck Jr., Civil Rights lecturer at the University of Pitt and an authority on black baseball essentially answered those questions by stating; "I think that if Robinson's arrival in the MLB had been a chaotic social disaster, it would have made it difficult for this country to change."

"A life is not important except in the impact it has on other's lives."

– Jackie Robinson

Jackie Robinson

Chapter 16

Minnie Forbes: The Last Living Negro Team Owner

*L*ittle has been written about the owners of Negro League baseball teams. The reasons why a person would commit their resources to own a Negro League baseball team are fascinating. I am sure that the life story of every Negro League owner is fascinating. Bob shares information about the influences in the life of the last living owner of a Negro League baseball team in this chapter.

One night while I was surfing the Internet, I stumbled upon an article about President Obama honoring three former players and an owner from the Negro Leagues. The only one that I was familiar with was Minnie Minoso. But the other Minnie caught my attention. Her name was Minnie Forbes. She was the former owner of the Detroit Stars. Ms. Forbes owned the team from 1956-58. Not only was she a woman, but I would learn that she was the last living owner of a Negro League team.[135]

Her Uncle Ted Rasberry influenced her interest in baseball[136]. When Minnie was a toddler, her uncle moved to Grand Rapids and she began working for him as a teenager. Her uncle owned the Grand Rapids Black Sox. When she turned sixteen, Minnie began playing softball on the same team with Ted's wife.

---

135 "Former Owner of Negro League Baseball team (on line), August 18, 2013
136 "Ted Rasberry," Negro League Payer Association May 31, 2012

Her Negro League career began when she became Ted's secretary at eighteen years old. Minnie did all of the office work concerning baseball matters, like sending out contracts, booking the games, and basically marketing the team. Since she was the oldest of Ted's nieces, Minnie became her uncle's 'gal Friday.' This experience prepared her for becoming the owner of the Detroit Stars. Eventually, at twenty-four, she became the owner of the Detroit Stars. After selling the Detroit Stars, Minnie went on to become the fourth woman to play in the Negro Leagues for the Detroit Stars against the Kansas City Monarchs. To be honest, it was essentially a publicity stunt. Satchel Paige and the Kansas City Monarchs were coming to Grand Rapids in 1958. Minnie's Uncle Ted wanted to cash in on the opportunity of selling a lot of tickets so he publicized that a woman would play in the game, à la Toni Stone and Mamie Johnson who had played in the Negro Leagues. He decided to play Minnie, his niece, whose heroes were Stone and Johnson. Minnie started at third base and played a couple of innings. Accounts of the game indicated that no balls came in her direction. On top of that, she did not get a chance to bat because each of the two innings she played, the Stars were retired in order. No one could accuse Ted Rasberry of false advertising[137].

Times were rough for the league during the period that Minnie Forbes owned the Stars, causing her to sell the team in 1958. She moved onto a life without baseball. She went into retail to work, becoming an office manager for thirty-nine years at Jacobson's, a large retail store. She also did some modeling.[138]

Ms. Forbes forgot about her life in the former Negro League baseball. For many years, the Negro League was nothing more than a distant memory for her. But it seemed that each year someone called, pestering her to partake in a celebration honoring the defunct league. She felt that it was a part of her life over fifty years ago, but since she was in her eighties, Minnie did not want to be bothered.

---

137 Minnie Forbes, interview, December 13, 2015
138 Ibid.

Still, organizers like Louis Manley Jr. were persistent. He was also a well-known Detroit historian and the President of the Michigan Chapter of Negro League Baseball. Minnie finally relented and agreed to participate. It started in 2011 when she threw out the first pitch before a Tigers game. Because of her experience at the Tigers event, her interest became revived. She found that she enjoyed signing autographs and answering the fans' questions. She began to understand the importance of her Negro League baseball experience. It was also an opportunity to catch up with the former players from her time with the Stars.[139]

She enjoyed sharing stories with the fans about the Negro League and she also told the fans about the challenges players faced, like racism. Not only did it happen in places like Birmingham or Memphis, racial prejudice was also prevalent up North around Detroit. Minnie remembered providing a place for opposing players to stay when they came to play the Stars.

One of the players that Minnie caught up with was Pedro Sierra, who was one of her favorites. Sierra played for the Stars when she owned the team. Pedro came to America in 1954. He played for the Indianapolis Clowns from 1954-55, then the Detroit Stars from 1956-58. Afterward, he signed with the Washington Senators minor league system in 1959. His minor league career was interrupted by serving with the 4th Army. Pedro went on to play in the Canadian Provincial League from 1967-69, plus the Mexican and Dominican League. One of the main reasons that Minnie Forbes decided to leave the sport was its deterioration. Many have argued when the demise of the Negro League occurred. Some like to point to April 15, 1947, when Jackie Robinson made his major league debut with the Brooklyn Dodgers, thus breaking baseball's racial barrier.[140]

Others point to 1949 when the Negro National League folded. Several teams such as the Homestead Grays, Newark Eagles,

---

139 Ibid.
140 Ibid.

Philadelphia Stars and Baltimore Elite Giants switched to the Negro American League before leaving all together.

By 1955, the American league had shrunk to only six teams. It included the Birmingham Black Barons, Detroit Stars, Indianapolis Clowns, Kansas City Monarchs, Louisville Black Colonels and the Memphis Red Sox. Team owners sensing the leagues' weakened state began selling off star players to the major leagues. Tom Baird, the owner of the Monarchs sold eight of his players to the majors. He also let his manager Buck O'Neil go to the Chicago Cubs as a coach.

That team became a shell of its glory days. Tom Baird sold the Kansas City Monarchs to Ted Rasberry in 1955, which included the equipment, the team name and its franchise in the Negro American League. Baird turned his attention to scouting for the Kansas City Athletics, which meant that Rasberry now owned the Detroit Stars and the Kansas City Monarchs. Rasberry was also the former owner of the Grand Rapids Black Sox, a black semi-professional powerhouse in the Great Lakes area.

League officials cited a conflict of interest. For that reason, they would not approve his ownership of both teams. The 1956 season opened with Dr. J. B. Martin as the new league president. This is also when Ted Rasberry turned over the Detroit Stars to his niece and secretary, Minnie Forbes. When Minnie owned the Detroit Stars, her ball players were paid $150 every two weeks and $3.00 for lunch. Obviously, they played for the love of the game. Tickets for the game were $1.00 for the grandstand and $0.50 for the bleachers. When she became the team's owner, she was not treated any differently by her players, nor by her fellow team owners, mainly because she was a familiar face. Before she took over, Ms. Forbes was a regular attendee at the league meetings with her uncle. Ted always introduced her as his secretary. Minnie did not believe the other owners realized that she had become an owner.

As Minnie Forbes said, "There was never a lot of money in Negro League baseball, so Ted felt it was important to have as many teams in the Negro American League as possible; that is why he bought the Kansas City Monarchs."[141]

While Negro League baseball was an important part of the black community's economy, it also became a problem. Especially since the only source of income for many of the teams was the "paid gate." To achieve and maintain financial success required keeping expenses reasonable and playing well enough to attract fans. The situation was a dichotomy. While integration into the major leagues was good, it stole from the turnstiles of Negro League teams who desperately depended on it. To combat the loss of revenue, owners had to sell their best players as a way to replace the lost income. By removing talent from the team, they also tarnished the fans' attraction, leading to low attendance and thereby causing teams to have insufficient income.

The Detroit Stars were crowned the Negro American League champions in 1956. Surprisingly, in 1957 the league added two new teams. They were the Mobile/Havana Giants, and the New Orleans Crescent Bears. Both quickly folded after just one season.

In 1958, Goose Tatum became the owner of the Detroit Stars. Tatum played in the Negro Leagues before becoming a star basketball player for the Harlem Globetrotters. He was considered basketball's first "clown prince." He is credited with inventing the hook shoot. Goose had played first base for the Indianapolis Clowns and the Birmingham Black Barons.[142] Eventually, Detroit changed its name to the "Clowns" until they ceased operations in 1960.

An article appeared in the "Chicago Defender" on August 20, 1960, where Negro American League President Dr. Martin expressed that the Negro Leagues could play an important role in preparing young black players for Major League baseball. Unfortunately, this idea died due to the increase in integration. When minor league teams began accepting more African American players it eliminated the need for the Major League Baseball to have segregated farm systems. While

---

141 Ibid.

142 "Goose Tatum," The Encyclopedia of Arkansas History and Culture, www. encyclopediaofarkansas.net

it was Martin's hope to develop a financial relationship with the minor league system, the Philadelphia Phillies were the only team to show any interest. The future of the Negro Leagues sunk even deeper.

Negro League baseball's heart stopped pumping after the 1960 season. Sadly, its hallmark event, the annual East/ West All-Star game held at Chicago's Cominsky Park was played for the last time. Some teams hung on by playing independently by barnstorming, but the games were just a novelty. After 1960, there was no more Negro League.

Although, it did gain popularity again in the nineteen-nineties as Major League cities celebrated the league's existence. Once a year, MLB teams scheduled a game with an opponent where they both wore replica Negro League uniforms.

The acknowledgment of black baseball reached its apex on August 5, 2013, when President Barack Obama greeted Minnie Minoso, Pedro Sierra, Ron Teasley and Minnie Forbes at the White House. The President honored them for their contributions to athletics and the Civil Rights movement. When I spoke on the telephone with Minnie, I could hear the pride and joy in her voice when I asked about that day. For one thing, she never could imagine being invited to the White House, let alone meeting the President of the United States – especially an African American one. She was glad to see that players who formed the Negro Leagues were finally being recognized for their part in history. Ms. Forbes was thankful that nowadays all players can play for any team as long as they have the ability and the talent. They can stay and eat anywhere; in her mind, that is the greatest thing, which was not the case sixty years ago.

Of course seeing the Negro League get recognition was not the greatest thing she experienced; no, there was something better, "I got kissed by the President! I've been telling everybody. And to think, it all happened because of the Negro Leagues!"[143]

---

143 Ibid., Gibbons

Chapter 17

Baseball's Integration and the Exodus of Negro League Baseball

Jackie Robinson's play in White Major League Baseball was an important step toward integration in the United States. However, this integration has not always left Black communities and organizations better off. Segregation forced people to support local Black businesses, professionals and sports teams. In this chapter, Bob talks about the influence of integration on Negro League Baseball.

When President Lincoln signed the Emancipation Proclamation on January 1, 1863, he took the first step at ushering in racial integration. Then on April 15, 1947, Jackie Robinson pushed open the floodgates for equality by literally changing the complexion of the National Pastime when he made his debut with the Brooklyn Dodgers, an event that led to the Exodus of the Negro Leagues.[144]

The conflict or segregation of baseball began in 1887 when Cap Anson, a member of the Hall of Fame and whose career spanned from 1877-97 refused to play against a black pitcher named George Stovey in 1887. Later that year, the International League's Board of Directors voted not to approve any subsequent contracts with black players ... this became the birth of the infamous "gentlemen's agreement" which led to the total exclusion of black players from major league baseball for years until Jackie Robinson. Unable to play

---

144 "The Decline of the Negro Leagues," Peterson, Robert, www.britanica.com

professional baseball with the white players, Rube Foster founded the Negro National League in 1920, the first black baseball league. The league's demise would occur in 1931, for two reasons; first, because of Foster's death the preceding season and second, the Great Depression. The Great Depression hit black baseball harder than the white major leagues. Some black teams relied on barnstorming to survive, moving from town to town. At the end of the MLB season, the black and white teams would barnstorm against each other. Barnstorming in baseball consisted of exhibition games after the regular season. The black teams depended on the extra income.

As Buck O'Neil, former first baseman and manager of the Kansas City Monarchs explained, the MLB players were just playing for a payday, whereas the black players were there to prove they could play and that they were as good or better. This might explain why the black teams won a majority of the games. Records showed that the black teams beat the white squads 309 out of 438 times.

Before Jackie Robinson and Branch Rickey, there were some formidable owners in Negro baseball. Their names were Gus Greenlee (Pittsburgh Crawfords), Cum Posey (Homestead Grays) and a woman by the name of Effa Manly (Newark Eagles).

I mention these three because they were arguably the best-known owners in the Negro Leagues. Each is now in the Hall of Fame of baseball. Gus Greenlee was the one who picked up the ball after Foster's death and organized the Negro National League in 1933. His 1935 Pittsburgh Crawfords team showcased many of the greatest black players. That team had Satchel Paige, Josh Gibson, Cool Papa Bell, Judy Johnson and Oscar Charleston. Mr. Greenlee is arguably one of the most influential figures in the history of the Negro Leagues.

Gus was a businessman, politician, sportsman and a numbers banker. He also owned a stable of boxers which included light heavyweight champion John Henry Lewis. Gus ran a popular cabaret called the Crawford Grill. His linchpin was his baseball team, the Pittsburgh Crawfords.

Gus was born inside a log cabin in Marion, NC. He left North Carolina after his first year of college and then moved north to

Pittsburgh where he held jobs as a shoeshine boy, a steel mill worker and a taxi cab driver. He enlisted in the army serving overseas with the 367th Division during World War I. After returning to Pittsburgh, he became active in the black community. During Prohibition, he operated nightclubs as a front for his numbers and bootlegging operation. His Crawford Grill became a center of activity for jazz, booze, gambling and girls. In the 1930s, Gus also became a force in Pittsburgh politics.[145]

He was instrumental in the formation of the new Negro National League, serving as its president during its first five years. He worked at eliminating rowdy behavior and assaults on umpires. His greatest legacy was the creation of the East-West All-Star game. It was formed the same year as major league baseball's own mid-summer event. The annual East-West game became both a popular and profitable venture in black baseball.[146] Also in 1935, his Crawfords defeated the New York Cubans, making them the undisputed Negro League champions. Most historians consider that 1935 Crawfords team to be the greatest black baseball team of all time.[147]

Gus Greenlee was a wealthy man who was very generous to his players. In 1932, he built Greenlee Field, the only black-owned ballpark in the east. Unfortunately, between losing Paige and Gibson, and a big payoff on heavily played numbers, Gus had to divest himself from the team and razed Greenlee Field after the 1938 season.

In 1945, he attempted to return to an active role in black baseball. He and Branch Rickey sought to form the United States League; their desire was to find a black candidate to integrate baseball. The league lasted two seasons and never achieved MLB caliber.

Gus operated the Crawford Grill until 1951 when it was destroyed by fire, racketeers encroached on his numbers business and Federal

---

145 "Gus Greenlee," by Brian McKenna, SABR Bio Project
146 Lester, Larry, *Black Baseball's National Showcase* (Lincoln, Ne, University of Nebraska Press, 2001) 15
147 Ibid., McKenna

agents harassed him about back taxes. While in the midst of some bad luck William Augustus Greenlee died on July 10, 1952.[148]

Gus Greenlee's biggest adversary and competitor in Negro League baseball during the 1930s was Cumberland Willis Posey Jr., who owned the Homestead Grays.

Cum Posey was born June 20, 1890, in Homestead, a suburb of Pittsburgh. His career with the Grays stretched from 1911-46. He served as an outfielder, manager, officer, owner, and secretary of the NNL. He could easily be called the "father of the Homestead Grays. His roots ran from the team's inception and he is credited with making the team a success.

He was very fortunate that his parents were great role models. The Posey family was among the wealthiest black families in Western Pennsylvania. His father, Cumberland Posey Sr., was a riverboat engineer on the Ohio River, and later became the general manager of the Delta Coal Company. Posey's father enjoyed a career in both banking and real estate. Then there was his mother, Anna Posey, the first black graduate of Ohio State University and who taught at the college.[149]

Cum was an all-around athlete at Homestead high school. He went on to attend Pennsylvania State College from 1909-10, then Pittsburgh University in 1913 and Holy Ghost College (which became Duquesne University) in 1915.

At Duquesne, Cum Posey studied chemistry and pharmacy, enrolled under a fictitious name, Charles W. Cumbert. He led the school basketball team in scoring and was the captain of the golf team. He would eventually play baseball professionally. Cum started as a mail clerk when the Homestead Grays were formed in 1910 when they were a team of steelworkers playing on weekends. Posey joined them as an outfielder in 1911. Then in 1912, he began booking enough games for the players to play only baseball. Over the next decade, the Homestead Grays became the biggest attraction as an

---

148 Ibid.
149 "Cum Posey," by Brian McKenna, SABR Bio Project

independent team. In 1922, the Grays encountered raiding tactics by the Pittsburgh Keystones. Loyalty had never been a characteristic within black baseball; players went to wherever they were paid the most. Satchel Paige was frequently guilty of this. When the Keystones threatened to steal the Grays players, Posey brought in Charlie Walker as a partner; together they were able to squash the threat.

The Grays were an independent team in 1929 that accomplished a record of 140-13. It was also the year that Posey ended his playing career. It was also the same year the Homestead Grays entered the American Negro League until the league folded. The Grays returned to independent play in 1930. Posey was able to pick up Oscar Charleston, Josh Gibson and Judy Johnson. They defeated the New York Lincoln Stars for the Eastern championship. They improved to a 163-23 record to win the championship again in 1931.[150]

Cum turned over his managing responsibilities to Vic Harris in 1937 so he could concentrate on the team's business aspects. Under Posey's guidance, the Grays became a team of major league quality

But as the saying goes, "He, who lives by the sword, dies by the sword" and while Posey built his powerhouse teams by signing players away from other teams, his adversary in Pittsburgh, Gus Greenlee learned from him. The Homestead Grays lost Charleston, Gibson and Johnson to the Crawfords. Posey could not compete with the salary that Greenlee offered to them. During the Depression when Cum fell into financial difficulties he took on a co-owner named Rufus "Sonny man" Jackson. With new money Posey was able to bring back Gibson and Leonard.

Cumberland Willis Posey Jr. died of lung cancer in 1946 at Mercy Hospital in Pittsburgh.[151]

Over In Newark, New Jersey there was a married couple, Abe and Effa Manly. Effa holds the distinction of being the first female

---

150 Ibid.
151 Ibid.

owner of a Negro League team. She is also the only woman of any color enshrined in the Hall of Fame in Cooperstown, New York[152]:

Effa wore several hats at Newark; she was the Eagles' business manager, the team's house mother – especially to the younger players, the schedule maker and power broker within the Negro National League. Effa Manly was the lone woman in a world dominated by tough men, as writer Jerry Izenberg of the "Star Ledger" said, "She rarely lost arguments with much grace."

She never backed off. Or was never afraid to fight over rule changes, which she generally won, not because she was a beauty, but rather that she was right. For instance, the Baltimore Elite Giants moved their home games to Newark because no one promoted the game better than Effa Manly.

Abe Manly co-owned the Newark Eagles with his wife Effa from 1935-46. Many feel that Abe purchased the team as a mere hobby in 1935. He actually gave up his gambling pursuits to become a legitimate baseball team owner, but it was his wife who actually ran the team. Abe died on December 9, 1952, in Germantown, PA.[153]

At that time, Newark was a predominantly white city; it had the Newark Bears, a minor league team for the New York Yankees in the white major leagues.

The Eagles were made up of players who due to racial barriers had no hope of ever playing for the Yankees, the Giants, or even the Toledo Mud Hens. When the MLB broke the race barrier, it was driven by greed to acquire black stars and their fans. They did not feel guilty of racial injustice; all they cared about was getting cheap talent, and Branch Rickey, who had a reputation of being cheap, was the biggest culprit. He began raiding black players from several black teams at no cost to him. Rickey was very interested in Monte Irvin, who played for Effa Manly of the Newark Eagles.

---

152 "The Most Famous Woman in Baseball," by Mike Cook, 2012 Baseball Research Journal, SABR

153 Ibid

"Mrs. Manly, the Brooklyn Dodgers are going to do a great thing for your race. We have decided to sign Monte Irvin."

Effa replied, "Well, that sure does sound great, Mr. Rickey, and I know a lot of folks of my race will be very happy after you buy his contract."

"I don't think you understand." Branch replied.

So Effa explained, "I understand that this ball club wants $5,000 for his (Irvin's) contract."[154]

This didn't sit well with Mr. Rickey, who accused her of standing in the way of her race."

(In an interview with Mrs. Manly on October 19, 1977, Effa states that she and several of the Negro League owners knew that someone was going to break the racial barrier, and each felt that Monte Irvin was the perfect player to do it. She also said that did not mean to slight Jackie, because he was also a wonderful player.)[155]

While several MLB club owners began to steal players from the Negro Leagues. Cleveland's Bill Veeck was an exception. He admired Effa and was one of her biggest fans. He made sure to pay her for Larry Doby.[156] In that regard, Veeck was smarter than Branch Rickey.

After Rickey attempted to get Irvin for free from Manly, he informed Horace Stoneham that if he wanted Irvin, he should offer Effa $5,000. In fact, Stoneman paid Mrs. Manley the desired amount. Irvin went on to star for the Giants, winning two pennants for them while serving as a mentor to the impressionable Willie Mays.

When Monte heard about the $5,000, he told Mrs. Manly that he should get a cut of the money. Effa explained to her young player how that wasn't going to happen. As she explained, it went like this:

"Well, we have this nice young man who does our legal for free and I am planning to give him $2,500 for his hard work. And then

---

154 "In a League of Her Own," by Jerry Izenberg, "The Star Ledger," Newark, NJ, February 28, 2 – 6

155 Effa Manley, Interview- William Marshall (Louie B. Nunn Ctr. For oral history, University of Kentucky, October 19, 1977

156 Dickson, Paul, Bill Veeck: Baseball's Greatest Maverick (Walker & Co. NY, NY, 2012) 126

there is this fur stole in the window at Chesloff's. Monte, I never had a fur stole and his one is only $2,500. Son, now how much does that leave for me to give to you?" she smiled.

About forty years later at a Negro League reunion in Kentucky, Effa Manly, beautiful as ever, walked into the room.

Monte Irvin spotted his former boss and complimented her, "You look fine Mrs. Manly."

Effa smiled, "Monte, do you remember this fur? It's the one I bought at Chesloff's about four decades ago."

Ever the gentlemen, Monte responded, "Well, then you got a very good deal."

With her charming smile, "Not as good as the one Stoneman got."[157]

The pinnacle of every Negro League season was the EAST-WEST All-Star game, which was Gus Greenlee's creation. The inaugural event was played in 1933. Ironically it was the same year that Major League Baseball held their first All-Star game and it was also held at Comiskey Park in Chicago. It became the MOST important black sporting event in the country. Several MLB Hall of Fame members have played in both events, such as Ernie Banks, Roy Campanella, Larry Doby, Jackie Robinson, Satchel Paige. Black Baseball's National Showcase was played between 1933 and 1953.[158]

During the era of segregation, Negro League baseball played a critical role as a source of "black pride" It was a time that African Americans needed role models to emulate.

For all of the good that breaking the racial barrier brought to baseball, it also caused a downward spiral that effectively eliminated teams owned and supported by African Americans in baseball.

Along with the triumphs of Joe Louis in the boxing ring, and Jesse Owens in the Berlin Olympics of 1936 were also factors that contributed to the league's demise. Integration began to deplete the talent pool and made it difficult for the Negro leagues to field

157 Ibid., Manley interview
158 Ibid. Lester

competitive teams. Despite black baseball's prominence in the black community, the black fans were drawn more to see players like Hank Aaron and Willie Mays play in the MLB.

Black baseball's most successful league, the Negro National League, died of financial malnutrition in 1948. The Negro American League limped until 1960, continuing mostly by "barnstorming."

Monte Irvin wrote the foreword for the *Biography of the Negro Leagues* saying, "All of us were grateful that Jackie made it because he made it better for everybody. Not only athletically, but financially, socially, and politically… We'll always be grateful for the great pioneering job he did, and may God bless him forever."[159]

Since statistics, attendance and other numbers affiliated with the Negro Leagues are ambiguous, sketchy at best, it is hard to illustrate the demise of black baseball, so I will be using the attendance figures of the East-West All-Star game.

When Gus Greenlee originated the East-West game in 1933, there were 19,568 fans in attendance for the game. Then ten years later in 1943, attendance grew to 51,723. By the time of the last game in 1953, it had dwindled to a mere 10,000.

While Jackie Robinson's signing was great for American Society, unfortunately, it was the beginning of the end for the Negro Leagues.

---

159 Riley, James A., The Biographical Encyclopedia of the Negro League Baseball (Carroll & Graft Pub Inc., NY, NY, 1994) xiii

Section V
Team Influence

Chapter 18

1914 Boston Braves:
The Miracle Man and his Braves

*I*t is very easy to underestimate the influence of the manager in baseball. Even though these individuals sit or stand on the sidelines during the game, it does not seem like they have as much control over their team as the coaches in the National Basketball Association (NBA) do. These leaders seem to only get engaged in the game when there is a controversial call, an injury or a pitcher being taken out of the game. However, effective managers are the most influential people in the day-to-day success or failure of a baseball team. In this chapter, Bob tells the amazing story of the influence of one particular manager on the 1914 Boston Braves.

When Dale first asked me to become part of this book project, it occurred to me that the game of baseball was the perfect backdrop in exploring the role of influence in the game. So I started searching my baseball memory banks to come up with some stories about teams who were both successfully and unsuccessfully influenced. I kept in mind the how and why certain teams were successful. For some, it was due to an influential manager like Gil Hodges of the Mets of 1969, or Dick Williams' 67' Red Sox, or a failure such as Gene Mauch and the prodigious collapse of the Phillies in 1964. But I would be remiss to forget the ultimate story of a team defined by its manager's influence…. the 1914 Boston Braves, led by George Tweedy Stallings. Stallings would become known as the "Miracle Man." He guided the finest season ever enjoyed by the Boston Braves!

This comeback story is over a hundred years old, and it's one I hope that hardcore baseball fans never forget. The 1914 season might be the finest job that a major league manager has or will ever do. Like the way that Hollywood loves underdogs, the 1914 Boston Braves were the ultimate underdog story!

If we were to trace the origin of this story, we might start with the end of the 1912 season when James Gaffney, owner of the Boston Braves was sitting in the stands with George Tweedy Stallings, who would become the next manager for his team. Stallings had managed the New York Highlanders during the 1909 and 1910 seasons. After getting them to second place, he was fired and replaced by Hal Chase before the 1910 season was completed.[160]

While in the stands that afternoon, Gaffney asked Stallings his opinion about the Braves. Gaffney's new manager, not known to mince words, responded that he felt that the Braves were terrible. Gaffney reminded Stallings that he (Gaffney) was his new boss, and it was up to him to make the team better. Even so, Stallings reiterated that the Braves were the worst team that he was ever affiliated with.[161]

Two years later, Stallings' team would be hailed as the bravest of all in major league baseball! Their manager became known as the "Miracle Man." Some might suggest that Stallings did it with mirrors; to be honest, he employed psychology. Not only was he motivational, he was a brilliant strategist and tactician. His mantra was, "You can win, you must win and you will win!"[162]

Stallings began managing in 1893, and if not for the great job he did with the Braves in 1914, his managerial career would never be remembered. Stallings' lifetime managerial career record of 879-898 over thirteen seasons in the big leagues was below average; besides

---

160 "George Stallings,"by Martin Kohout, SABR Bio Project
161 Ibid.
162 Kaese, Harold, *The Boston Braves: 1871-1953* (Boston, Northeastern University Press, 2004) 136

that, his playing career was not memorable either. George Stallings had two hits in twenty lifetime at bats in major league baseball.[163]

"The Braves' Manager Stallings Preferred Mediocre Players that Hustled Instead of Loafing Star Players"

For some reason, players wanted to play for Stallings. He preferred mediocre players that hustled instead of loafing star players. Before Stallings came to Boston, the Braves had posted four consecutive last place finishes. Stallings practiced hard love, refusing to coddle his players. He had no tolerance for dumb plays and was known to give a tongue lashing to those when they committed one. Another of his favorite motivational ploys was to purposely place a chip on the players' shoulders. He built his players up, making them believe how good they were. Stallings felt that if a ball club had only mediocre ability, he could motivate them and they would become World Champions.

Many of his players considered it a privilege just to sit and listen to their skipper talk baseball. In fact, the feisty Johnny Evers felt that Stallings knew more about baseball than anyone who was connected with the game.

The 1914 Boston spring training camp was one filled with optimism. Unfortunately, the Boston Braves started off the 1914 season by winning only four out of their first twenty-six games. By early July, their record of futility was 6-40, which was unfortunately a common record for the Braves. One popular theory for their ascension occurred in early July when they suffered an embarrassing loss to a AAA team in Buffalo.[164] Because of the loss, Stallings instituted a couple of his theories. His first move was to bring Fred Mitchell to the Braves. George felt that Mitchell was the best judge

---

163 Simon, Tom (Ed.), *Dead Ball Stars of the National League* (Dulles, Va., Braxey's Inc., 2004) 323

164 "1914 Miracle Braves," This Great Game (website) www.thisgreat. com/1914-baseball-history-hml

of pitchers that he ever saw. Stallings carried a smaller pitching staff so that he could incorporate a platoon system.[165] The Braves used forty-six players during the 1914 season. Stallings was the first to use left-handed hitters to bat against right-hand pitchers and vice-versa. The weakest part of the team was the outfield, so he used eleven outfielders with only Joey Connolly playing full-time. He was also the only regular player to bat over .300. No other outfielder had over 400 at bats. Boston's only star player was the feisty Johnny Evers, who would become the MVP of the National League that season.

Whether it was coincidence or magic, the Braves went on to win twelve of their next sixteen games. The 1914 Boston Braves became the first team to win a pennant after being in last place on July 4th. They orchestrated one of the most memorable comebacks in baseball history going from last to first in the span of two months. Boston was 70-19 over the last 89 games. Not only did they finish 10 ½ games over the favorite New York Giants, they swept the heavily favored Philadelphia A's who had a legendary $100,000 infield. It consisted of Stuffy McInnis, Eddie Collins, Jack Berry and Frank Baker. They were teammates from 1910-1914. The $100,000 infield nickname reflected the purported combined market value of the foursome at the time, which is the equivalent of about $2.7 million in 2019.

After the World Series, Connie Mack complimented the Braves and began dismantling his team during the off-season.

It is easy for the skeptics to claim that Stallings accomplished the 1914 season because of luck; but in truth, Boston had on excellent pitching staff, with Dick Rudolph and Bill James each winning 26 games and Lefty Tyler chipping in 16 more. They also got solid play from their keystone combination of Evers and Maranville. The duo led the National League in double plays that season.

The 1914 Boston Braves were the poster child for underdogs. Stallings kept them hustling even after they clinched the pennant.

---

165 Ibid

Giants' catcher Chief Meyers observed that most of the people in the country were pulling for the Braves and rooting against McGraw.

The story of the 1914 Boston Braves provides an excellent example of how a manager's motivation and influence relate to a baseball team's success.

Chapter 19

1964 Philadelphia Phillies: Gene Mauch and the Year of the Blue Snow

Bob holding a copy of SABR's
The Year of the Blue Snow

Baseball is filled with amazing stories about unique events that made baseball history. The sport's historians have traditionally come up with some interesting names that were used to memorialize a historic baseball event. In this chapter, Bob tells the story of Gene Mauch and the "Blue Snow."

The Philadelphia Phillies have been a futile baseball franchise for most of their history, although they have been more successful over the past twenty-five years. The Philadelphia Phillies were founded in 1883 and have the distinction of being the oldest continuous, one-name, one-city franchise in all of professional sports. The team's origin can be traced back to the Worcester Ruby Legs, which disbanded before moving to Philadelphia where they became a member of the National League.[166]

Al Reach was not the first professional player as popularly claimed; instead, he was the first openly professional player. He was also the founder of the Philadelphia Phillies.[167] Before 1964, the Phillies' history was filled with mediocrity. They would not win their first National League pennant until 1915 and did not win another until the "Whiz Kids" of 1950. So who could blame Phillies fans for getting excited about the 1964 team?

The Phillies planted the seed for emergence from the second division on opening day in 1960. The incumbent manager Eddie Sawyer resigned after the Phils lost 9-4 to Cincinnati after the first game of the season. He explained that he was forty-nine years old and hoped to be fifty someday.[168] Apparently, he was not confident about that possibility if he remained as the Phillies manager. Up in Minneapolis, Gene Mauch was gearing up for another season as the manager of the Minneapolis Millers, who were affiliated with the Boston Red Sox, when he received a phone call from John Quinn. Quinn offered Mauch the Phillies manager job and Mauch accepted. So Gene basically has Eddie Sawyer to thank for his major league managerial career.

Ever since he was an eighteen-year-old rookie with the Brooklyn Dodgers, Gene wanted to be a manager. Red Smith, the famous baseball columnist, recalled something Branch Rickey said, "Mauch

166 "Worcester Ruby Legs," www.baseball.reference.com/teams/WOR/index.shtml

167 "A.J. Reach & Company," www.baseball-reference.com/A.J._Reach_Company

168 "Eddie Sawyer," by Ralph Berger, SABR Bio Project

looked sixteen years old, but after talking with him, he seemed twenty-six, and when you talk about baseball with him, you would swear he is thirty-six."

Mauch cited his former manager Leo Durocher as his managerial inspiration. He received his baseball education by sitting on the bench watching Leo. Since he never played in more than seventy-three games in a season, Gene had plenty of time to study the game and the managers that he played for.[169]

The 1961 Phillies lost 107 games, which included a streak of twenty-three losses, one short of the major league record. Still, Mauch kept his job. The team began turning the corner after the 1962 season. The Phils finished the season at 81-80. Mauch won the "Manager of the Year" in the National League that season. He followed up that season with a fourth-place finish (87-75) record in 1963.

The phrase "Year of the Blue Snow" that described the Phillies' 1964 season was coined by Gus Triandos, a Phillies backup catcher. At first, it described the Phillies' place in the National league's pennant race. The Phillies being in a pennant race was surprising to most, except the hardcore Phillies fans. While the team had finished in either last or next to last place during Mauch's first three seasons, the 1964 season was different, and the Phillies moved into first place during the middle of July. Phillies fans got "cocky," believing that they would never relinquish that lead. But when the losses began piling up at the end of the season the phrase took on a negative meaning. The Phillies watched a 6-½ game lead evaporate over their last twelve games. One of the biggest collapses in baseball history, as Triandos called it, "The Year of the Blue Snow."[170]

Handling players was not Mauch's best suit. He was an intense manager who expected his players to be cut from the same cloth as him. Mauch felt that his players should want to win as badly as he did. Gene was obviously a tactical genius, but he did not have a clue how

169 "Gene Mauch," by John Vorperian, SABR Bio Project
170 "The Year of the Blue Snow," Wulf, Steven, Sports Illustrated, September 25, 1984

to use pitchers. Some claim that he could not understand when his pitchers were injured or slumping.

No one ever questioned Mauch's baseball knowledge. Bobby Wine, one of his former players, felt that no one was a better strategist. Wine felt that his former manager knew the rules better than the umpires. For instance, there was a game where Jim Bunning was having problems with a baseball and asked for a new one. The umpires refused to give him another, so Gene came out to the mound, dropped the ball on the ground, and then stepped on it. Bunning got a new ball.[171]

Gene Mauch created the "double switch." This is when a manager makes a pitching substitution and then simultaneously places the incoming pitcher in a favorable spot in the batting order. Mauch became known for his "small-ball" style, which emphasized defense, speed and base-to-base tactics on offense, rather than power hitting. His teams generally played better in ballparks that were not conducive for homerun hitters.

Several things arguably led up to the great collapse of the Phillies' 1964 season, such as Gene Mauch's penchant for "small ball," his lack of understanding of how to handle pitchers and combining his great desire to "play-to-win," attitude. The Phillies started off fast by winning nine of their first eleven games in 1964. On July 16 they moved into first place and gradually built a seven and one half point lead. The question was no longer If the Phils were good enough to win the pennant. Management began printing World Series tickets by mid-September.

The Phillies were sitting in first place on September 20th with a six and a half game lead and twelve games left to play Many felt that they were a lock to play in the World Series but then the unthinkable happened; they lost eight games in the standings in ten days! September 21, 1964, is etched in the minds of many long time Phillies fans. Chico Ruiz, a utility infielder on the Cincinnati Reds

---

171 Marmer, Mel, and Nowlin, Bill (Eds.), The Year of the Blue Snow: 1964 Philadelphia Phillies (Phoenix, Az, SABR, 2013) 250

stood on third base as Art Mahaffey waited for a sign from his catcher Clay Dalrymple during the sixth inning Mahaffey concentrated on home plate and ignored the runner on third base. Mahaffey had two strikes on Frank Robinson with two outs. Ruiz took off and stole home. Years later, Pete Rose said that it was the dumbest play he ever saw. It was the only run the Reds needed as the Reds won 1-0. The infamous collapse had begun.[172]

Many blamed the collapse on Mauch for over using his two best pitchers, Bunning and Short. Down the stretch, they pitched on two days' rest instead of the normal three during the streak. In all fairness to Mauch, it should be noted that half of his preferred pitching rotation was fighting injuries. Dennis Bennett had a sore shoulder and Ray Culp had not pitched since mid-August.[173]

Many written accounts portrayed the Phillies manager becoming increasingly panicked, lashing out at his players while over managing in an attempt to salvage the pennant. It is true that Gene became desperate; however, it should also be noted that the team would not have been in contention for first place without him. It did not hurt that the Phils beat up on the weaker teams. They were 28-8 against Houston and New York, both 1962 expansion teams. However, Philadelphia was only 64-62 against everyone else.

Only three players: Richie (Dick) Allen, Johnny Callison and Tony Taylor were regularly penciled in the lineup. The only other position player with one hundred games was catcher Clay Dalrymple who shared time with Gus Triandos behind the plate. Mauch incorporated a platoon system at most positions. Philadelphia's pitching rotation was not considered on par with the other National League teams until they traded for Jim Bunning.[174]

Hindsight is 20/20; you can have your choice of Gene Mauch's blunders for the collapse. The first one occurred on September 16. Mauch decided to start Jim Bunning, his pitching ace, against Houston

172 Ibid., 27-31
173 Ibid.
174 Ibid., 330-332

with only two days' rest, considered the first sign of panic from the Phillies manager. Houston was in second to last place, and a team that Philadelphia had dominated. Why throw your best pitcher against them? Especially on short rest. The Phillies lost 6-5. From then on, Mauch seemed to favor pitching Bunning in every series down the stretch.[175]

The next day in Los Angeles he made another move that might be construed as impatience or panic. Mauch started rookie pitcher Rick Wise, who had just turned 19. It was only Wise's eighth major league start. Wise went into the bottom of the first inning with a 3-0 lead. He gave up two singles and a walk before a ground out that resulted in two runs. Mauch panicked, pulling out his young pitcher. He brought in veteran Bobby Shantz who pitched into the eighth inning and the Phils won 4-3. So instead of showing faith and confidence in the youngster, he deflated it. Wise would never appear in another game again that season.[176]

Of course, most Philadelphia fans point to the Chico Ruiz game (September 24, 1964) as the start of the collapse. It was not the first time an opposing player stole homeplate against the Phillies that season. On September 19th; Willie Davis stole home with two outs in the sixteenth inning. Mauch also made a questionable move during the fourteenth inning that might have cost the Phillies the game. Callison led off with a single, bringing up Allen, the "clean-up" hitter. Allen was to be followed by weak hitting Bobby Wine, pinch-hitting for the pitcher in the batting order. Allen came up with nobody out; he was enjoying a fine rookie season and had 26 homers. He had two singles and a walk; his previous plate appearances in the game so far. Mauch, a proponent of "small-ball," had Allen bunt to move Callison over to second. Since Allen had been successful at driving in runs fifty percent of the time with runners in scoring position, many question why did Mauch want to take the bat out of Allen's hand – especially when followed by the team's weakest hitter? Wine flied out for the second out and Callison was picked off second for the third out.

---

175 Ibid., 330-336
176 Ibid., 340-344

Over the last twelve games, the Phillies played against Cincinnati five times, and St. Louis three games. All three teams had an opportunity to control their destiny.

On September 21st, the Phillies lost 1-0. The only run was Ruiz's steal of home plate. What is rarely mentioned is how Mauch once again took the bat out of Allen's hands in the first inning by bunting Gonzalez to second. Allen's bunt was followed with both Callison and Covington grounding out to end the inning. Because of this game, Mauch lost faith in Mahaffey, who actually pitched a decent game. Mauch would only use him only one more time that year.[177]

Short was roughed up 9-2 the following day. Philadelphia failed to take even one game in a series against the Reds and it cost them dearly. Their lead was now three and a half.

The Phillies went on to lose ten games in a row. During the Phils ten game losing streak, Bunning and Short both lost three times. They both won in their final starts of the season, but by then it was a little too late.

"Mauch Over-managed and Did Not Trust His Players' Abilities and Instinct – He was his Team's biggest Negative Influence"

In conclusion, while Gene Mauch can be questioned on the way he used Bunning and Short, the poor physical status of his pitching rotation greatly influenced his decision. Gene prided himself on his knowledge of the game, but it was his "hands on" approach that was also to blame. He simply over-managed. This did not indicate brilliance, but rather the manager's overwhelming desire to control the game. Mauch's style could also have indicated his distrust in his players' abilities and instincts.

Mauch's biggest problem was his impatience over winning the pennant and his over-reaction to a string of defeats. Gene Mauch was his team's biggest negative influence.

---

177 Ibid., 324-26

Chapter 20

1967 Boston Red Sox: Dick Williams and the Impossible Dream

As a young child growing up in Boston, I was influenced to believe that the only baseball team that mattered was the Boston Red Sox. However, unfortunately for the first six years of my life from 1960 to 1966, this team underperformed. Fans had to lower their expectations because the team was not a winner. However, in 1967 everything changed because of the influence based leadership of a manager named Dick Williams. In this chapter, Bob tells the interesting story of how Dick Williams turned around the Red Sox franchise in 1967.

In 1967, the Boston Red Sox performed a turnaround that ranks as one of the best in baseball history. So this team was referred to as the Impossible Dream, named after a song from the musical "Man of La Mancha," which was based on Cervantes' *The Ingenious Gentleman Don Quixote of La Mancha*. This novel is considered one of the best literary works ever written.

The Red Sox were founded in 1901. They dominated the American League during the beginning of the century. In 1903, they defeated the Pittsburgh Pirates in the first World Series. Boston won three more championships before 1919.

After their 1918 World Series victory over the Chicago Cubs, they experienced the longest championship draught in the American League's history. It was popular to feel it began on December 26,

147

1919, when Harry Frazee sold Babe Ruth to the New York Yankees. Ruth began as a standout pitcher but turned into one of the most prolific sluggers in baseball. In 1919, when he became a full-time outfielder he broke the single season homerun record with 29.[178]

The popular belief is that Frazee sold Ruth to finance a Broadway musical called "No, No Nanette" which debuted in 1925 – but actually the money from the trade financed a non-musical called "My Lady Friends," on which "No, No Nanette" was based. The sale of the Babe became known as the "The Curse of the Bambino."

Frazee then sold the team in 1923 to Bob Quinn. Between 1925 and 1932, the Red Sox averaged 100 losses per season. When Tom Yawkey bought the team in 1933, he acquired ace pitcher Wes Ferrell to go along with Lefty Grove. He also purchased future Hall of Fame members Joe Cronin and sluggers Jimmie Foxx and Ted Williams. The Red Sox were very competitive in the 1940s, going to the World Series in 1946, but losing to the St. Louis Cardinals. The Boston Red Sox finished in second place in both 1948 and 49.

During the 1950s, the team was popularly called Ted Williams and the seven dwarfs and played at the .500 level. When Ted retired in 1960, the team finished second to last with a 65-89 record.

After Williams retired, the Red Sox became the definition of "underachievers" during the sixties.

The 1965 squad under Billy Herman finished with an embarrassing 62-100 record. The team became known as a Country Club. Many felt that he was to blame. Herman was known to join his players for drinks and never forgot to bring his golf clubs on road trips.

The Boston front office was also weak. Yawkey liked to surround himself with "drinking buddies" and "yes" men. However, one of the best moves he ever made was hiring Dick O'Connell as the team's general manager to succeed Pinky Higgins. O'Connell was instrumental in promoting several black players that formed the

---

178 Golenbock, Peter, *Red Sox Nation: An Unexpurgated History of the Boston Red Sox* (Chicago, Triumph Books, 2005) 58

nucleus of the 1967 team.[179] Former manager and long-time Red Sox employee Johnny Pesky felt that Dick O'Connell was responsible for turning the team around. The roster was crowded with superior young players such as Yaz, Conigliaro, Lonborg, and Petrocelli. Joe Foy, the MVP at Toronto in 1965, and George Scott who won the "Triple crown" at AA Pittstown the same year, joined the Red Sox causing the team to turn around. Then, before the 1967 season, O'Connell traded three fringe players for Jose Tartabull, a useful outfielder along with ace relief pitcher, John Wyatt. During the season, he acquired Ken Harrelson, Jerry Adair, Elston Howard, and Gary Bell, all valuable pieces of the Red Sox puzzle. But the most important move made by O'Connell was promoting Dick Williams, a minor league manager, to Red Sox manager. The groundwork occurred at a Boston banquet at the end of the 1966 season when O'Connell spent time with Williams. After their conversation, the general manager hired Williams.[180]

Williams played for the Red Sox in 1963 and 64. He detested the "country club" atmosphere. So when he took over, he changed the Red Sox's spring training to become the antithesis of a "country club."[181] Williams expected his players to be in shape before they arrived at camp. He did not feel that spring training was meant for his players to sweat themselves into shape. Instead, he devoted the camp to drills and training of fundamentals. The veteran players seemed to welcome the new approach and worked hard. Writers waited to see if Williams would "kowtow" to Boston's two best players, Tony Conigliaro, and Carl Yastrzemski. Dick Williams addressed this early by stripping Yaz of his captaincy.[182]

Dick Williams felt there were too many players that felt they were in charge. He ended that, assuring them that he was the only one in charge. When the camp was finished, Williams guaranteed that the

---

179 Petroceli, Rico and Scoggins, Chaz, *Rico Petrocelli's Tales from the Impossible Dream* (Sports Publishing LLC, 2007) 207

180 "Dick Williams," by Jeff Angus, SABR Bio Project

181 "Dick O'Connell," by Kerry Keene

182 Ibid., Petrocelli, 5

Red Sox would win more than they lost. Las Vegas odds makers put them at 100-1 to win the American League pennant.

The first indication that the team had potential occurred during the second game of the 1967 season. Whitey Ford, the Yankee legend and future Hall of Fame pitcher squared off against Billy Rohr, the twenty-five-year-old Red Sox rookie. Rohr took a no-hitter with two outs and two strikes in the ninth. Elston Howard, who ironically played for Boston by the end of the year, broke up the gem with a single to right-center. The young pitcher finished his major league debut with a one-hitter.[183] By the end of April, the Red Sox were tied for first place at 11-10, then eventually slipped into sixth place with an 18-20 on May 27th.

Dick Williams explained that after the first two months, he was not managing a team but making a point. Williams was all business. What you saw is what you got.

The Red Sox manager did not care how much a player was earning. He was there to win games, so no favors. His rules were the same for rookies and veterans, if a player was not hitting or pitching, he was not in the line-up.

Dick Williams was a practitioner of tough love. One example occurred after a game that Jim Lonborg pitched. He lost a no-hitter, and then he lost his shutout, and eventually lost the game by a score of 2-1. When people began consoling the pitcher for tough luck after a loss, Williams replied in no uncertain terms, that it was a loss.[184]

Fans and players pointed to several games where the name "Impossible Dream" could have originated. The most popular choice was a game played on June 15th. On that date, the third place Red Sox were at Fenway playing the first place White Sox. The series was knotted up one game apiece. The game was scoreless for the first ten innings. Chicago took a 1-0 lead at the top of the eleventh, but Joe Foy singled at the bottom of the inning to bring up Tony Conigliaro. Tony was in an 11-49 funk before stepping into the batter's box. With

183 Ibid, 55
184 Ibid., 55

one swing, Conigliaro hit a two-run homer to win the game. The Red Sox went into third place alone, and only four games out of first. The following day the "Boston Globe" referred to the team's season as the "Impossible Dream."[185]

Shortly afterward, the team fell quickly into fourth place by losing three out of four games to the Washington Senators and then regrouped on June 21st. To many, this is the day that the Red Sox turned in their "country club" membership. On the evening of June 20th, Boston beat the Yankees 7-1 at Yankee Stadium, highlighted by Joe Foy's grand slam. Then the next game they jumped on the Yankees' rookie pitcher Thad Tillotson for four runs in the first inning. When Foy came up the next inning with men on first and second, Tillotson threw three fastballs high and tight and then hit Foy just above the left temple. Fortunately, Joe was not hurt. He dusted himself off, glaring at the pitcher while he trotted down the first base line. When the Yankee pitcher came up in the bottom half of the inning with a man on second, Lonborg drilled him between the shoulder blades. As he walked down to first, he pointed threateningly at the pitcher. Foy raced over from third base challenging him to a fight. Umpire Nestor Chylak followed him ready to restore order, but both benches emptied. Amazingly, no one was thrown out. When Lonborg batted in the third, he was plunked. The benches cleared again. Boston went on to win 8-1. The game indicated that the Boston Red Sox were no longer a group of individuals but a team. This had been Dick Williams' goal since the start of the season.[186]

Dick Williams quipped, "I had to look both ways to see if I was getting it (punches) more from my own players than the Yankees."[187]

Williams' sarcasm was probably due to his managerial style. He was known for making bed checks on the road, even by walking inside of players' rooms. All season long, he benched Foy and Scott because of weight issues. Dick was not afraid to sit players for not

---

185 Ibid., 65-66
186 Ibid., 99-102
187 Ibid., 101

hitting, even Yaz, the eventual Triple Crown winner, did not escape the manager's wrath. Williams was a stickler for hustle and did not tolerate mental blunders.

As gruff as the Boston skipper seemed, he had a warm understanding side. Williams was good at handling his players' personal situations. He had a gift for consoling players after a death in their family or domestic problems. Still, Williams was a stickler for the rules he set. One policy in particular was a weight limit for Joe Foy and especially George "Boomer" Scott. Part of the reason, it was motivational – as "Boomer" had a tendency to get complacent. As far as Williams was concerned, it did not matter if the Red Sox were fighting for a place in standings or not. He lived by his rules. Williams benched him for the first game of a series with the Angels because he was four pounds over his weight limit, even though George was the team's best hitter against California that season. He had three homers off of Jim McGlothlin, the Angels' starting pitcher of the first game that season. Initially, the Red Sox players were dismayed. Williams' explanation for benching his slugger was how much did he weigh when he hit the homers off of McGlothlin? George Scott respected his manager and accepted his punishment without complaint.

Williams had a rule of punishing players for exceeding their determined weight limit. He operated within this rule all year so he was not going to change it because George Scott was the team's best hitter and they were in a tight pennant race.

Scott was able to sweat off five pounds in twenty-four hours to return to the lineup the next game. He drove in the only Boston run during a 2-1 loss to California.

The American League pennant race was shaping up to be one of the greatest of all time and would intensify that July. But before the games played on July 1st the White Sox had built a comfortable 4 1/2 game lead over the second place Tigers and 5 ½ over the Red Sox. Boston and Detroit were tied the following day. Two weeks later the Red Sox were in fifth place, six games behind. Then on July 14th, Boston began a ten game winning streak and by July 23rd climbed into second place a half of a game out. After the streak, they won nine out of their next twenty-one games. On August 15th the Red Sox were back in 5th place, but very much in contention and only three games back.

The standings changed daily and in some cases, hourly. Then on August 18th, something occurred that could have psychologically eliminated the Red Sox from the pennant race. Tony Conigliaro, whose walk-off homer inspired the "Impossible Dream,"[188] and the youngest player to lead the American League in homeruns – also the second youngest major league player to reach 100 career homeruns, who at the time was also leading the American League with 20 dingers, stepped into the batter's box to face Jack Hamilton of the California Angels. Hamilton had given up one hit over the first three innings, a single to Conigliaro. Tony was known for crowding the plate; he also had a blind spot. He never saw it coming and the ball crashed into the left side of his face, ending his season and possibly ending Boston's dream.[189]

As luck might have it, general manager O'Connell was able to purchase Ken "Hawk" Harrelson who had just been released by the Kansas City A's over a verbal spat with his old boss Charlie Finely. Harrelson played in only twenty-three games for Boston, batting .200, with three homers; it was his presence in the lineup that kept Yaz and kept Boston's dream alive after Conigliaro's beaning.

After the loss of their top slugger, the team won seven in a row, four against the Angels that allowed them to move into second place. Their record for August was 14-5. Boston found themselves in first place. The Red Sox won as many as they lost in September, spending most days in either first or second. On September 26 they were in third place with four games to go. They lost on September 26 and 27. The White Sox were eliminated with a 1-0 loss to the Washington Senators. It was now a three-team race with the Twins, Tigers, and Red Sox.

After losing two games to Cleveland, Boston was left with two games against Minnesota. Detroit had four to play, back-to-back

---

188 Ibid., 98
189 Ibid., 134-36

double headers against the Angels. If the Tigers swept and the Red Sox split with the Twins, or if Detroit took three out of four and Boston won both games against the Twins, Detroit would win the pennant. The Red Sox had two days to prepare for the Twins.

Yaz probably won Red Sox MVP honors based on his performance over the last ten games. During that span, he went 20-37, with a .541 batting average. During the first eight games before the Twins' series he hit four homers, three doubles, driving in fourteen runs and scored eleven.

Many expected that Williams would start his ace Jim Lonborg for the first game against the Twins; instead, he stuck to his pitching rotation and used the gritty Jose' Santiago. The manager's choice paid off, as they won 6-4.[190]

After 162 games, it came down to a final game in Boston. It featured aces Dean Chance of the Twins against Jim Lonborg of the Red Sox. Boston was down 2-0 before scoring five in the bottom of the sixth. Yaz drove in two and also scored. Boston won the game 5-3 and the American League pennant![191]

The Red Sox played the St. Louis Cardinals in the World Series, the same team that Boston faced their last time (1946) in the "Fall Classic." The Red Sox lost four games to three that season. The seventh game of the 1967 series featured both team's ace players, Bob Gibson and Jim Lonborg. The Cardinals won 2-0 to capture the series in seven games.

The Red Sox season is considered <u>one</u> of the greatest turnarounds in baseball history during the twentieth century.

There are several reasons that could be credited for the Red Sox' great season, such as their young talent, or career years by Yaz and Jim Lonborg. Who could deny the job that General Manager Dick O'Connell did with his acquisitions before and during the season. But no one could argue that Dick Williams' influence inspired the team to believe in the "Impossible Dream."

190 Ibid., 183-84
191 Ibid., 170-79

Chapter 21

1969 New York Mets:
Gil Hodges and the Miracle Mets

*O*ne of the most interesting baseball stories that has taken place during my lifetime relates to the team of overachievers dubbed the "Miracle Mets." Clearly, as a Red Sox fan, the 2004 come back of the Boston Red Sox against the Yankees in the 2004 American League Championship Series (ALCS) means more to me. However, the story of the 1969 Mets' comeback and the influences that led to that amazing turnaround is one of the most incredible stories in sports history. Bob tells the story of the influences that led to this miraculous turnaround in this chapter.

While standing at the podium, the young President from Boston, Massachusetts delivered the following dream to Congress. "This nation should commit itself to achieving the goal, before the decade is out, of landing a man on the moon and returning him safely to Earth." John F. Kennedy's prophecy became a reality on July 20, 1969, when Neil Armstrong stepped on the moon's surface and uttered, "This is one small step for man, one great leap for mankind."

The running joke among Mets' fans claimed that our country would land a man on the moon before the Mets won a World Championship. The Mets almost laid the joke to rest; they missed by three months. That was the moment Cleon Jones caught the final out of the 1969 season, erasing all of the last place seasons suffered by the New York Mets. On that October 16th afternoon, Davey Johnson flied out to left field, and the improbable occurred. The "Amazin'" Mets" defeated the mighty Baltimore Orioles four games to one to become the World Champions of baseball!

At one time, there were three major league teams in New York; the Dodgers, the Giants and the Yankees. In May of 1957, National League owners voted that both the Dodgers and the Giants could move west. The city's baseball triumvirate started cracking shortly after the Brooklyn Dodgers finally beat the Yankees in the 1955 World Series. Both the Dodgers and the Giants blamed their decaying ballparks and deteriorating neighborhoods for lower attendance. A little more than two years later, Horace Stoneman, the owner of the New York Giants, and Walter O'Malley of the Dodgers joined together to move their rivalry to California. This left New York City with only the Yankees.

The migration west might have been motivated by lagging attendance in New York City, but ironically the National League's overall attendance did not benefit from the Dodgers' and Giants' relocation either to the west coast in 1958. Oddly, after the move, the American League's attendance also suffered. Robert Wagner, New York City's mayor at the time, formed a committee to return National League baseball to New York.[192] At about the same time, baseball icon Branch Rickey entered the picture; the same Rickey who created the minor league farm system while in St. Louis, and the one who broke down baseball's unwritten racial barrier when he signed Jackie Robinson.

An article appeared in the "Sporting News" on May 21, 1958, where Branch Rickey stated how the time was right for major league baseball to expand, suggesting that expansion could occur under the present two-league format or with the creation of a third league. When Rickey felt that Major League baseball had been dragging its feet long enough, he established the Continental League consisting of eight

---

192 Lowenfish, Lee, *Branch Rickey: Baseball's Ferocious Gentleman* (Lincoln, Ne, University of Nebraska Press, 2007) 545

teams on August 18, 1959.[193] The teams were located in New York City, Houston, Toronto, Denver, Minneapolis-St. Paul, Dallas-Fort Worth, Atlanta and Buffalo. All but Buffalo would eventually have MLB teams. Only Buffalo is still AAA (as of 2019).

Because of Branch Rickey's Continental League, Major League baseball was pushed toward the thought of expansion. Existing team owners invited the Continental League owners to a meeting in Chicago on August 2, 1960, to discuss the mechanics of expansion. The expansion was agreed upon on August 17, 1960. The Continental League teams from Houston and New York joined the expanded National League in 1962.

Joan Whitney Payson, a former minor partner of the New York Giants, plus a big baseball fan, became the new owner of the New York Mets. The Mets' management saw an opportunity – New York's return to the National League, so they packed their roster with former Brooklyn Dodger and New York Giants players. In fact, their baseball cap incorporated each team's colors and insignias. They also signed Casey Stengel, the former manager of the Yankees, with hopes of winning over disgruntled fans still upset about the Yankees firing the "old professor."[194]

At first, it was fun for Mets fans to embrace their team as the "lovable losers." Eventually, their affection for losing wore thin. They became tired of the constant last place finishes. Manager Wes Westrum resigned before the end of 1967 and Salty Parker finished the season. The club began making changes during the off-season with hopes of bringing back a winner to the "big city."[195] They started by promoting young pitching talents like Seaver, Koosman, Gentry, McAndrew, McGraw and Ryan; then they made trades for veteran pitchers like Don Caldwell from Pittsburgh, Cal Koonce from the

---

193 Ibid.
194 "Joan Payson," by Joan M. Thomas, SABR Bio Project
195 Clavin, Tom and Peary, Danny, *Gil Hodges: The Brooklyn Bums, The Miracle Mets, and the Extraordinary Life of a Baseball Legend* (NY, NY, New American Library, 2012) 303

Chicago Cubs and Ron Taylor from Houston. The Mets had great pitching and decent defense, but very little in the way of offense.

Management understood the need for more trades. However, the most important trade did not involve a player. Instead, it involved the acquisition of a new manager. They essentially traded for Gil Hodges from Washington for $100,000 and an obscure pitcher named Bill Denehy.[196] Bing Devine, the club's General Manager, coveted Hodges as the Mets' next manager. So, it became official during the third game of the 1967 World Series on November 27, 1967.[197]

Hodges was a man who went quietly about his business. He made few demands with only small suggestions, like recommending getting Tommy Agee from the Chicago White Sox. Tommy was a former "Rookie of the Year" in the American League.[198] Agee's first season as a Met did not look promising, as he was hit in the head by a Bob Gibson pitch.[199] Agee put up paltry numbers that first season batting only 217 with 5 homers. Still, Gil felt he was the leadoff batter the team needed. Hodges' faith was rewarded as Agee bounced back in 1969.[200]

Hodges proved to be a savvy manager with a knack for improving the teams that he managed. Bud Harrelson, the shortstop for the Mets, said Gil knew the rules better than the umpires. Hodges was also adept at using a platoon system, which kept his team fresh. In 1969, he used a left-right combo in right field of Art Shamsky, a left handed power hitter, and Ron Swoboda. Art proved his worth in August by batting .350. He was a major reason the Mets went from 9½ games back on August 13th to first on September 10th. That season only eleven players appeared in one hundred games and only two, Agee and Cleon Jones, played in more than 125.

196 "69' Mets: finally got serious under Gil Hodges," by Mark Hermann, Newsday, September 24, 2009
197 "Gil Hodges," by John Saccoman, SABR Bio Project
198 Ibid., Clavin 29
199 Allen, Maury, After the Miracle: The Amazin' Mets Twenty Years Later,(NY, NY, Franklin Watts, 1989) 30
200 Agee batted .271, 26 homers and 76 RBIs in 149 games

"He walked in and his physical presence changed what was going on immediately. Then he spoke it changed even more. When you looked at the size of his hands, it changed even more." – Tom Seaver, Cy Young winner in 1969.[201]

Gil did not outwardly demand his player's respect, he earned it!

Art Shamsky felt that acquiring Donn Clendenon from Montreal on June 15th was very significant.[202] Clendenon's contribution was not limited to his on-field production but also his unifying presence in the clubhouse; he eased tensions by lightening the mood on a team that was unaccustomed to contending. Ron Swoboda felt he was a catalyst, doubting that the Mets could have won without Clendenon.

While most Mets fans can point to several reasons for the miracle 1969 season, such as timely hitting, stellar defense and great pitching; it did not hurt that Agee and Jones had career years at the plate, the way that Jerry Grote was adept at handling the talented, young pitching staff, how Tug McGraw, a former starting pitcher became a bullpen stalwart or the Clendenon trade. All Mets players were in agreement about who was most responsible for the miracle season, it was Gil Hodges.

Gil's players were always prepared. Donn Clendenon explained the reason for the Mets' success was their manager, and every guy on the team knew his job.[203]

Ken Boswell said, "Gil was the smartest man I ever met in baseball. He was really the creator of that team. He wasn't the friendliest guy around the club. He often seemed distracted. He was just a quiet, strong leader. He could get mad and yell. Yell at umpires or scream at any of us when things went badly. He seemed to be leaning forward on the bench all the time thinking ahead to moves."[204]

---

201 Ibid. Hermann
202 Golenbock, Peter, Amazin': the Miraculous History of the New York Mets (NY, NY, St. Martin's Press, 2002) 224
203 Ibid., Allen 65
204 Ibid., Allen 77

There is one particular incident that spoke volumes about Gil Hodges; it occurred on July 30th and that earned him his players' respect. The Mets played a double-header with the Houston Astros. During the ninth inning of the first game, relief pitchers Cal Koonce and Ron Taylor surrendered eleven runs. Then in the second game, Gary Gentry gave up seven before Nolan Ryan came on to relieve. Johnny Edwards sliced a ball to left field. The burly catcher was not known for his speed; he was able to pull into second "standing up" because of Cleon Jones' non-hustle. With Edwards at second base, the Mets manager slowly walked out of the dugout toward the field. Nolan Ryan thought that Hodges was coming out to see him, but once Hodges stepped over the third base line, he made a left turn out to where Cleon Jones was playing. Gil asked his star player if he was okay. Whatever Jones' response was, his manager quietly escorted him back to the dugout. He then sent Ron Swoboda out onto the field. Other managers might have felt that Jones showed him up, but not Gil. The Jones confrontation verified the players' opinions of their manager. Years after the incident, when Jones was at the 20th celebration of the 1969 team, he said that the 1969 Mets would not have won if not for Gil Hodges.[205]

Gil Hodges had a certain unique non-verbal influence. There is a story from when he managed the Washington Senators. Ryne Duran was one of his pitchers. Duran was nearing the end of his career. Duran slowly sunk into the bottle, to the point where Gil was called to a bridge only to find his pitcher was contemplating jumping. No one knows what Hodges said, but the fact is Ryne Duran did not jump; instead, he cleaned up his habit and became an advocate against alcoholism.[206]

On September 8th, the Chicago Cubs came into town for a two game set with the Mets. At the time the Mets were 2 ½ games in back of the Cubs. Bill Hands faced Jerry Koosman in the first

---

205 "Good Ships runs aground; Defensive Lapses take Big Toll," by Jack Lang, The Sporting News, August 16, 1969, 15
206 Ibid., Clavin 294

game. Hands let loose a fastball at Tommie Agee's head in the bottom half of the first. When Ron Santo came up in the top of the second, Koosman drilled Santo to lead off the inning. Mets' coach Joe Pignatono stated that hitting Santo was the reason the Mets won the pennant.[207] Ironically, Hodges did not say a word to Koosman about hitting Santo, because he did not need to. While the game against the Cubs was the third game of a winning streak, the Mets went on to win seven more in a row. Then from September 21 to October 1, the Mets strung together nine more in a row. They won 38 of their last 49. Jim Gosger, who was a late season call up, earning a promotion after a good season at Tidewater, remembered how big a thrill it was to be a part of it. Gosger only played in ten games, batting fifteen times with two hits, both doubles.

"The whole place, the town just went crazy...we were celebrities, but I was just happy to be a part of it."[208]

When they clinched the NL East against St. Louis, the Mets earned the right to face the Atlanta Braves in the playoffs. New York was considered underdogs, even though they won seven more games than Atlanta during the season and took eight of twelve games in their "head to head" series. The baseball world still expected Cinderella's carriage to turn into a pumpkin. New York shocked the odds makers by sweeping the Braves in three games. The Mets were going to the World Series. Their opponent was the highly favored Baltimore Orioles.

During the first game, Don Buford, the Orioles' leadoff man, hit the second pitch from Mets ace Tom Seaver over the outfield fence and Baltimore won the first game 4-1. It appeared that the Mets miracle had finally burst. Instead, the Mets regrouped and won the next four games to capture the first World Series in their young history!

---

207 Ibid, Clavin 103-04
208 Jim Gosger interview with author on April 22, 2014

Many books have been written about this team. But Mets fans refer to the season as a miracle while others simply called them amazing. The New York Mets became the first expansion team to win a World Championship.

The Mets were a team built with defense and pitching. But their fate was arguably constructed by the influence of Gil Hodges.

Chapter 22

1971 Pittsburgh Pirates: The Team That Changed Baseball

The significance of Jackie Robinson becoming a Major League Baseball star cannot be overstated. He was the right person at the right time. However, there were other racial firsts that had significant influence on the diversification of professional baseball. In this chapter, Bob talks about the extremely important role that the 1971 Pittsburgh Pirates played in accelerating the diversity of baseball.

**Steve Blass and Manny Sanguillen, the battery
for the 7th game of the 1971 World Series**

In the opinion of many baseball fans, baseball's racial barrier ended when Jackie Robinson debuted with the Brooklyn Dodgers on April 15, 1947. Next was Bill Veeck's signing of Larry Doby the following July for the Cleveland Indians. Unfortunately, each was only an introduction. Only four black players played in the majors that year. The other two were Hank Thompson and Willard Brown of the St. Louis Browns. After that initial integration, only two other players entered the league during the rest of the decade – Satchel Paige and Monte Irvin. Why was integration so slow? Before Jackie broke the racial barrier, owners had a "gentleman's agreement," and they were suspected of having a secret quota. There was also another quota among owners during the nineteen-fifties. John Lardner[209] in 1953 claimed that a 50 percent color line existed in the Major Leagues, meaning that a M.L. team could only play four blacks out of the nine on field at a time. The ratio of 5 whites to 4 blacks substantiated white supremacy.[210] By 1955, there were only twelve blacks in the major leagues; that number included a dark-skinned Latino named Roberto Clemente.

During the 1960 World Series between the Yankees and the Pirates, they combined to have eleven minority players, four on the Yankees and seven on the Pirates, which seemed like a great improvement – until you consider that it had been thirteen years since the signing of Jackie Robinson.

While most major league teams still seemed to be dragging their feet, the 1970 Pirates had fifteen minority players play alongside twenty-one Caucasians. The Pirates featured non-white stars like Clemente, Matty Alou, Willie Stargell and Manny Sanguillen. This team captured the eastern division of the National League.

The following year, Pirates' manager Danny Murtaugh wrote out the following line-up for a September 1, 1971, game against the

209 John Lardner, "a forgotten giant of sports writing world," by Scott Tinley, Sports Illustrated, October 14, 2010.
210 Kahn, Roger, *The Boys of Summer* (New York, NY, Harper & Row 1971) p172.

Philadelphia Phillies.[211] He did not realize that it was historic. The line-up consisted of only African-American and Latino players.

Rennie Stennett, 2B
Gene Clines, CF
Roberto Clemente, RF
Willie Stargell, LF
Manny Sanguillen, C
Dave Cash, 3B
Al Oliver, 1B
Jackie Hernandez, SS
Dock Ellis, P

When the line-up's significance was brought to the manager's attention, he responded, "Did I have nine blacks in there? I thought I had nine Pirates out there on the field. Once a man puts on a Pirate uniform, I don't notice the color of his skin."[212]

"Once a man puts on a Pirate uniform, I don't notice the color of his skin."
– Manager Danny Murtaugh

Murtaugh's response should not surprise anyone. The Pittsburgh Pirates were considered the most racially progressive team in major league baseball. The 1971 Championship team was loaded with talent. It consisted of future Hall of Famers like Roberto Clemente, Willie Stargell, and Bill Mazeroski. Each of them became team leaders on the field and in the clubhouse; Clemente a Latino, Stargell an African American, and Mazeroski, a Caucasian.[213] Instead of each

---

211 Markusen, Bruce, *The Team that Changed Baseball: Roberto Clemente and the 1971 Pittsburgh Pirates* (Yardly, Pa., Westholme Publishing, 2006), 108

212 Ibid., 109

213 Blass, Steve and Sherman, Erick, Steve Blass: A Pirate for Life (Chicago, Triumph Books, 2012) 120-22

leading only those from their racial class or ethnicity, they led ALL of their teammates by example. The 1971 Pirates were baseball's true "melting pot."

Young Latino players on the Pirates and on opposing teams gravitated toward Clemente for advice. Roberto advised them on how to act and dress in their new country.[214] Something that was not available to him when he came up in 1955. His stature was elevated in the late sixties to early seventies. He inspired players of all backgrounds. Roberto took Manny Sanguillen, a young catcher from Panama under his wing and treated him like a younger brother; others learned from his behavior on and off of the field. Al Oliver, a young black player, admired Clemente's hustle and work ethic. Young white players such as Steve Blass and Dave Guisti loved bantering with Clemente in the clubhouse.[215] Kidding aside, they both looked up to him as a team leader.

Clemente also mentored Willie Stargell, an African American who was another leader on the team. Roberto knew how to relax his teammates. Stargell loved to watch Roberto play; he learned so much from Clemente. Clemente was the strong, silent type, but his mannerisms had a powerful knack of teaching others about life inside and outside of baseball. When Willie struggled during the 1971 series, Roberto told him not to press, that he (Roberto) would carry the team on his back.[216] Clemente went on to bat .414 for the series and hit safely in every game. He was voted the MVP of that series. Eight years later Stargell became the driving force behind the 1979 "We Are Family" Pirates; he credits Clemente's example.

Bill Mazeroski led by example, but was also a quiet teacher. A white player, he also led by example. Willie Stargell was very grateful for Maz because he taught him the values of patience and consistency. Willie learned that you needed consistency to enjoy a long career.

---

214 Herb Rayborn interview with author on 8/13/2012
215 Ibid., 123
216 Markusen, Bruce, *Roberto Clemente: The Great One* (Sports Publishing LLC, 2001) 250

Consistency was the key to patience. Maz was also a major influence on Dave Cash, the Pirates' young African American second baseman. Cash felt that he learned how to be a major league second baseman because of Bill's help. All the while, Maz knew that Cash was a threat to take his job, but this did not prevent him from helping Cash become a better player.[217] Maz felt the 1971 Pirates were the strongest team he ever played for, stronger than the 1960 World Series championship team that he played on.[218]

"The key to the team's success was how every man on the roster picked each other up."
– Dave Guisti

In a conversation I had with Dave Guisti, he felt that the key to the team's success was how every man on the roster picked each other up. It began in the clubhouse. Everyone liked each other… It did not matter if you were black or white or Latino. [219] Everyone put being a teammate first. As Dave Cash claimed, you could put all of our names in a hat and whatever you pulled out would have a great chance of winning any ballgame.

The 1971 Pirates were more than a very good baseball team, which they needed to be in order to beat a great Oriole team. The Baltimore Orioles featured four pitchers that won twenty games, and had Hall of Famers Brooks and Frank Robinson. While they were arguably one of the best championship teams, they should also be remembered as a team that ushered racial balance into the game.

But, the 1971 Pittsburgh Pirates was the team that truly changed baseball!

---

217 Ibid., Markusen (2006), 26-7
218 Ibid., Markusen (2006), 23
219 Ibid., 53-54

Chapter 23

1979 Pittsburgh Pirates:
Pops And We Are Family

Extraordinary professional baseball teams often have leaders who go above *and beyond the call of duty to inspire their teammates. These individuals inspire every member of the team to get the most out of their skills and abilities possible. In this chapter, Bob talks about the amazing influence of Willie Stargell on the 1979 Pittsburgh Pirates.*

In 1979, America was experiencing double-digit inflation, a near disaster at Three Mile Island and a hostage crisis in Iran. However, through all of the gloom, a team in Pittsburgh provided a ray of sunshine, evoking a feeling that the actor James Earl Jones spoke of in the movie *Field of Dreams*: "Baseball has marked the time. This field, this game, is a part of our past ... It reminds us of all that once was good, and could be again ..."

The beginning of the 1970s was kind to the Pittsburgh Pirates. From 1970-75 they won the Eastern division four out of five years, advancing and winning the World Series in 1971. Unfortunately, between 1976 and 1978 another Pennsylvania team, the Philadelphia Phillies, won the Eastern Division. The Pirates finished second to them in each of those years. The Phils won 101 games in both 1976 and 1977, but in 1978 the Pirates came back from 15 ½ to play for first place to challenge them on the final weekend of the season. The Pirates needed to sweep a four game series in order to win the division. They won the first two but were eliminated with a loss on Sunday, September 30th. They bounced back and won on the last day of the season to finish 1 ½ out of first. This gave Pirates fans hope for 1979.[220]

The Pirates got off to a slow start in 1979. They lost four out of the first five games. Then with the help of John Milner's hot bat and some stellar pitching from Don Robinson, Jim Bibby, Ed Whitson and Kent Tekulve, they were able to reach a respectable 4-4 won and lost record. Still, the defense continued to be erratic causing them to lose the following series to the Phillies. Both General Manager Harding Peterson and the Pirates' manager Chuck Tanner, had seen enough, and pulled the trigger on an unpopular trade. They traded Frank Tavares, who was their starting shortstop, known more for his speed on the base paths than for his defense, for Tim Foli, a back-up shortstop for the Mets.[221]

While Foli was a solid defensive player, his personality did not endear him to people in baseball. He was known for his unpredictable temper, both on the field and in the clubhouse. Fortunately, all of this seemed to change when he came to Pittsburgh. The first teammate to greet him was Willie Stargell. Pops had a "one to one" conversation with his new teammate. Pops explained to Foli that he was not joining a new baseball team but a family.

With a new lease on life, Foli contributed to his new team in various ways, like hitting to the right side to advance the runner, taking a pitch to allow a teammate to steal second, or laying down a sacrifice bunt. He enjoyed one of his best seasons in 1979. That season, he batted .291 with 65 runs batted in. He went on to bat .333 in the World Series while setting a record of not striking out in 33 plate appearances.

---

220 Finoli, David, and Ranier,Bill, *The Pittsburgh Pirates Encyclopedia* (Sports Publisher LLC, 2003) 583

221 McCollister,John, Tales from the 1979 Pittsburgh Pirates: Remembering "The Fam-A-Lee," (Sports Publishing LLC, 2005) 17

"Willie Stargell was a spiritual leader in the clubhouse."

No one will deny that Willie Stargell was a great influence on the 1979 Pirates. At thirty-nine years old, he was still a feared bat in the lineup. But more importantly, he was a spiritual leader in the clubhouse. Willie had a way of taking a player under his wing, then talking to him in a fatherly way. It made sense that he was affectionately called "Pops" by his younger teammates. Phil Garner gave Pops the greatest compliment when he said, "When my sons grow up to be men, I hope they will be like Willie Stargell."[222] Opponents also echoed this admiration. Joe Morgan, the Hall of Fame member of the Cincinnati Reds chipped in, "He was my hero. He's the reason I wore number 8."[223]

On Memorial Day of 1979, the Pirates found themselves 6 ½ games behind the Expos.

Management felt the team needed another potent bat. They felt that Willie Stargell and Dave Parker were not enough.

So, Peterson pulled off another unpopular acquisition by bringing the unhappy Bill Madlock into the Pirates' fold. The team's clubhouse buzzed with apprehension. "Mad Dog," as Madlock was known, had a bad reputation around baseball. This did not concern Dave Parker, who figured that once Pops had a conversation with him, everything would be fine.

Many felt that the Madlock deal was the key to the Pirates' magical season. He solidified the Pittsburgh defensive alignment; one used the rest of the season and into the NLCS and World Series.[224]

Madlock was moved to third base, his natural position after playing at second in San Francisco, which meant Garner replaced Rennie Stennett at second base, his natural position. Pittsburgh was in third place on the day they traded for Madlock. On July 28th, they moved into first place for the first time. Then on August 5th, they

---

222 Ibid., 49
223 Ibid., 47
224 Ibid., 3

spent significant time at the top of the Eastern Division, remaining there until September 20th. Then the Pirates and the Expos had a showdown with Montreal September 24-26, and the Pirates won three out of four. They finally clinched the division on the last day of the season.[225]

Pops dispensed gold felt stars that acknowledged a player's accomplishments. Pirates' players vied to earn them. Pitcher Bert Blyleven felt his teammates not only wanted to win games, but earn a 'Stargell Star.'"[226]

Willie Stargell felt the team needed a rallying cry or song, so they adopted "We Are Family," the team's catchy theme song for the 1979 season. As Stargell tells it, the team was sitting in the dugout during a rain delay against St. Louis, when he heard a Sister Sledge's song entitled "We Are Family" over the loudspeakers.

It was the birth of a tradition; during 1979 the Pirates played the song after victories and defeats. The celebratory song became the team's rallying cry![227]

The 1979 Pirates finished the season with a record of 98-64, winning the East by two games ahead of the Montreal Expos. They went on and swept their old nemesis, the Cincinnati Reds in three games.

It was an exciting season. Willie Stargell finally stepped out from Roberto Clemente's shadow. Stargell's quiet confidence was never as evident as on October 13th. The Pirates had lost their third game of the World Series, putting them down three games to one. Stargell sat in the dugout with Teke, Parker and Garner. Pops looked at his downcast teammates and told them even if they lost, it was their obligation to show everyone how the Buccos played baseball. This seemed to inspire the Pirates to come came back and win the series in seven games.

225 Nowlin, Bill and Wolf, Gregory, *When Pops Led the Family: The 1979 Pittsburgh Pirates* (SABR, Phoenix, 2016) 53-54

226 Ibid., McCollister, 36

227 Ibid., Nowlin, 346

Kent Tekulve enjoys telling about the seventh game of the World Series. The Orioles loaded the bases and were trying to rally when Eddie Murray, a future Hall of Famer, stepped up to the plate. For the first time, Teke showed a little anxiety, more than normal. Stargell could see it. So he called for time, and he walked out to the mound.

Stargell looked at the tall, skinny reliever and informed him if he was afraid to pitch to Murray, let him have the ball so he could pitch, and Teke could play first.[228] The words seemed to calm down the Pirates' closer and he got Murray to hit a lazy fly ball to Parker to end the inning. The Pirates would win the seventh and deciding game of the 1979 series, completing a remarkable comeback after being down three games to one.

While it was a miracle season for the Pittsburgh Pirates, it was a magical one for Willie Stargell.[229] Willie was the MVP of the NLCS, MVP of the World Series and then tied Keith Hernandez as MVP of the National League. He did this at the ripe old age of thirty-nine. He became the oldest player to win each award and the only one to win all three during the same season. 1979 was special for Sister Sledge. Their song "We are family" not only reached number one on the Disco Charts, but also the Rhythm and Blues Charts. It made it as high as number two on the Pop charts. It became a gold record and won the singing group a Grammy in 1979 for the best R&B performance by a duo group with vocals. Sister Sledge is still performing globally, but has had only moderate success since that magical year of 1979

Willie Stargell, leader of the "We Are Family" Pirates died on April 9, 2001, at the age of 61. For the 2001 season, current Pirate players wore a two and a half inch black circle honoring him. The Pirates have also erected a bronze statue of Willie outside the left field entrance to PNC Park in Pittsburgh.

---

228 Ibid., 221

229 He batted .282, 32 homers, and 82 RBIs. His .997 fielding percentage was the best of all first basemen in the NL.

Section VI
Player Influence

Chapter 24

Wally Westlake: 1947-1956

S *ome of the most interesting baseball stories are about the influences of players who were not stars. Many of these individuals feel extremely lucky to have had the chance to play their favorite sport professionally. In this chapter, Bob tells the little known story of the positive and negative influences in the life of professional baseball player Wally Westlake.*

Wally Westlake with large fish

Wally Westlake was born on November 8, 1920, in Gridley, Ca. He was originally signed by the Brooklyn Dodgers as a free agent in 1940 and made his major league debut in 1947. Westlake played for

Pittsburgh between 1947 and 1951. During that span, he averaged a little more than twenty home runs a year. Westlake has the distinction of hitting for the cycle twice, once in 1948 and then in 1949. When Branch Rickey traded Wally to Saint Louis, Wally blamed Rickey for hurting his self-confidence. Before the trade, he was on his way to having quite a career. Westlake would make stops in St. Louis, Cincinnati, Cleveland, Baltimore and finally Philadelphia during his career. He was an All-Star in 1951 and played in a World Series for the Cleveland Indians in 1954.

Wally began playing sandlot baseball while in grammar school. At the time, organized baseball was not available for younger players. He played every chance he got. His dad was very supportive about him playing and always encouraged him.

Wally made the baseball team at Christian Brothers High School, then played summer ball with the Manhart American Legion team. The Manhart team had been around since 1935, and was considered THE summer travel team in California during the 1930s! Manhart ended up playing the Long Beach Legion team for the state championship. They played in the championship at an old Pacific Coast League Park that Wally could not remember the name of. He remembered hitting with the bases loaded in the bottom of the ninth. Wally hit a single to right field that brought in the tying and the winning run.

After that game, he thought, "Damn it, I'd like to get some more of this!"

It was around that time that Wally began to think about a baseball career. Wally played every chance he could get. The Brooklyn Dodgers signed him after he graduated high school on June 14, 1940. Then they farmed him out to Dayton, Ohio of the class "C" Mid Atlantic League. He was paid $425 a month. His family had just survived the Great Depression, a time which made poverty a reality. Still, he could not believe he was being paid to play a game – especially one that he loved! Unfortunately, he did not do well at first.[230] They released him, giving him the following advice:

---

230 He batted .176 with only two homers in thirty-one games

"Here is your outright release and a bus ticket home. Our advice to you is to forget baseball. It's apparent that you don't have the talent to play the game. Go home and don't waste your time on baseball and find yourself a good job!"

So Wally rode the bus home that evening and when the bus passed the ballpark, its lights were still on. He can remember the boiling feeling in his gut and he re-thought quitting.

He promised himself, "If you think you're going to make me quit, you sure as Hell better think about it again!"

So he went home and looked up the fellow that managed his old American Legion team. His old manager had become a "bird dog" scout for the Oakland Oaks of the Pacific Coast League.

Wally first played for Merced Bears of the new California League in 1941. They gave him $100 per month; Westlake batted .265 with eighteen homers. Then, in 1942, he went on to sign a contract with the Oaks.[231]

When World War II interrupted his baseball career at the age of twenty-two, Wally was drafted, serving in the Army between 1943 and 45. Unlike his father, who saw action in Europe during WW I, Wally stayed stateside. He took joy in referring to himself as a "Broadway Soldier."

After completing his time in the service, he returned to Oakland. He was now twenty-five and felt that he was running out of time. Fortunately, he had one thing in his favor; a quirky guy by the name of Casey Stengel. Casey was his manager with the Oaks. One day during pre-game warm-ups, Stengel called Wally over into the dugout.

"Sit down here, young fellow. Young fellow, you know, you have pretty good talent. Now I'm going to teach you how to play this game."

Casey did just that for the next five months. He taught his young outfielder all of the things that you cannot learn from a book. Wally learned the little things that helped you win baseball games. With only one year under Casey's tutelage, he batted .268, seven homers

---

231 where he hit .269, with seven homers, and drove in seventy-four runs in 169 games.

and drove in seventy-four runs, and Casey sold him to the Pittsburgh Pirates. After playing two weeks at Spring training, Wally thought, "Hell, I can play with these guys, and even out play some of them!" Wally Westlake made his major league debut on April 15, 1947, at twenty-six years old.

While on the Pirates he met Hank Greenberg, the future Hall of Fame player. Later in his career, Hank became the General Manager when he played for the Cleveland Indians. Wally indicated that "big old Henry" gave him some tidbits of information. Although he admitted that Greenberg spent most of his time working with Ralph Kiner, he also helped with Westlake's swing. He felt that Hank Greenberg was a first class gentleman.

But to this day Wally Westlake thanks Casey Stengel for helping him reach his dream of playing in the big leagues![232]

---

232 Westlake's career statistics were 127 home runs, 539 RBIs and a .272 average for ten seasons.

Chapter 25

Bob Friend: 1951-1966

B*ob Friend is yet another player with a story that is more interesting and dynamic than his professional baseball career. In this chapter, Bob describes the influences that made Bob Friend the person and player that he was.*

Pittsburgh Pirates, New York Mets, Yankees

Bob Friend pitched during most of his career for the Pittsburgh Pirates. He has the distinction of being the first pitcher on a losing team in 1955 to lead the National League in earned run average. His best year in the MLB was 1958.[233] That year, he was selected to his second All Star team. He also finished fourth in the MVP race, and third for the Cy Young award. Friend finished his career with a losing record of 197-230, which is understandable since he played most of his career on the awful Pirates' teams of the 1950s. Bob had a winning record for only five of his sixteen seasons in the big leagues.

One of his older brothers got him started playing baseball as an eight-year-old in West Lafayette, Indiana. While Indiana was mostly known for basketball, it also had a pretty good youth baseball program.

Bob Friend played a significant role in my baseball passion. After church, one Sunday, I was sitting in the family car waiting for my father to buy the Sunday paper; that is when he bought me my first pack of baseball cards. I can remember opening up my first Topps wax pack with curiosity and excitement. There was a Bob Friend card

---

233 Friend had a pitching record of 22-14, and a 3.68 Era

in the pack. Although I did not know anything about him, I saw that he played for the Pirates. My dad was from Pittsburgh, so I became a Pirates fan because of that. From that point on, Friend's card held a special place in my heart. Unfortunately, as I got older, my baseball cards became less important and I lost the card. Years later there was a baseball card collecting show in the 1990s. At a card show, I found the same Bob Friend card that was in that first pack. Back in the mid-sixties, a card cost just a penny, but the one at the show cost five dollars. I had the card blown up to 8" by "10 and when I met Friend at an autograph show at Three Rivers Stadium in Pittsburgh, I asked him to sign it.

Several years later during a phone conversation I had with Bob, he shared his influences during his career. He listed George Sisler, Clyde Sukeforth, Robin Roberts, Murry Dickson and Branch Rickey as influential early in his career. When I mentioned my relationship with Wally Westlake, he replied that Wally was one of the nice guys, both him and Kiner. Each of them showed kindness and encouraged each of the young players like him (Friend).

George Sisler, who is in the Hall of Fame, guided Bob on how to act like a professional. Clyde Sukeforth assisted Friend by fine tuning his pitching strategy. Both men and Bob were loyal followers of Branch Rickey. One of Rickey's favorite characterizations of pitching was, "Pitching is the art of deception." He felt that pitching success could be achieved by changing location and speeds. The two pitchers that made an impression on him when he began pitching were Robin Roberts of the Phillies and Murray Dickson, a teammate on the Pirates.

The great thing about Bob Friend was his outlook on life; he was just happy that he got to play major league baseball. Plus, he was not shy about giving credit to anyone who influenced him. From what I can tell, Bob Friend is one of the nice guys, too! (Bob Friend died February 3, 2019)

Chapter 26

Frank "The Original" Thomas: 1951-1966

B *ob is a fan's fan who has spent much of his life reaching out to players during and after their Major League career. In this chapter, he shares stories about the influences in Frank Thomas' life and the way in which he influenced Bob's interest in becoming a baseball writer.*

Frank Thomas Christmas Card

Pittsburgh Pirates, Cincinnati Reds, Milwaukee Braves, Chicago Cubs, New York Mets, Philadelphia Phillies and Houston Astros

The first time that I met Frank was at a Pittsburgh Pirates Dream Week camp in 1993. He was one of my coaches along with Kent Tekulve. Out of all the former players in the camp, I knew the least about Frank. But it was a letter that I wrote to him that began our twenty plus year friendship.

It all started when I saw a Moss Klein article about Frank Thomas of the White Sox, in the Newark "Star-Ledger." It was entitled "The Original One." I thought that Frank would like to see it, so I sent it to him. I am now the proud owner of over 150 personal letters from Frank. I have visited Frank anytime I am in Pittsburgh, and we occasionally speak on the phone. Frank is one of the biggest influences in my baseball writing. I had just became a member of the "Society of American Baseball Research" (SABR) and I soon became a member of the "Bio Project," which was a group with the auspicious goal of writing a bio for every former major league player. Frank was the subject of the first one that I wrote. Our friendship enabled me to reach out to him and use him as a source of information for other writing projects.

Frank John Thomas was born in Pittsburgh on June 11, 1929. He signed his first professional baseball contract with the Pirates in 1947. Before he began his baseball career he planned on entering the priesthood. Frank, a devout Catholic, started off by going into the seminary, but because of his love for baseball, plus a "God given talent," influenced him to become a ball player.

Frank claims his love for baseball began in the crib. According to Frank's mom, he would not go to bed unless there was a baseball and a glove in the crib with him. Just another reason that Frank felt he was destined to play.

As a youngster, Frank always played with kids older than him. He remembers walking up a hill to ask some older boys if he could play; they grudgingly allowed him, but he was always picked last. But after seeing him play, he got picked first from that time on.

Frank loved to hit baseballs. He bragged to me that he was swinging from the dugout to the batter's box. Jack Rothrock, his first manager when he was at Tallahassee, Florida told him, "You can't get to the big leagues by walking!" During his sixteen years in the majors, he walked only 484 times in 6,915 plate appearances while still having a decent career batting average of .266. Frank also likes to point out that he never struck out one hundred times in any season that he played.

Frank felt when he reached the majors that Lenny Levy was his first influence. Levy used to own a local car dealership as well as coaching third base for the Pirates. Lenny also played an important role in Bill Mazerosk'si walk-off homerun during the 1960 World Series. He was the coach who told Mazeroski that it was his turn to bat in the bottom of the ninth. Any Pirate fan can tell you that Maz hit Terry's second pitch for a homerun that ended the series.

Lenny's advice to Frank was "be quick with your hands."

In 1959, Frank was traded for Smokey Burgess, Harvey Haddix and Don Hoak. All three players played a significant role in the 1960 World Series season. Frank often jokes how he should get more credit for helping the Pirates' winning that year.

Another of Frank's influences was Frankie Gustine, who also is a Pittsburgh native. Gustine was like a father to Frank. Frankie Gustine was also a native of Pittsburgh, and he always had time to talk with Frank when he was a young player. Gustine shared advice about playing the game and how to act when away from the ball field.

Frank is proud that he has never ignored a kid who wanted an autograph. Frank can remember when he was playing youth organized baseball and he waited around for autographs from the players. Many of them would push the kids aside or not pay any attention to them, but not Gustine or Rip Sewell. One day, Sewell noticed Frank's torn pants, and then asked how they were torn? When Frank told him was playing ball all day, Rip smiled. Rip always made time for kids. That is something that influenced Frank when he made it to the majors. To this day, he still reads and signs his fan mail. All because of the way Rip Sewell treated him as a kid.

Frank hit over 30 homeruns during three separate seasons. He also hit 20 homers nine times. Frank Thomas was an All Star three times, each time as a Pittsburgh Pirate during his 16-year career.[234] Although Pittsburgh is his hometown and he still lives there, he is very fond of the New York/New Jersey area from the days when he was an "Original" New York Met.

Frank with Harry Zeiser playing for the Tallahassee Pirates of Florida-Georgia State League

234 Frank Thomas appeared in 1,766 games, with 1,671 hits, 286 homers and 962 RBIs the latter two were impressive for the era that he played during.

Chapter 27

Ernie Banks: 1953-1971

*M**y** Father, Reverend Gilbert H. Caldwell Jr., knew and marched with Dr. Martin Luther King, Jr. He is on the left in the picture below standing next to Ralph Abernathy and Dr. Martin Luther King, Jr. This picture was taken during a press conference before a march to integrate the Boston Public Schools. Even though he knew and marched with Dr. King, my Father's favorite memories are playing sandlot touch football with the legendary Ernie Banks in Texas. In this chapter, Bob discusses the influences in the life of one of the best individuals and players to ever compete in the sport of baseball – Ernie Banks.*

Chicago Cubs

On January 23, 2015, baseball lost an iconic figure. Ernie Banks died of a heart attack at eighty-three years old. He played nineteen years in the MLB, all of them with the Chicago Cubs, earning him the moniker of "Mr. Cub." Mr. Banks was best known for his enthusiastic quote, "It's a beautiful day for a ballgame … Let's play two!" Unfortunately, Ernie was also known for the most games (2,528) without playing in the post season. He loved the game, never losing his passion. Ernie was known as "Mr. Sunshine."

When I was growing up, the Cubs were really bad. Luckily, they had Ernie Banks, their young African American slugger. Ernie was the first African American to play for the Cubs. For the majority of the sixties, he was the only thing worth remembering from the "Windy City."

185

I first learned about Banks because this 1963 Topps baseball card my Aunt Linda gave me when my family was out for a visit in Pittsburgh that summer. I was only six years old at the time; my reading consisted of the *Dick and Jane* books, but at that early age, I was able to decipher the statistics on the back of baseball cards. I became aware of how much of an accomplishment it was for someone to hit 37 home runs and drive in 104 runs for a team that finished next to last place. I remember thinking, who is this guy?

That guy was Ernest "Ernie" Banks, born on January 31, 1931, in Dallas, Texas to Eddie and Essie Banks. He weighed five pounds and two ounces at birth. The Banks would have twelve children in all. Ernie was the oldest son.

Eddie Banks worked for the Works Progress Administration (WPA) and held several additional jobs. The banks were poor, and struggled to make ends meet in the segregated South. Ernie's dad worked seven days a week. Later on, he became a warehouse loader for a grocery store chain. This meant that he didn't work on Sundays. So, Sunday dinners became very important. It was the only time that their father Eddie Banks could eat with his family. While his father did everything within his means to support the large family, it was his mother who deserved the majority of credit for raising their children. Essie stressed the importance of cleanliness to her children. Ernie's parents taught their children to love and to have right thinking.

Since Ernie was the oldest son in the family, he did most of the chores, like making sure that all of the kerosene lamps were filled in the house. He chopped wood and brought it into the wood burning stoves that heated the house. Ernie pumped water from an outside pump. Mr. Banks might not have been aware of it, but those days shaped his attitude in life.

When Ernie attended Booker T. Washington High School, he developed a new interest, sports. He played softball, basketball and football.

When he was a child, Reverend Gil Caldwell lived across the street from the high school. His father was the minister at a Methodist church. Gil told me that he got to know the Cubs legend a bit. He can remember playing touch football with Banks and his father. Both Eddie and Ernie Banks felt he had skill because of his soft hands. Gil remembers watching the Banks playing a lot of softball in the schoolyard. After Ernie's first softball game, recreation director Woody Culton convinced him to play shortstop. He eventually played for J.W. Worlds, the community's best fast-pitch softball team. Bill Blair, a scout for the Monarchs, discovered him when Ernie was only seventeen. So, Blair started him off playing for the Amarillo Colts. They played games around Texas, New Mexico, Kansas and Oklahoma. Essie Banks supported any sport that her son decided to play as long as it did not interfere with his schooling.

When Ernie played for Amarillo, he met Negro Leagues legend Cool Papa Bell, and it was because of that meeting that the Monarchs became interested in him. This was also when he met the respected evaluator and Monarch manager Buck O'Neil. He did not seem to have a choice but to sign with the Kansas City Monarchs. In 1950, Ernie was paid $300 a month, but the following year he was drafted by the army.

When he came back to play with the Monarchs, he attracted the attention of the Chicago Cubs. The Cubs purchased Banks' contract for $15,000 and brought Ernie to the city where he would forever be linked.

Banks was not supposed to be the Cubs' first African American player; that honor was intended for Gene Baker. But when Baker and Banks arrived at Wrigley Field on September 14, 1953, Baker was nursing a minor injury so Ernie became the first to play. On September 17th, he started a game against the Philadelphia Phillies, for which he played shortstop and batted seventh. Banks did not get a hit in three times to the plate. Ernie went on to play in ten games during 1953, finishing with a batting average of .314 with two homers.

Ernie Banks' career numbers helped him into baseball's Hall of Fame. He was named the MVP of the NL for two consecutive years in both the 1958 and the 1959 seasons. This was quite impressive because he played shortstop for a fifth place team. He became a feared slugger, hitting twenty or more home runs a season thirteen times. He drove in over one hundred runs eight times. Banks was voted into baseball's Hall of Fame on the first ballot in 1977.[235] In 2013, President Obama presented him with the prestigious Medal of Honor, which Chicago Mayor Rahm Emanuel said was Banks' proudest moment. After the President presented him with the distinguished medal, Ernie presented a bat that once belonged to Jackie Robinson to Barack Obama, the first black President. It was a way of passing the torch across generations.

Ernie Banks was a great ambassador for baseball. He always had time for younger players, much like veterans Monte Irvin, Jackie Robinson, Hank Thompson, Richie Ashburn and Ralph Kiner had for him.

Phillip Wrigley, the owner of the Chicago Cubs, was a big influence on Ernie, and it literally paid off. The Cubs' owner advised his star player to invest. Banks bought several businesses during his playing career and he accumulated four million dollars in assets by the time he was fifty-five years old. Ernie was very active in the Chicago community, setting up several charitable organizations. While many Chicago fans know Banks as their team's first African American player, he was also the first person of color to own a Ford Motor dealership in the United States. In 1969, Banks was appointed to the Board of Directors of the Chicago Transit Authority.

In his eulogy for his friend, mentor and teammate, fellow Hall of Fame player Billy Williams said, "Ernie has been the cornerstone not only to the Chicago Cubs, but the city of Chicago … When Ernie walked up to you he acted like he knew you for years."

A true Cubs fan named Maria Starnas described meeting Banks by chance in the lobby of a suburban hotel. He immediately showed a deep interest in her, asking about her goals and dreams and then helped her draft a plan to achieve them.

"We talked for about an hour and a half, it was as if we were long-lost friends."

---

235 He finished his career with 512 home runs and 1636 runs batted in.

This author personally feels that Ernie Banks reminds me of Dr. Martin Luther King Jr. as far as race relations were concerned. He did not preach or practice militancy, but patience.

"My philosophy about race relations is that I'm the man and I'll set my own patterns in life. I don't rely on anyone else's opinion. I look at a man as a human being; I don't care about his color. Some people feel that because you are black you will never be treated fairly, and that you should voice your opinions, be a militant. I don't feel that way. You can't convince a fool against his will... If a man doesn't like me because I'm black, that's fine, I'll go elsewhere, but I'm not going to let him change my life." – Ernie Banks

Jesus Christ said, "So whatever you wish that others do to you, do also to them, for this is the law of the prophets." (Matthew 7:12) Or to many, "The Golden Rule."

Ernie Banks also believed, "Treat people the way you want to be treated and be forgiving. Listen to those who are more experienced. And don't be afraid to dream big."

When describing the life of Mr. Banks, his numbers have never fallen short in describing his true greatness as a baseball player. Ernie Banks was known as much for his off-field demeanor as his on-the-field performance.

Joe Torre, former opponent and admirer of Banks, spoke eloquently of Ernie. "Ernie Banks was living proof that you don't have to wear a championship ring on your finger in order to be a pillar of baseball and a champion in life. He made the confines of Wrigley Field friendly, he made the Cubs lovable, and he was one of the pivotal people during a vital time in our history who made a great game worthy of being our national pastime... you don't need to wear a championship ring on your finger to be a Champion in Life!"

Chapter 28

Vernon Law: 1954-1967

E*very person who ever played Major League Baseball or Negro League Baseball has an interesting life story. They had some fascinating influences in their life that were strong and positive enough to propel them into a short or long career in the competitive sport of professional baseball. Bob tells the little known story of Vernon Law in this chapter.*

Pittsburgh Pirates

Vernon Law played a significant role in my life. Vernon was the first player that I ever wrote a fan letter to. He became my first autograph. I still have it today.

Vernon Law was promoted in 1950 after a quick climb up the ladder to the major leagues. He played a full season, and then served in the military between 1951 and 54. Vernon was unfortunate to be a very good pitcher on some very bad major league teams. The pinnacle of his career occurred in 1960.[236] Law made the All Star team in 1960 won the Cy Young award and went on to win two games against the mighty New York Yankees.

Unfortunately, Law's career was ended by an injury that he sustained on a bus trip when the Pirates were celebrating clinching the 1960 season. He finished his major league career with a 162-147 record. He won the prestigious "Lou Gehrig" award for his contributions both on and off the field in 1965. This is an award that Vern is most

---

236 Vernon was 20-9, 3.08 ERA, and led the league in complete games.

proud of. He was brought up as a deeply Christian man and earned the nickname during his career as "Deacon." This moniker was given to him by Wally Westlake, a former teammate. Wally used to call Law "Preacher" until Vernon corrected him by saying that he was not a preacher but a Deacon. So, Wally changed Vernon's nickname to "Deacon."

Law did not get a lot of endorsements like his Pirate teammates; he was mostly asked to speak at churches and other religious organizations. He felt honored when Bob Prince asked him to come back to Pittsburgh to speak at his church about "tithing." Vernon and his wife always tithed. He was thankful for Branch Rickey, whom he got along with fine; tithing got him out of a difficult situation because he gave 10% to his church. One season when he had to choose between tithing or paying his rent, he chose to give the money to his church, which left them in the hole. Suddenly, a check for $1,500 came from Rickey in the mail. It was a bonus for his hard work. Vern noted that while Rickey always had the knock on him of being tight with money, Law never saw that side of him.

When you talk to Vernon Law, there is no question that God was his biggest influence inside and outside of baseball, but if he was to choose one person who played an important role in his career it was a former player, coach, and scout by the name of Bill Burwell. Bill Burwell pitched two years for the St. Louis Browns and one for the Pirates during the twenties. He also accumulated 239 victories during his minor league career. Law was a raw talent, and naïve about pitching. Vern had a fastball and a curveball. He was told that he needed to add a change up to his repertoire. In 1949, Bill Burwell who was his pitching coach and manager for the Davenport Pirates, taught him how to throw one. Vern also credited Burwell for teaching him how to pitch.

After Law's playing career, he coached for the Pirates, in Japan, high school and Brigham Young College. During his two years in Japan, he taught Japanese pitchers about pitching inside. Before that, the pitchers from that country threw predominately outside.

Because of my conversation with Vernon Law, I learned that influence went both ways for him. He was influenced by others and a great influence to many of the younger Pirates' pitchers that were his teammates, like Steve Blass and Bob Veale. He influenced them by setting an example with his work ethic, and by setting an example as the consummate professional ball player.

Chapter 29

Earl Averill, Jr.: 1956-1963

arl Averill, Jr. never reached the level of professional baseball success that his father achieved. However, he was an interesting person who, because of his influences, made history in a small way. Bob shares some information about the influences in Earl Averill, Jr.'s life in this chapter.

Cleveland Indians, Chicago Cubs, Los Angeles Angels, and Philadelphia Phillies

Earl's career never made him a "household" name but his family's lineage did. Earl's dad was the Hall of Fame Outfielder Earl Averill Sr.

Earl's dad played centerfield for three different teams during a career that spanned thirteen years, from 1929-41. [237] He was selected for the All Star team six times and was the first American League player to homer in his first major league at bat.

Earl Jr. never enjoyed the same career as his father; but was able to play eight seasons as a catcher, a third baseman and an outfielder. He played for five different teams. In 1961, he became the first starting catcher for the expansion Los Angeles Angels. That was also his best year in the big leagues with 21 home runs and a .266 average.

Aside from his dad, his favorite players were DiMaggio and Gehrig. When I asked Earl at what age he began playing baseball,

---

237 *Earl Sr. had over 2,000 hits, 400 doubles, 100 triples, .268 home runs for a .318 average in his career.*

he admitted that was a tough question because he grew up around the game. Several players dropped by to visit his dad like Freddie Hutchinson and Earl Torgenson. Young Averill's passion for the game was influenced by the conversations between his dad and his dad's former teammates. When Dad and Hutchinson played together, they used to carpool. Earl would make Freddie play catch with him before they left for the ballpark.

Fred Hutchinson is better known for the Cancer Research Center named after him than for his major league career. He enjoyed an eleven year career with the Detroit Tigers. As a pitcher, he won ninety-five games in eleven years. Hutchinson also managed in the majors for the Detroit Tigers, St. Louis Cardinals and Cincinnati Reds.

When Earl Jr. became a professional player, baseball icons such as Red Ruffing, Bill Mckecknie and Red Cress pitched batting practice to him. Earl had several major influences aside from his dad. He could not think of any coach or manager in the big leagues that had provided guidance or help. The only advice he remembers getting from his former manager Al Lopez was, "If you reach out you might get the ball before it hits the dirt." This is surprising when you consider that Lopez was a longtime catcher and the former record holder for most games caught.

Earl and his wife are recently retired from an upholstery business that they ran for years. He is proud of his dad but also of his own career.

(Earl died May 13, 2015)

Chapter 30

Dave Giusti: 1962-1977

*M*any *of the baseball players that we focus on in this book are not superstars. They are the players that played the sport in the shadows of legends. However, they each have one or more unique accomplishments. We live in a time when multi-million dollar baseball contracts are commonplace. Dave Giusti made salary history at a time when most baseball players did not make much money. Giusti benefitted from many positive influences that enabled him to gain the distinction of being the first relief pitcher to earn $100,000 a year.*

Houston Astros St. Louis Cardinals, Pittsburgh Pirates, Oakland A's, Chicago Cubs

I first met Dave while attending Pirates Dream week in 1993. While all of the ex-Pirates were friendly, Dave was especially nice. Most of the time, he served as Steve Blass's straight man. Years later, I wrote his bio for SABR and we have spoken on the phone numerous times. He has always been happy to discuss incidents in Pirates baseball from his perspective. Every time we do speak, I remind him how happy my father and I were when the Pirates traded for him!

On April 20, 1970, Dave Giusti became a relief pitcher, due to a sub-par spring training camp. Murtaugh, with his uncanny wisdom, made him a relief pitcher. Before arriving in Pittsburgh he had spent the first seven years as a starting pitcher for the Houston baseball club. It was the 1966 season that Dave had his breakout season for the Astros. He went 15-14, 4.20 as Houston finished in eighth place.

One of the season's highlights was pitching a one-hitter against Juan Marichal that year.

While he did not create the role of "closer," he certainly helped define it. While in this newly created role, Giusti started the 1970 season with a record of 8-0 with 14 saves. He was chosen for the All Star team. Because of Dave's dominance, he became the first relief pitcher to earn $100,000 a season.

Dave Giusti was six years old when he was first exposed to the game of baseball. It was his Uncle John, who played football at Syracuse University that got him started. His dad helped as much as possible, but since he worked a lot his Uncle John was a surrogate mentor.

Like many youngsters of his age, Dave began his baseball journey by playing Little League. Because of Dave's facial hair, his coaches were forced to carry his birth certificate with them at all times to prove his young age. Dave began shaving at twelve years old.

The first time he experienced success occurred when his little league team went to the sectionals. A couple of years later, when he was fifteen, his Babe Ruth team lost the New York state championship by a score of 1-0. The winning pitcher was a kid name Carl Yastrzemski, who would go on to star with the Red Sox and be enshrined into baseball's Hall of Fame.

As a senior, he played on the Syracuse University team that made the NCAA tournament. The Orangemen went to the College World Series after beating Saint Johns University. Syracuse went on to defeat Colorado State, Western Michigan, until losing to Oklahoma State. Dave played third base in that game.

After playing at Syracuse University, both the St. Louis Cardinals and Houston 45's showed interest in him. He chose Houston because he felt it would be a quicker way to the major leagues. On June 16, 1961, Dave signed with the Houston Colt 45's becoming Houston's first bonus baby. He used the money to purchase a large insurance policy. He also paid off his parents' medical bills. While playing for Houston, he met Robin Roberts, a future member of the Hall of Fame who became his mentor. They were not teammates for that long, but Roberts influenced him greatly as a young Houston pitcher. This was during a time when older teammates were not as forthcoming with advice because they were worried about someone taking their job, but Roberts was different.

Dave earned a Bachelor's Degree at Syracuse University and he also learned how to throw the "palm ball" while playing for the baseball team there. The palm ball is a type of "changeup." The proper grip is when the ball is placed tightly in the palm and thrown with the same pitching motion as a fastball. This grip causes the ball to have a natural sinking motion. In some circles, it is known as a "slowball." Ted Kleinhaus, the school's pitching coach, taught it to him. Jim Konstanty, who is best known for that pitch, was also a Syracuse graduate, but Dave learned it from Kleinhaus. It was Giusti's out pitch for his 15-year career. He claimed to throw it 30-40 % of the time.

Arguably the best period of Dave's career was when he played for the Pirates, from 1970-76. During that time the team went to five NLCS and won the World Series against the Baltimore Orioles in 1971.

He finished his career as one of the most dominant relief pitchers of his playing days; he was a "Closer" before the term became popular.

Chapter 31

Al Ferrara: 1963-1971

Frequently, pro baseball players are talented human beings who have more than one gift. Al Ferrara was a talented piano player in Brooklyn who was influenced (by playing sandlot baseball with the likes of Joe Torre and Joe Pepitone) to develop a passion for baseball and the Brooklyn Dodgers. He never had a chance to play in Brooklyn. However, he did play for the Los Angeles Dodgers. After his baseball playing days ended, Ferrara did some acting, developed his own business and worked in community relations for the Dodgers.

LA Dodgers, San Diego, Cincinnati

Al Ferrara grew up in Brooklyn during the 1950s with the same dream most boys from Brooklyn had – to play for the Brooklyn Dodgers, and why not? Most of the team lived in the neighborhood. Players like Snider, Hodges and Furillo were his neighbors in the borough. Al said that he used to go to Ebbetts Field all of the time. The inner sanctums of Ebbetts was a microcosm of Brooklyn. It was also filled with such characters like Hilda Chester with her cowbell, or the not so symphonic "Dodger Sym-phony."

Al shared with me that he dreamt of playing for the Dodgers and he did play for the Dodgers – just not in Brooklyn. In 1963, Al realized the dream by playing for the Dodgers. If they had a Hall of Fame for his activities outside of baseball Ferrara would be a "shoe-in." Aside from catching or hitting a baseball, Al had other talents outside the game. He was a classically trained pianist and performed at Carnegie Hall. Ferrara also acted in TV sitcoms like "F-Troop." He appeared on screen with such notable actresses as Tallulah Bankhead and Zsa Zsa Gabor.

When Al was growing up in Brooklyn, he often appeared on Happy Felton's "Knothole Gang." Felton had the local kids come on the field and Dodger players would join them for the show. A young Al appeared often and went to Ebbetts Field all of the time. The group of boys he hung around devised creative ways of hustling to get in, such as saving the wrappers from ice cream Popsicles. You could get one Dodger ticket for five wrappers. His buddies would send Al in. He would sit at the top of the centerfield bleachers and point his comrades to the direction of where balls were hit out of the park during batting practice. Ferrara said that a ball was worth a ticket or two. The gang tried to work it so they got everyone inside for the game.

When Ferrara was a sophomore at Lafayette HS, Johnny Podres beat the Yankees in the seventh game of the 1955 World Series. Ironically, Podres was his first roommate when he reached the big leagues. Al and Johnny became lifelong friends. In fact, when Ferrara returned to his high school for a reunion of his sophomore class, Podres asked if he could come. They were thrilled to meet Podres!

When I asked if he had any major influences as he climbed the ladder of professional baseball, Al replied that you were pretty much on your own in those days. Although he mentioned Kenny Myers, who was a certain scout he confided in. Myers was the youngest player to sign a major league baseball contract at the age of fifteen. Kenny Meyers holds a minor league record for hitting four homeruns in one game; two of them were grand slams. Unfortunately, an injury during WWII ended his career. As a scout, Meyers discovered Willie Davis, who played for the Dodgers. Former San Francisco Giant Manager Roger Craig credited Meyers: "He helped me more than anyone else in baseball." Former Dodger catcher John Roseboro wrote in his autobiography: "Myers was sensational; he had revolutionary ideas about batting."

For Al, if something was not working well for him, he could go to Kenny to talk about it. Ferrara said if anyone was his mentor, it was Kenny Meyers. Duke Snider was his last manager in the minors, and also helped quite a bit. Of course, when you reached the "bigs," you depended on your teammates. During Al's era, ball players sat in the clubhouse for an hour or two after the games, having a couple of beers and talking baseball. Many times he sat talking with his teammate Ron Fairly about batting or whatever. It was not advice or coaching, just conversations about the game. Baseball was different during the sixties. We hung out and did things together. Now many players go their own ways. Back then there were players that you looked up to and they set examples. Al felt seeing the competitiveness of Maury Wills was a bit of an influence on him, plus witnessing the grit of Sandy Koufax's competitiveness.

Al Ferrara admitted that things have changed a lot since he was playing, but much of it for the good of baseball. He does not always agree with the changes, as long as it is good for the game[238]!

---

238 Al Ferrara played eight years in the MLB, with a lifetime batting average of .259, 51 homers in 574 games for the Los Angelos Dodgers, San Diego Padres, and Cincinnati Reds.

Chapter 32

Denny McLain: 1963-1972

*O*ne of the most fascinating things about influence is how different people *respond differently to various types of influence. Dennis Dale McLain overcame the emotional and physical trauma he faced as a child to become a talented musician and star pitcher for the Detroit Tigers. However, that trauma did not protect him from working with organized crime and serving time in prison. Bob shares the fascinating story of Denny McLain in this chapter.*

Detroit Tigers, Washington Senators, Oakland A's and Atlanta Braves

Denny McLain was a former pitcher in the major leagues. He pitched from 1963-72. McLain pitched for the Detroit Tigers, Washington Senators and Oakland A's before finishing with the Atlanta Braves. Denny won one hundred games before he was twenty-five years old. He averaged 268 innings and nineteen complete games per season between 1965 and 1969. He will probably be the last pitcher to ever win over thirty games in a single season, which he accomplished in 1968 while leading his Tigers to the World Series against the St. Louis Cardinals.

His exploits on the baseball diamond were rivaled by his controversy off of the diamond. In his book *I Told You I Wasn't Perfect*, Denny documented how he had served time in prison for embezzlement and being associated with organized crime on different occasions.

Many of the players that I have spoken to have interesting stories about what influenced them, but admittedly McLain's was the most unusual. Like others, Denny claimed that without his dad he would not have been successful in baseball. "Without Tom McLain, I never would have been a baseball player. He wanted me to be the player he wasn't able to be."

The reason I found this odd was that Denny's father, Tom McLain was an intimidating man who stood 6'3" and weighed 250 pounds with huge, powerful hands. He beat his two sons with a strap. Tom had been a talented shortstop in the Chicago area and the Cubs wanted to sign him. Unfortunately, Tom's future wife forced him to choose between her and baseball. Tom ended up getting married and then entering the military in World War II. When he returned from the war, he needed to work two jobs to support his young family.

Tom McLain led a stressful life; he smoked between three and four packs of cigarettes each day, and always had a can of beer between his legs every time he was driving his car. Despite his father's smoking, drinking and intimidation, Denny believed his dad loved him. As a coach, Tom McLain was not the cheerleader type. He did not jump up and down or shower his son with superlatives. There was never a hug, a kiss or even a handshake. Denny considered himself lucky if he heard,"Nice going', or Good game" from his father.

Tom McLain pushed his son to do well at baseball, schoolwork and playing the piano. If Denny slipped up he would face of his father's strap.

His father's top priority was Denny's development as a baseball player. Tom arranged his work schedule to accommodate his son's practices and games. As a 14-year-old freshman in 1958, Denny made the starting rotation at Mt. Carmel. One day, when he did not see his father at his usual spot in the stands on May 4, 1959, he knew right away that something was wrong. His father never missed a game when he was pitching. He even waited around after the game for him before taking the bus home. Denny learned that his dad had suffered a heart attack while driving to the game. Tom McLain pulled over to the curb and died, slumped onto his steering wheel. He was only 36 years old.

Because of Denny's success pitching at Mount Carmel high school, he received offers from the Yankees, the Phillies and the White Sox. McLain decided to sign with the hometown Chicago White Sox. He began at Clinton of class D of the Mid West League. Ira Hutchinson was his manager. Denny liked Hutchinson. He also appreciated that his manager tried to teach him how to throw the curve ball. Somehow, Denny could never get the knack of it. Since the White Sox' pitching staff were in a numbers game, having three pitchers but only two rotation spots, McLain was the odd pitcher out. Fortunately for him, Ed Katalinas, a scout for the Detroit Tigers saw him pitch and liked him. He signed Denny off of waivers on April 8, 1963. McLain moved quickly through the Tiger farm system. McLain's Major League debut was on September 21, 1963.

Charlie Dressen influenced him when he played for the Tigers. Dressen who was his first major league manager and had showed confidence in his ability to pitch at the major league level. Unfortunately on August 10, 1966, Dressen suffered his third heart attack and died. Denny loved Dressen for believing in him as a 19-year-old, helping him become a major league pitcher. Two years after Charlie Dressen died, Denny won back-to-back CY Young awards.

Another influence in McLain's career was Johnny Sain. He was considered by many as the finest pitching coach ever in the major leagues. Sain's mantra was, "If you maintain proper mechanics, you can really protect your arm from damage."

After ten years in the 'bigs' McLain finished with a 131-91 won-lost record. He made three All-Star game appearances, won two CY Young awards and won an MVP award. He also spent time in prison for embezzlement, mail fraud and conspiracy, but Denny says that is behind him.

Chapter 33
Jim Gosger: 1963-1974

Baseball experts focus most of their research on studying the history of the sport's superstars. However, there are many unknown players whose overlooked careers provide valuable insight into the secrets of success in life. Jim Gosger is one of those special players whose work effort kept him in the Major Leagues for a decade. Most people don't have the equivalent of Willie Mays' talent in their chosen profession. However, everyone can work just as hard as Jim Gosger to succeed.

Boston, Kansas City Athletics, Oakland A's, Seattle Pilots, New York Mets and Montreal Expos

Many fans know Jim Gosger as Jim Bouton's teammate in the controversial book *Ball Four*, yet he went on to enjoy a "serviceable" career in the major leagues.

Jim Gosger was born November 6, 1942, in Port Huron, Michigan, and signed as a free agent with the Boston Red Sox on January 6, 1962. He debuted on May 4, 1963. Jim's career lasted ten seasons between 1963 and 1974, playing for the Kansas City Athletics, Montreal Expos, Boston Red Sox, New York Mets and Seattle Pilots. His best years were 1965 with the Red Sox, when he batted .256 with nine homers, and in 1966 he batted .234 with ten homers while splitting time between Boston and Kansas City.

Gosger was known as a hustling, hardworking player. He was a solid fourth outfielder that played good defense and could come off the bench to pinch-hit. Alvin Dark, his former manager said,

"The thing about Gosger is he never lets his troubles at the plate hurt his fielding." Jim also complimented Dark as the best manager he ever played for.

He grew up in the small town of Port Huron, Michigan, where he played all of the sports all night and day. When he graduated from St. Stephens High School in 1960, Jim played a year of semi-pro. This is where a scout for the Boston Red Sox saw him and signed him to a contract. The scout was actually his dad's friend. His father was a decent catcher and had a chance to also play professionally until being drafted into the service.

When Jim signed that first contract, his father let him know, "I kicked your little butt for one reason. I wanted you to be a ball player."

When he started in Boston, he was fortunate to have Ted Williams as a batting instructor at his first camp; but it was his first manager that shaped his style of play. Eddie Popowski was a fiery little guy at 5'4," and a great manager who demanded that you always play hard. One day he pulled Jim aside to share a little advice.

"Listen, you want to make the big leagues?"

Jim nodded.

"I want you to run in and off the field, and every time you hit the ball you run hard."

Jim nodded again.

"That was my biggest influence. It got me to the big leagues. It really did. Because I had this ability to be at the right place at the right time and I hustled."

Jim stuck around the major leagues for a decade, which a lot of players cannot say – especially those with a .226 lifetime batting average.

Joe Adcock paid him a compliment that defined the type of player he was. One day Jim was playing for the Indians and Cleveland's catcher Duke Sims told him that their manager Joe Adcock felt if he had nine Jim Gosgers, the Indians would win it all!

Maybe Eddie Popowski's advice was right!

Chapter 34

Gary Kroll: 1964-1969

W*e decided to write this book because of the fascinating stories of everyone who was ever involved in major league baseball. We discovered that most of the former major league ball players who were successful in life were not stars on the field. They learned how to utilize their intensity and mental and physical gifts to make a lot of money in professions unrelated to baseball. Gary Kroll is one of those special people who had some interesting influences that got him to the big leagues, but found tremendous success after pro baseball.*

Philadelphia, NY Mets, Houston, Cleveland

I interviewed Gary Kroll on May 7, 2014. Gary won the first major league game that I saw at Connie Mack Stadium in Philadelphia on July 31, 1965.

The game started as a pitching duel between the Mets' Jack Fisher and Chris Short of the Phillies. The two seasoned veteran pitchers battled for nine innings before giving way to the bullpen with a 3-3 score. Kroll came in to pitch a scoreless tenth inning; the Mets scored a run at the top of the eleventh. Gordie Richardson closed out the game by tossing a scoreless eleventh inning to earn the save, making Gary Kroll the winning pitcher.

Gary Kroll will always hold a significant place in my becoming a baseball fan. So, I wanted to include him in this book. After several attempts by mail and telephone, I received a call from him. "May I speak to Mr. Hart?" I replied that I was Bob Hurte. "This is Gary Kroll." He informed me that his wife told him that I called. We chatted briefly; since I was in my car for work, I called him back when I got home that evening.

Gary has lived in Tulsa, Oklahoma since this is where he ended his baseball career. After his baseball career, he got into the insurance business and became very successful. It led to him starting an "insurance lead" business and he eventually became the owner of seven businesses. Kroll is especially proud of a resort he owns called "Dream Catcher Point Resort." It is located on the shores of Grand Lake in Northeast Oklahoma. It would become the location for the World Series of Bass fishing. Gary bought the house for $281,000 and then turned it into a resort. The house is now worth 3.2 million dollars.

Gary's path to becoming a pitcher in professional baseball was unique. He never pitched while in high school because he was a talented outfielder. A Phillies scout saw him working out in Los Angeles and signed him as a pitcher. Kroll explained to the scout that he never pitched, so the scout sent him to the instructional league in Florida. Gary did well, finishing third in both strikeouts and ERA. The following year he threw a no-hitter and had over 300 strikeouts. Then in 1962, he won twelve in a row. The Phillies brought him up in 1964, but he was traded later in the season for Frank Thomas of the Mets – the same Frank Thomas that I would become friends with.

I asked Gary whether he missed his baseball career. To my surprise, he replied that he did not. This was followed by forty-five minutes during which he regaled me with stories about his career. He remembered names and the details of situations as if they just happened. It is obvious that somewhere deep inside, he still missed playing the game.

He felt that the Mets coaching staff was poor when he played there. Mel Harder was his first pitching coach. Harder might have been a standout pitcher in his day, but he only got the job because he was a friend of Casey Stengel. He did not know how to communicate or help young pitchers make adjustments. Warren Spahn was his pitching coach at Tulsa during his last year of professional baseball. He was also Gary's roommate with the Mets. He felt Spahn had the capability to explain things – something he could have used when he first began pitching.

In 1971, he went to spring training with the St. Louis Cardinals. He threw well and had the best stat's of any pitcher at camp. Unfortunately, it was a numbers game and he was the third best pitcher of a trio with legendary pitchers Bob Gibson and Steve Carlton. After his last season at Tulsa, he decided to go in a different direction. He answered a $1,000 ad to sell insurance. While I cannot say for sure, in my opinion, Gary Kroll's success in business was influenced by his experience of playing professional baseball. Many athletes succeed in business and especially in sales because of their thirst for competitiveness. Gary demonstrated a tireless drive and tenacity for achieving his baseball goal of being a major league player. He applied this relentlessness to his business career. As a professional baseball pitcher, he pushed himself to achieve; he did the same as an insurance salesman. The company that he worked for recommended that he sell one policy per week. Gary felt that there was not anything preventing him from selling five times as much during that span. Then five became twenty until he sold between 700-800 policies. He eventually started an advertising firm, then began a "sales lead" generation company.

While Kroll's post career was obviously more successful than his baseball-playing career and he became a millionaire, he did consider himself lucky to pitch against Hall of Fame players like Aaron, Banks, Matthews and Mays. Gary said he would not trade that experience for any amount of money, which was good since the most he ever made in the majors was $7,000 a season. Kroll played before the big money of free agency.

Kroll felt he played during the glory years. While he insists he does not miss it, he was able to talk about his career as if it was yesterday, like a game against the Chicago Cubs. It was the eighth inning and Billy Williams was up with a man on second. Gary got behind in the count and threw a curve, which Williams hit over the fence. For the life of him, Kroll could not understand how Williams knew what he was going to throw. He determined that the man on second stole the signal!

Or, how he thought he knew how to pitch to Willies Mays. Mays did not get a hit off of him the first twelve times Willie batted against him. Gene Mauch, his manager in Philadelphia, explained that since Mays did not know much about Kroll he just took his swings. Mays did this until the game was on the line and then Mays blasted one out of the park. I asked Kroll what he thought of Mauch. He said he did not play for him long enough to form an opinion.

Like many young boys, Kroll started playing Little League baseball when he was eight. His stepfather liked baseball and got Gary into playing, although he never went to any of his games. Gary Kroll claims he does not miss playing; he is too busy with his businesses, but apparently, the young man deep inside of him still does. Gary completed four MLB years, with a career record of 6-7, in 71 games, 138 strikeouts and 4.24 ERA. He played for the New York Mets, Philadelphia Phillies, Houston Astros and Cleveland Indians.

Chapter 35

Steve Blass: 1964-1974

*T*he highs and lows of professional sports are incredible. Everyone loves reading *about the story of the person who, seemingly overnight, defied the odds and went from being an average athlete to an extraordinary one. Few people hear about those individuals who, seemingly overnight, went from being an extraordinary athlete to an average athlete. Steve Blass was an extraordinary athlete who finished second to Roberto Clemente in the voting for World Series MVP one year and became a struggling player two years later.*

**Steve Blass at Three Rivers Stadium,
Pittsburgh, courtesy of Sally O'Leary**

Unfortunately, Steve's playing career ended prematurely in 1973 when he could no longer find the strike zone. His malady became known as "Steve Blass Disease." Being a humorous guy Steve likes to point out, "Who are the two former major league baseball players that have diseases named after them?" The answer: "Lou Gehrig and me!" I can remember crying as a sixteen-year-old when I heard Steve was retiring from baseball.

Years later in 1993, we first met at Pirates Dream Week, and years after that we became close because of a mutual friend Nellie King, the former Pirates pitcher and broadcaster. Steve guessed he began playing baseball when he was either six or eight. Steve's father was his coach when he started youth baseball.

Steve has always loved baseball. In fact, when he was a boy, his favorite Christmas present each year was a brand new, shiny white baseball. Sure, he got other presents, but a new ball was a Christmas tradition. He looked forward to getting one each year. Blass was born in 1942, a simpler time and there were not a lot of toys or gadgets for children back then,. He remembers getting a new black Nakoma glove one Christmas. He never had new spikes; they were always "hand me downs." But he always looked forward to getting that new baseball.

Steve told me that as an eight or nine-year-old, he would wake up and run to the window to see what the weather was like and if it was good enough to play baseball. He used to throw a pink ball against a small red barn on his parents' property. He would play a simulated baseball game; it was always the Indians against the Yankees and he kept score on a card that he created. He always rooted for the Indians, his favorite team. Although they did not win every time because you never knew how the ball was going to bounce. As a youngster, he also listened to the Indians playing the Yankees on the family radio. He also kept the score. The voices of announcers Les Kieter, Jim Woods and Mel Allen entertained him through the speaker of the Blass family's console radio in the living room.

Although his father coached his Little League team, Steve considered Jerry Fallon his first coach. Fallon taught Steve and his teammates an important lesson, to have fun! Jerry promised that they would also learn a little about playing baseball.

When he attended Housatonic Valley Regional high school, Ed Kirby was his coach. Ed was a big influence. He prepared Steve for professional baseball. Kirby ended up coaching three future major leaguers. They were Blass, John Lamb and Tom Parsons. Kirby was extremely tough on him because he saw Steve's potential. Kirby indicated to his star pitcher that he would face some real challenges, and was tough on him so that he would be able to handle them.

Bob Whalen was another person who helped Steve. Whalen was a Pirates scout. He worked with Steve on his windup. He would throw down his pack of cigarettes in front of Steve, then instruct him to stride far enough that he could pick them up. Whalen eventually became Director of Scouting in the Pirates' organization.

Steve said two veterans were his mentors during his career, Bob Friend at the beginning and Jim Bunning toward the end of his career. Bob was Steve's first roommate in the majors. He taught Steve how to handle himself, what to do and not to do, where to eat and where not to eat. In fact, Friend helped Steve and his wife find their first apartment in Pittsburgh.

Jim Bunning pitched for the Pirates in 1968 and part of 1969. He told Steve to never get too high or low. Blass responded with what he feels was his best season in 1968 when he was 18-6 with seven shutouts. Bunning was a tough, hard nosed pitcher who pitched when he was hurt. He said to Steve that anytime you have a chance to start a game take it; do not miss a turn over a hang nail or similar injury.

Steve played for Danny Murtaugh. Murtaugh was his baseball father. When you were doing your job, he left you alone. But if you messed up, he let you know about it. Steve also liked playing for Bill Virdon.

Steve had many mentors in the broadcast booth such as Bob Prince, Lanny Frattare, John Sanders, Mike Lange and Greg Brown. While Brown is younger than Steve, he considers him both a friend and mentor. Each of his fellow broadcasters stressed to Steve on being himself, and never too analytical, which was easy; Steve was not a fan of analytics. The Hall of Fme baseball announcer Bob Prince gave Steve the following advice when he started his broadcasting career:

"You're not going to change the world; you're a baseball player. Just make sure you have a tight close to your talk. Don't stumble around at the end, finish up neat and tidy.[239]"

Steve pitched for ten years in the majors, all with the Pittsburgh Pirates. He had a career record of 103-76, 3.63 ERA, won two World Series games in 1971 (finishing second to Roberto Clemente in the World Series MVP voting), pitched in the All Star game in 1972 and was runner up to Steve Carlton for the Cy Young award in 1972.

In 2012, Blass' book *A Pirate for Life* came out, a title that aptly describes this man. He is a Pirate for life! However, late in his career, his inability to find the strike zone ruined his professional baseball career. He has become famous for his sudden unexplainable loss of control as a pitcher after the 1972 MLB season. In 1973 his ERA climbed to 9.85. He had a horrible year, walking 84 batters in 88 2/3 innings and struck out only 27 batters. He spent the 1974 season in the minors and retired from baseball in 1975. His inexplicable loss of accuracy was referred to as the "Steve Blass Disease." It is used to refer to a talented baseball player who went from being an accurate pitcher to losing his ability to throw a baseball accurately.

---

239 *We Had Them All the Way*, Jim O'brien, James P. O'brien Publishing, Pittsburgh, Pa, 1998, p 248

**Bob with Steve Blass at the
press entrance at PNC Park**

(At the end of 2019, Blass retired after sixty years of affiliation with the Pittsburgh Pirates.)

Chapter 36

Dick Drago: 1969-1981

*I*t *is easy to overlook the importance of the early influences in our lives. Many people still believe the ridiculous myth of the self-made man or woman. No human being has ever been self-made. There is always someone who influences a person to get the most out of their skills. Dick Drago's father played a critical baseball influence role in his life. Without his father's influence, he would not have made it to professional baseball.*

Kansas City Royals, Boston, California, Seattle, and Baltimore

Dick Drago was both born and played youth baseball in Toledo, Ohio. He attended Woodward high school, where he lettered in basketball, bowling and baseball. Drago posted an 18-3 record and had two no-hitters his senior year. Dick went to the University of Detroit on a baseball scholarship. He lasted one year in college before he signed a professional contract with the Detroit Tigers in 1965. Dick began a climb up the minor league ladder; his final year in the minors was spent pitching for the Toledo Mud Hens in 1968, where he was selected on the International All-Star team. Dick felt that he would be promoted to the parent club. Instead, he was left unprotected and was selected by the Kansas City Royals in the expansion draft.

Dick Drago cannot remember not playing baseball. He spent most of his childhood playing outside. Dick can remember getting his first baseball glove. It was his reward for being so brave after having some baby teeth pulled at the dentist. He became hooked on the game when his family moved to Asbury Park, Ohio. His family lived across from a Junior High school which had a painted baseball diamond on its blacktop. Dick became a loyal Tiger's fan when he turned eight and tried to listen to every Detroit Tigers' game on the radio. His father was the reason he loved baseball. They played catch constantly. When his dad was not around he threw a baseball against a school wall until he wore the ball out. Dick was not always a pitcher. When he was ten he was playing Little League, and his coach did not expect a lot from him so he sent him out to right field.

His father was at practice one day, watching all of the pitchers on the mound. He then sought out his son's coach to inform him that his son could throw better than anyone he had on the mound. The coach figured he was just another father bragging about his kid, but he decided to let Dick pitch. After that first time on the mound, Dick became the team's best pitcher.

Drago learned control from his game of catch with his father. When he made an errant throw, his dad made him run after it. After a while Dick got tired of chasing his wild throws, forcing him to develop control. His father was his baseball coach from the age of ten until fifteen when he entered high school.

In the summer, Drago played in the Connie Mack League, and then the Knothole League. Eventually, Dick hung around an adult team called the Dunbar Drillers. The team's coach was a 'bird-dog' scout for the Tigers. The coach let Dick shag balls in the outfield and sometimes pitched batting practice. MLB scouts began to come around to speak with his father. This was in 1964 and the last year before the free agent player draft. Back then, scouts came over to your house, sat in your living room, talked with your parents and then offered professional contracts. The Boston Red Sox offered the most money. However, Dick wanted to play for the Tigers. He went to college for just one year. Since he was a freshman, he could not play; he could only work out with the team. After the school year, the Tigers came by and signed him to a contract.

Dick Drago's dad was his biggest influence until he reached professional baseball, then that important role was taken by Johnny

Sain. Each spring Sain came down to work with the young pitchers in the instructional league. Sain felt that it was important to throw often. At the time, Dick did not really have a breaking pitch, so Sain taught him the slider. Sain preached movement of the ball. He also showed him the cutter, a version of the fastball made popular by Yankees' closer Mariano Rivera.

A fellow pitcher that also helped Dick was Moe Drabowsky, plus Galen Cisco who eventually became a pitching coach in the majors. Dick felt that after a while you were on your own. At Boston, he got mental pointers from Louie Tiant. Bob Lemon, his manager with the Royals taught him how to pitch under pressure.

Dick Drago pitched thirteen years in the MLB.[240] Half of his career was as a starting pitcher before finishing his career as a spot starter/reliever. His best year was 1971 when he was 17-11, 2.98 with the Royals. Kansas City finished in second place in the American League West

Dick had a satisfying career, but is enjoying retirement. He plays a lot of golf and does things with the MLB alumni and fantasy camps.

---

240 Dick Drago's MLB career pitching record of 108-117 and earned run average of 3.62

Chapter 37
Steve Braun: 1971-1985

O*ne of the most amazing things about influence is how one statement or one impactful word can change another person's life. Steve Braun is one of those rare major league ball players who had the chance to be influenced by legendary players like Rod Carew, Harmon Killebrew and Tony Oliva. Even though he never became a legendary player himself, he was a very positive influence to many players and at least one fan. Bob summarizes the Steve Braun story in this chapter.*

Minnesota Twins, Seattle Mariners,
Kansas City Royals, St. Louis Cardinals

I met Steve Braun at a community day in Stewartsville, NJ, where I live. Steve played fifteen years at the major league level finishing as a member of the 1982 World Champion St. Louis Cardinals. He began his career as a second baseman but changed because he had to compete with the legendary Rod Carew. Steve is one of the few players to have 100 career pinch hits. After finishing his playing career he spent twenty years as a batting coach, first in the minors, then with the Cardinals, then with the Red Sox before finishing up with the Yankees.

Steve grew up in a small town, north of Trenton, NJ, called Washington's Crossing, NJ. This is the spot where General Washington crossed the Delaware River to fight the "Battle of Trenton." Steve has read all the books about the battle and spent a lot of time in the park.

He began playing organized ball at seven. Although you needed to be nine to play Little League, his father convinced the officials that his son was good enough. His father was his biggest influence. He got Steve out there playing every night. When Steve did not have a league game, his family went down to the park. Steve had eight brothers and sisters and they all liked to play.

Another person who was a major influence in his life when he became a professional baseball player was Jesse Flores, a dynamic pitching coach and scout. He gave Steve advice about hitting from a pitcher's perspective. When asked, Steve could not think of any veteran teammates that provided influence, although he admired Harmon Killebrew, who was more the silent leader type. The slugger never discussed hitting with him because they were different types of hitters. Instead, he influenced Steve in a different way. When Steve was very young he jumped from class A to the MLB. Harmon showed him how to act like a major leaguer. For instance, one time after a game where the Twins got beaten up pretty badly, Steve rushed to get out of the ballpark. When Killebrew and Steve stood in front of the mirror in the locker room, Harmon said to him without looking over, "First one out of the ballpark is the first one out of the league." Killebrew's words made an impact; in his own way the Twins star was telling the rookie that he needed to have respect for the game. From that day on, Braun did not rush out of the clubhouse. Killebrew's lesson was in a nice and easy manner. Harmon's words drove home the point to him.

He learned a lot from watching other pro ball players and he had great examples to observe while playing with the Twins, Killebrew, Carew and Oliva.

One young player that Braun influenced was David Eckstein, who played predominately with the Angels and Cardinals. He taught Eckstein about the importance of understanding the pitch count. Steve stressed strike zone discipline, fouling off balls until you get your pitch. One of Eckstein's proudest accomplishments was having a ten pitch at bat. Eckstein became a World Series MVP in 2006. Steven also loaned his hitting manual to Jason Varitek whose average and on base percentage went up when Steve coached him. Then there was Vince Coleman who Steve got to think of like a leadoff batter.

During Vince's last year with the Cards, he increased his on base percentage by thirty percent.

Steve played fifteen years in the MLB for the Minnesota Twins, the Seattle Mariners, the Kansas City Royals, the Toronto Blue Jays and the St. Louis Cardinals. He enjoyed a productive baseball career, but not one deserving enshrinement in baseball's Hall of Fame.[241] However, he was a Hall of Famer when it came to influencing and being influenced by others. Steve, unlike many other major leaguers, understands the critical importance of influencing others and being influenced. Steve Braun's many different influences had the most impact on my understanding of the power of influence.

---

241 Steve Braun's lifetime batting average is .271 with 52 homers

Chapter 38

Tom Walker: 1972-1977

Most people take influence for granted. They rarely think of the many ways that they are influenced every day of their life. People almost never think that a person's words can help someone avoid tragedy. Sometimes a person can influence someone to do something (or not do something) that saves their life. Tom Walker was the beneficiary of this type of influence from one of the greatest people and players to ever play professional sports – Roberto Clemente.

Montreal Expos, Detroit Tigers, St. Louis Cardinals and California Angels

Tom Walker and I became friends because of Bill Mazeroski (Maz) when I was writing his bio for a SABR's book called *Sweet*

60. This fascinating book tells the story of the 1960 World Series Champion Pittsburgh Pirates. Dave Giusti, a mutual friend, suggested that I speak with Tom because of the relationship his son Neil had with Maz. Initially, we spoke about the influence that Maz had on his son's learning to play second base. I then learned about the interesting journey that Tom took to become a major league player.

Tom's life has been carefully shaped by the game of baseball. After completing his first year of playing in the Majors, he went down to Puerto Rico with Balor Moore, his teammate from the Expos. They played on a team coached by Roberto Clemente. Tom actually volunteered to go to Nicaragua with Clemente to deliver supplies to earthquake victims, but Roberto told him to stay on the island and enjoy the New Year's Eve celebration. Unfortunately, Clemente's words proved to be fateful for Tom. Roberto Clemente influenced Walker to stay in Puerto Rico and, consequently, it saved his life. Clemente took the plane to Nicaragua and died when the plane crashed that evening. It is hard to justify even now that a person who was such a great athlete and human being would die so suddenly doing such good things.

Tom Walker began playing baseball at the tender age of six while living in Florida. It was his Uncle Dudley that got him into playing. Dudley was the first to help him become a better ball player. He lived with Tom's family while serving in the Air Force. Tom was always waiting for his uncle to come home so they could have a game of catch. Uncle Dudley also seemed to look forward to their games of catch and played a pivotal role in influencing Tom to love baseball.

When Walker began his professional baseball career, his biggest influence was Cal Ripken Sr. Cal was his manager at Dallas–Fort Worth of AA. Tom said that Ripkin Sr felt that it was about work. He took a no-nonsense approach. Cal Sr. taught you to push yourself to limits you did not realize you had. As we described in the earlier chapter on the Ripkens, later this philosophy became known as the Ripken way – and with his profound influence on his team, it also was known as the Orioles' Way.

Steve Garvey, a former high school teammate, also influenced him, but not in a traditional sense. Walker did not try emulating Garvey but he was motivated by him to become the best he could be. Garvey became such a talent that big league scouts began to fight to watch him play. On the other hand, Tom needed to work real hard to make sure that he played very well for the scouts on the days when he pitched.

When he finally reached the Montreal Expos, Tom's biggest influence was Gene Mauch, his first major league manager. Gene knew the game better than most people. There were times when Walker admitted that he really disliked him. Mauch could push the right buttons to get a player's best performance out of him. Mauch preferred older to younger players. Whatever the case, you could learn from him, unless you were in his "dog house."

Tom was a first round draft pick by the Baltimore Orioles; thirty-two years later his son Neil became a first round draft choice by the Pittsburgh Pirates. As of 2020, there have only been ten other such combinations.[242] They are the Grieve, Burroughs, Mayberrys, Swishers, Walkers, DeShields, Boxbergers, Nevins, Witts and Soderstrom.

Bob with Tom Walker at PNC Park

---

242 Tom Walker pitched six seasons in the major leagues, had a career record of 18-23, 3.87 with 17 saves. He spent them as a reliever and spot starter.

Chapter 39

Carolyn King: 1973 Little League

*I*t is amazing how simple, seemingly mundane activities can influence a country forever. Carolyn King was a young girl with blonde pony tails who, unintentionally, became a world-wide celebrity and changed Little League baseball. Baseball's role as "America's Pastime" has given the sport heightened visibility when barriers of race or gender are broken. Carolyn's story is yet another example of how baseball has influenced the perspectives and beliefs of millions of Americans.

Ypsilanti Orioles Little League

What began as a simple bicycle ride with her brother to the nearby Bowen Field House to sign up for Little League, turned into a major social challenge! Never did Carolyn figure that her trip would lead the fight to break down the gender barriers or the American institution of Little League baseball! Carolyn King was a 5'4" blonde, twelve-year-old with ponytails and braces; all she wanted was to play baseball with her brother and friends from the neighborhood.

Carolyn became the centerpiece in a baseball "battle of the sexes — "one she did not want to become. All she wanted to do was simply to play baseball. When I spoke with her, Ms. King admitted that she was very uncomfortable at being touted a "trailblazer." *People* magazine had her sharing the cover with such notables as Sandra Day-O'Connor, Billy Jean King, and the astronaut Sally Ride. Each of them were known as icons of women's rights.

The Ypsilanti chapter of the Little League was formed in 1939. It held the oldest Little League charter in the state of Michigan.

When Carolyn went to the tryouts, Bill Anhut came up to her to inform her that girls were not allowed to play. Then moments later, Anhut apparently had a change of mind and ran after her to pin a number on her back. He asked her if she was serious about trying out. Carolyn nodded.

"I'm going to give you a shot," he replied.

The Ypsilanti Orioles chose Carolyn in the eighth round. Later the league held a special meeting after the draft, and decided to kick Carolyn off of the Orioles before she had the chance to show her skills. Next, the town council stepped in to inform the league that if Carolyn could not play the league would not be allowed to use their fields. This of course forced the Ypsilanti Little League to reverse its decision on May 10, 1973, and Carolyn became an official member of the Orioles.

When Carolyn first stepped onto the grass of Candy Cane Park, it was packed with thousands of people with cameras in hand. The media was there in full force. However, Carolyn was also greeted by jeers, like "Why don't you go home and play with dolls?"

Carolyn was not influenced by any one person outside her family to play baseball. She simply yearned to play baseball with her brother and the other neighborhood kids, who all happened to be boys. She grew up across the street from a park and considered herself a "tomboy" who just wanted to have fun playing baseball. When her brother went down to Bowen Field house, she followed.

Carolyn King made history by becoming one of the first girls to ever to play Little League Baseball. She became the most prominent girl to play the "boys' " sport. She also became the centerpiece of a groundbreaking gender discrimination lawsuit in 1974. Before the court decision, Ypsilanti, Michigan Little League had a rule that specifically prohibited girls from trying out. Not many people paid attention when Bill Anhut broke the rules by allowing her to try out. However, to everyone's surprise, Carolyn beat out 15 boys for a starting position and she was selected for the Orioles team.

This was followed by Little League International, based in Williamsport, Pennsylvania, that planned to remove the Ypsilanti

American Little League's charter if Carolyn was allowed to play in a Little League baseball game. She was removed from the Orioles' roster. However, as we indicated, the Ypsilanti City Council stated that if Carolyn was not allowed to play, Little League could not use any of the baseball fields in the city. The League was stuck between a "rock and a hard place." It had to make a very tough decision that would impact the future of the organization. So, they decided to allow Carolyn to play on May 10, 1973, at Candy Cane Park. The world-wide press made Carolyn's first baseball game national news. The stands were packed with television cameras and crowds. It became the biggest story ever to reach Ypsilanti, Michigan. Little did they know that the story was about to get much bigger.

Little League International pulled the Ypsilanti American League's charter simply because they allowed a little girl to play in a baseball game. Lawyers representing Carolyn and the City of Ypsilanti filed a gender discrimination lawsuit against Little League International. Unbelievably, Little League International won the lawsuit. The following year in 1975, after thinking about it Little League baseball allowed girls to play Little League Baseball for the first time in history. This amazing story was the subject of a documentary called "The Girl in Centerfield."

Because Carolyn was persistent, she got her wish to play baseball. However, this simple wish changed her life in ways she would never have imagined. Carolyn's participation in baseball made her a national hero to some and a target to others. Before she began playing Little League Baseball, Carolyn was a normal girl from a traditional middle class Michigan family. It all changed because she simply wanted to play baseball. She became a celebrity who was the subject of news stories by the legendary Walter Cronkite on the evening news.

Clearly, her story was what the country needed at the time. Carolyn's unintended "Battle of the Sexes" took place when the nation was dealing with the tragic story of Watergate that forced President Richard Nixon to resign in disgrace. Clearly, the country was in need of a "feel good" story. As a cute little blonde girl with a pony tail, Carolyn's story about breaking through a gender barrier was the perfect story at the perfect time in America.

She did not set out to make history or to influence an entire sport. In an interview years later, Carolyn King stated that "There isn't anything her daughter should not be able to do athletically if she has the talent! Or for that matter, any girl." It is amazing how simple things done to average people can influence the world forever.

Chapter 40
Billy Sample: 1978-1986

O*ne of the most interesting things about writing this book is learning how the* sport of baseball influenced the entire lives of former professional baseball *players who did not have Hall of Fame baseball careers. Billy Sample is a former major leaguer who has used baseball to have as much fun with the sport after his retirement as he did when he played.*

Texas, New York Yankees and Atlanta

**Billy Sample with Bob at a
Billy Staple's Hot Stove event**

William Amos Sample, better known as Billy Sample, graduated from Andrew Lewey High School in Salem, Virginia in 1973. He was a standout player in three sports in school – baseball, basketball and football. His high school football team was so good that they lost a state championship to T.C. Williams – the legendary school that was loosely depicted in the popular movie *Remember the Titans.*

Billy played nine years at the major league level, where he was known for his speed and defensive prowess in the outfield. Sample is a fascinating individual who used his considerable talents in a variety of jobs after his baseball career ended. He has been a broadcaster for both the Seattle Mariners and California Angels, as well as a contributor on radio for NPR and CBS. In addition, Sample was a columnist for "USA Today's" Baseball Weekly column and has written extensively for the online publications of ESPN and MLB.com, He has also been published in the "New York Times" and *Sports Illustrated.*

As a three year-old, Sample began watching baseball shows on television like the "Game of the Week" with Dizzy Dean and Pewee Reese. Surprisingly, he did not play a lot of baseball until he was eleven years old. Unfortunately, public schools in his community did not allow black and white students to go to school together until he was in the sixth grade. The popular soft drink company Dr. Pepper sponsored the first baseball team he played for. It had previously been an all-white team, so it was quite an adjustment for everyone when the team became integrated. Sample remembers his first baseball coach, Junior Epperly, as a tough leader, a taskmaster who demanded a lot from his players. Fortunately, they had a pretty good team that included future pro player Sandy Hill, who eventually played with the Pittsburgh Pirates.

Although he got bigger and stronger in high school and became a great football player, Billy realized at age 15 that he was a much more talented baseball player than a football or a basketball player, so his future was in baseball. After high school, he began going to tryout camps for professional teams. Because he lived in a town that had a minor league team, he was able to gauge how good he was or needed to be. This gave him the confidence to try out for minor league teams where he ended up playing with or against future MLB players like Mario Mendoza, Dave Parker, and Ed Ott.

Sample felt that a lot of people influenced his baseball career, but no one person was a main influence. Although he remembers having an influential conversation with Doyle Alexander, both of them were at the end of their careers in Atlanta. Doyle pointed out how John Tudor pitched to Sample. Alexander went over Tudor's pitching pattern in detail and told Sample how to hit a Tudor pitch. The next time he faced Tudor, Sample hit a single after the hitting instructions Doyle gave him. This convinced Sample that he should have spent much more time getting advice from pitchers earlier in his career.

> *"When you watch an incredible player, you stopped being a teammate and become a fan."*
>
> **– Billy Sample**

Sample also felt you could be influenced through osmosis. He had the opportunity to be teammates with the legendary Al Oliver while playing with the Texas Rangers. Billy felt that when you watch an incredible player like Oliver, you stopped being a teammate and become a fan.

Billy Sample was born in 1955 and played nine years in the majors. He was an outfielder who, between 1978 and 1986, played for the Texas Rangers, the New York Yankees and the Atlanta Braves. Sample had the distinction of hitting a single on his first major league pitch in 1978. He had 684 hits, 46 homers, 230 RBIs and 98 stolen bases. He made the Topps All Rookie Team in 1979. Almost half of his career stolen bases came in 1983 when he stole 44 and was fifth in the American League, which was impressive – until Rickey Henderson stole over 100!

While Sample was not a Hall of Fame baseball player, he has led a very successful life after baseball. In 2016, he published the book *A Year in Pinstripes … And Then Some,* which talked about his life and his baseball career. In addition to broadcasting and writing, he was a baseball consultant for the Showtime documentary about the Yankees' 1996 baseball season entitled "Joe Torre: Curveballs Along the Way." He wrote the screenplay *Reunion 108*, which won the Best Unproduced Screenplay Award at the 2011 Hoboken Film Festival. The critical acclaim of this film led him to produce the screenplay into the movie *Reunion 108*, which tells the entertaining fictional story of two generations of baseball players returning to the site of their minor league championship. Baseball has clearly been one of the major influences in every aspect of Billy Sample's life. Billy played nine years in the MLB, for three teams: the Texas Rangers, the New York Yankees and the Atlanta Braves.[243]

---

243 He played in 826 games, hit 46 career homers ane a lifetime batting average of .272.

Chapter 41
Paul Mirabella: 1978-1990

*I*n examining the careers and the lives of the baseball players we interviewed and researched, we discovered how important good or bad fortunes are in the careers of most people. Sometimes people find themselves in their dream position, but the influence of bad luck leads to their failure — just when they wanted to succeed more than ever. Paul Mirabella's career as a Yankee is a perfect example of this reality.

Milwaukee Brewers/ Seattle Mariners/
Texas Rangers/ Toronto Blue Jays/
New York Yankees

Paul began playing Little League baseball at eight years old. His parents were very supportive but they did not push him into playing. Paul really enjoyed the game of baseball and, because he was good at it, determined that it was his favorite sport. His brother played football so he decided to focus on a different sport. His early experiences in baseball were very positive so he, like most other good young baseball players, dreamed about becoming a major leaguer.

Paul had many different coaches throughout his life that played an influential role in his development as a baseball player. However, he was heavily influenced by the legendary players he had the opportunity to play with over the years. The roster of amazing players who influenced him include: Catfish Hunter, Ron Guidry, Louie Tiant, Gossage, Graig Nettles and Thurman Munson.

When I spoke to Paul, he made it clear that the two players that had the greatest influence on him were Munson and Nettles because of their openness in speaking with him and how they focused on excellence.

They were two of the on-field leaders of the Yankees' World Series championship teams of the 1970s. They exhibited the fighting and winning attitude of those teams. They were clutch hitters, aside from what they did on the baseball diamond. Nettles was considered one of the best fielding third basemen of his era, while Thurman was able to elevate the Yankee pitching staff by getting the best performance out of them.

Nettles played 22 MLB seasons, half of them in Yankee pinstripes, until he returned to San Diego to play with the Padres. Thurman played his entire eleven year career with the Yankees, but died tragically in a plane crash in 1979.

Paul stated that both Nettles and Munson were consummate professionals. When he was on the Yankees, he was used out of the bullpen. While sitting in the pen, he had several opportunities to talk with Goose Gossage. He took full advantage of picking the brain of the future Hall of Fame player. Paul made his major league debut as a Texas Ranger on July 28, 1978, where he got his first win against the Chicago White Sox. It was the perfect beginning to his major league career.

However, shortly after that win, he was part of a deal where the Yankees traded several players, shipping him with Sparky Lyle and another player that he could not remember, off to the Rangers in exchange for Dave Righetti, with Paul and another. Becoming a reliever for the Yankees was a dream come true for Paul. He could potentially take advantage of this opportunity to exceed his expectations in the most public baseball marketplace in the world. Playing for the Yankees was the break he needed and the chance of a lifetime. He made his Yankee debut on April 10, 1979, coming into the game as a reliever and blew the save after Goose Gossage had loaded the bases. Unfortunately, he was continually being put in extremely difficult situations, which made him appear like a mediocre pitcher at best. Some would say it was bad luck. Unfortunately, as a Yankee, Paul could never gain traction and had a disappointing record as a Yankee reliever or occasional starting pitcher with an 8.79 ERA.

The good news is that Paul fared much better on other baseball teams. Paul was traded to the Toronto Blue Jays with Chris Chambliss, which resulted in rejuvenating his career. He was not a Hall of Fame type of baseball player; however, he was a good athlete who had a chance to live out his dream of being a professional baseball player on many different teams. Paul played for the Texas Rangers in 1978 and 1982, the New York Yankees in 1979, the Toronto Blue Jays from 1980 to 1981, the Baltimore Orioles in 1983, the Seattle Mariners from 1984 to 1985 and the Milwaukee Brewers from 1987 to 1990. Paul pitched for a total of thirteen years in the MLB and appeared in 298 games. According to the *Baseball Records Play Index* and the *Baseball Almanac*, he was the starting pitcher in 33 games, completing three of them and one was a shutout.

Paul Mirabella was a much better pitcher than his record with the Yankees indicates.[244] However, he either had bad luck or was not ready for the biggest stage in the sport. Even though he never became a superstar, Paul is thankful that he had a chance to live out his baseball dreams. He now owns a wholesale tire business and is living happily ever after.

---

244 Paul pitched 499 innings, faced 2,236 batters and struck out 258 of them. His overall win and lost record was 19-29, with an earned run average of 4.45.

Chapter 42

Jim Campanis: 1989-1994
Minor Leagues

I always laugh when I hear the saying, "If I didn't have bad luck I would have no luck at all." When you examine the lives of as many different people as we have, you learn how important the influence of luck is to making careers. Sometimes the luck of being the right person at the right time leads to a Hall of Fame career. Unfortunately, sometimes people start their baseball career with luck on their side but bad luck hits them at the wrong time in their career. Jim Campanis, Jr. was born into a baseball family. He was a great player destined to be the third generation of professional baseball players. Jim seemingly had everything he needed to become a major league baseball player. However, he was sidelined with bad luck at the exact wrong time in his career.

He was a member of the 1985 USA Junior National Team and Team USA in 1988, third round draft pick by the Seattle Mariners, played in the minors 1989-94

Jim Campanis, Jr. was born into a major league family. His dad, Jim Sr. played catcher for six years in the majors with the Los Angeles Dodgers, the Kansas City Royals and the Pittsburgh Pirates. His grandfather, Al Campanis had a "cup of coffee" with the Brooklyn Dodgers in 1943 after playing seven years on Dodger minor league teams. While playing for the Dodger's triple A minor league team, the Montreal Royals in 1946, Branch Rickey asked Jim's grandfather to teach Jackie Robinson how to play second base. Al was Robinson's friend and teammate. He was also Jackie's roommate during his team's barnstorming tour. He went on to become a high-ranking executive in the Dodgers organization, serving as Vice President of player personnel and General Manager.

Unfortunately, Al Campanis became the face of racial insensitivity after doing an interview on Ted Koppel's" Nightline" program on April 6, 1987. When Koppel asked him why more African Americans were not on the field as managers or general managers he replied: "'No, I don't believe its prejudice. I truly believe that they may not have some of the necessities to be, let's say, a field manager or perhaps a general manager."

It was a poor choice to make a point, and it proved to be a disaster to his long, storied baseball career. As negative as Campanis's comments were, they ended up having a positive influence on baseball. After the controversy, the game made it a priority to hire minority executives, and after two years Bill White became the National League President. White was followed by several other African Americans to serve in the front office of MLB teams.

Jim Campanis Jr. says that he cannot remember a time when he was not playing baseball. He spent his childhood around the game at the professional level during his father's playing days. Jim began to play little league when he was eight. One of his greatest experiences was shagging balls during the Pittsburgh Pirates' batting practice. He remembers with pride that he once caught a fly ball hit by Willie Stargell.

Campanis played baseball in college at the University Of Southern California (USC). He was college teammates with several sons of former major league players like Brett Boone and Daemon Buford. He also played on the team with the children of celebrities such as Harrison Ford and Barry White's sons. During his junior year at college, Jim batted .392, with 23 homers and 92 runs batted in. He was so good that he received All-American Honors and was selected to be a member of the 1985 USA Junior National Team and Team USA in 1988. His twenty-three homers were second to the future legendary pro baseball player Mark McGwire at USC. Jim Jr. was signed by the Seattle Mariners as a third round draft pick. He roomed with Ken Griffey Jr. in the minors. However, on the day that he was told that he would become a major league ball player with the Seattle Mariners, he broke his wrist. This injury led to several other injuries which forced him to leave professional baseball. He played six years of professional baseball, three at single A and three at the double A level. His career totals were a .254 batting average, 56 homeruns and 239 runs batted in.

While Jim felt that he had the honor of playing for several "world class" coaches in the minors and in college, he still went to his father for playing advice. His father was able to make suggestions on his son's batting just by listening to Jim describe his problems over the phone.

It was very tough for Jim when he realized that his baseball playing career was over. At one point he entertained the idea of coaching, but instead decided to go back to school and embark on a different career journey. He got involved with selling advertising and became very successful in that profession. He went on to own his own firm, Campy Media, which develops advertising campaigns for clients. Jim is a talented writer and has written several baseball stories on his experience around the game, and in 2016 published the book, *Born into Baseball: Laughter and Heartbreak from the Edge of the Show.* Jim had the great fortune of being born into a legendary baseball family. However, he had the bad luck of having career ending injuries just when his career was getting started.

Chapter 43

Chris Hammond: 1990-2006

I find the popular saying, "Where there is a will there is a way" to be very motivational for me. This saying tells me that if I have enough of a desire to do something I can find a way to do it. Chris Hammond clearly has both strong values and a strong will. His "values" convinced him to leave professional baseball completely to support his wife. His "will" and the influence and support of his wife enabled him to return as a major league pitcher in spite of not playing baseball for two full years. Bob shares the incredible story of Chris Hammond in this chapter.

1990-2006: Florida Marlins/ Cincinnati Reds/ Atlanta Braves/ New York Yankees/ San Diego Padres

Chris Hammond played between 1990 and 2006, pitching for fourteen years in the MLB. Hammond was a starting pitcher for the first part of his career while playing for the Reds, Marlins and Red Sox. Then Chris retired after the 1998 season due to his wife's difficult pregnancy. He did not pitch during the 1999 or 2000 season. After two years away from the game of baseball, he decided to return to the sport. His wife Lynne borrowed a radar gun from a highway patrolman to clock his fastball. Incredibly, in 2001, even after his absence from baseball, Chris was able to get his pitching speed up and made it back to the majors at the age of 36. In 2002, Hammond was able to accomplish something only three other pitchers did before him. He ended the season with an earned run average under 1.00 while pitching 70+ innings. Chris Hammonds established himself as a late inning left handed set up guy. He signed as a free agent for the

Yankees, then the Padres, then finished his career with the Reds and then retired in July of 2006.

Both his father and his brothers were his big baseball influences. They encouraged Chris to play T-ball when he was only four years old. He went on to play youth baseball his entire childhood. After graduating high school, he was awarded a scholarship to attend the University of Birmingham. He was not a great student, and transferred to Gulf Coast Community College in Florida because of his lackluster academic performance. Because of his pitching ability, the Cincinnati Reds selected him during the sixth round of the 1986 Amateur baseball draft. Chris moved quickly through the minors with stops at Tampa, Chattanooga and Nashville. He ended up with the Reds during their World Series of 1990 but did not play in it. After three years at Cincinnati, he went on to pitch for the Marlins during their inaugural season. Rene Lachman was his first manager while at the Marlins and also a big influence. Lachman was able to get him to believe in himself as a major league player. Chris also credited Rene's brother Marcel for teaching him to focus on the mound. He cannot remember a specific teammate that mentored him, although when pitching in Atlanta he watched Glavine, Maddux and Smoltz pitch while playing in Atlanta.

When he finally retired for good, he became a full-time father. Chris loves kids and started the Chris Hammond Foundation to help rural kids in Alabama with the supplies they need both for life and to play baseball. Like most nonprofits, his Foundation relies on fundraising, so Chris holds an annual celebrity golf tournament each year. He is able to raise a lot of money by getting some of his better known former teammates to participate in the tournament. In 2013, Chris had Tommy Glavine, John Smoltz and Greg Maddux as sponsors. He is also active in his Christian faith, a regular attendee at Bible studies and he is a frequent speaker at church functions.

Chris finished with a career record of 66-62 and an ERA of 4.14. He now lives in Wedowee, Alabama where he spends most of his time running the Chris Hammond Youth Foundation, spreading the word about Christianity and living life on his terms.

Section VII
Baseball in Players' Lives

Chapter 44

Meeting Bobby Thomson[245]

*O*ne *of the most interesting things about baseball is how one pitch or one hit can change a person's life forever. In this chapter, Bob tells the story of Bobby Thomson, who hit "The Shot Heard Around the World." We naturally focus most of our attention on the hero who hit the game winning home run. However, it is also important to remember how a legendary "walk off" home run changes the life of the pitcher who gave up that decisive hit. Ralph Branca, the person who pitched to Bobby Thomson, had to live with that one pitch for the rest of his life – as did Ralph Terry, who pitched to Bill Mazeroski when he hit the walk off 1960 World Series Game 7 home run. It is easy to overlook the extraordinary power of influence in any given situation. However, it is truly amazing how throwing a ball to someone with a bat one time can generate sufficient influence to change lives ... and even the world!*

Bobby Thomson is a baseball icon. Even if he never did anything else in his career besides hitting his homerun to help the New York Giants win the third game of the 1951 playoff game against the Brooklyn Dodgers, it would have been enough to insure his place in baseball lore.

---

245 His lifetime numbers were 264 homers, 1,026 RBIs and a .270 average.

**Bob with Bobby Thomson at Knights of
Columbus event in Martinsville, NJ**

Legendary sportswriter Walter Wellesley "Red" Smith described the aftermath of Thomson's home run in a "New York Herald Tribune" column this way: "Now it is done. Now the story ends. And there is no way to tell it. The art of fiction is dead. Reality has strangled invention. Only the utterly impossible, the inexpressibly fantastic, can ever be plausible again."

Bobby Thomson's game winning home run was considered the most famous "walk off" home run in history until Bill Mazeroski's walk off home run in game 7 of the 1960 World Series. The home run was particularly meaningful because it was the first nationally televised game in baseball history. Thomson's legendary home run took place six years before I was born. Little did I know that our paths would cross each other on several occasions over the years!

In the mid-nineteen sixties, when my father worked as a part-time bartender at the Plainfield Country Club in Edison, New Jersey, he had a chance to meet various sports personalities. He would often come home and tell me whom he had served drinks to. These stories were all the more meaningful because he often brought me a personalized autograph from one of the stars that he met. I got even more excited because my dad would be so excited over whom he met. However, many times I had no idea who they were. I was influenced by my dad's enthusiasm to be excited about these people who I had not heard of.

One day, he told me that Pete Gogolak, who was fine field goal kicker for the New York football Giants, came into the country club's bar. Gogolak had the distinction of being the first soccer style field goal kicker. Gogolak was someone I actually recognized because he was still playing. Then there was Ralph Terry. Terry, who was a former Yankee pitcher, had the misfortune of surrendering Mazeroski's home run in the 1960 World Series. I still have his autograph and remember a story that he told my father. It seems Ralph got married right after the World Series and he and his bride honeymooned in Mexico. The next morning he spotted a local paper. While it was in Spanish he could make out one word, "Mazeroski!" He realized that no matter where he went he could not hide from that one pitch.

The one guy that my dad got the most excited about was Bobby Thomson! I can remember my father proudly giving me Mr. Thomson's autograph. It was on the back of a blank bar receipt. I feigned excitement, but at the same time, it meant nothing to me because I had no idea who this guy was. My father explained how Bobby hit one of the biggest homeruns in baseball history on October 3, 1951. He explained to me how he was captivated by Russ Hodges' famous home run call on the radio.[246] I had mentioned it earlier in the book, a young Willie Mays was on the on deck circle.

It seems that before the 1951 season, most experts felt that the Brooklyn Dodgers were unstoppable. This expectation was true for most of the season. By August 10th, the Dodgers were ahead of the Giants by 12 ½ games. But this was about the time the Giants began to sneak back, winning 37 of the last 44 games. At one point they won 16 in a row. When the regular season was completed, both the Dodgers and the Giants had identical records. This meant for the second time in National League history, a best of three play-offs was needed to determine the pennant winner. The last time was in 1946, when Brooklyn lost to St. Louis.

---

246 Personal remembrances with my father

With two teams winning one game apiece, the pitching matchup for the deciding game pitted Sal Maglie (Giants) against Don Newcombe (Dodgers). The game was deadlocked at 1-1 going into the top of the eighth inning. The Dodgers scored three times to go up 4-1. Then at the bottom of the ninth inning, the stage was set for what was referred to as, "The Miracle of Coogan's Bluff" or "The Shot Heard Around the World!" Alvin Dark started the inning off with a single, which was followed with another by Don Mueller, sending Dark to third. Then Monte Irvin, the NL's RBI leader popped out. Whitey Lockman hit a double to bring in Dark, but Mueller injured himself sliding into third and was replaced by Clint Hartung. The Giants were now down 4-2 with men on second and third, bringing Bobby Thomson to the plate to meet history!

Charlie Dressen decided that Newcombe had enough and went to the mound to make a pitching change. He had Ralph Branca and Carl Erskine in the bullpen. On the advice of Clyde Sukeforth, he elected to have Branca pitch to Thomson. Branca's first pitch was a fastball down the pipe for a strike. His second was up and in, with the intention of setting up for a breaking ball down and away. Bobby yanked it down the short leftfield line and over a seventeen-foot wall to end the game!

At 3:58 PM that afternoon Russ Hodges screamed over the airwaves: "Giants win the pennant! The Giants win the pennant!" Bobby Thomson would later admit: "I knew it was a homerun as soon as I hit it. A homerun, upper deck, that's what, went through my mind. Then all of a sudden, the ball started to sink, and for a split second, I thought it was going to hit the wall. Then it disappeared. I had never hit a ball like that before."

Thomson retired after the 1960-season with an impressive career. He was a three time All-Star, all with the Giants. Thomson hit over 20 homeruns eight times, and drove in over 100 runs four times. Arguably, 1951 was his best season: 32 homeruns, 101 RBIs and a batting average of .293. Years later, when I was working at AT&T, I almost crossed paths with Mr. Thomson. It seemed that he lived in Berkley Heights, New Jersey and was a golfing buddy of my Division

Manager. One afternoon, he came to my workplace to have lunch. My Division manager brought him to my work cube to introduce us, but I was home because my son was sick. He left an autograph for me, "To Bobby, Best wishes your friend Bobby Thomson, 'The Shot Heard around the world!'"

I was disappointed that I missed a chance to meet the man that I heard so much about. I figured that was it; I missed my chance. Several years later, my brother-in-law Joe called me up to invite me to a Knights of Columbus luncheon. I can still hear him say, "You know more about baseball history than I do; the speaker is some old ball player, and you probably heard of, some guy named Bobby Thomson?" Well, you can imagine my reaction. I jumped at the chance to meet him. I am happy to say, that Bobby Thompson did not disappoint. He was both entertaining and informative. I had a blast.

I can remember Bobby recalling something Carl Erskine said. He quoted Erskine recalling when he was asked what his best pitch was, he replied, "The curveball I bounced in the bullpen at the Polo Grounds back in 1951!"[247]

After Bobby finished speaking, the audience was invited to come up and meet him. I finally shook hands with him. Sure, I already had a couple of his autographs but I wanted to finally shake his hand. I also brought along a book about him for him to sign.[248]

What could be more appropriate than a copy of *The Giants Win the Pennant, The Giants Win the Pennant: The Real Story of Bobby Thomson*? (Author's Note: Bobby Thomson died on August 16, 2010)

---

247 37th Family Communion Breakfast, Knights of Columbus, Martinsville, NJ, January 18, 2004
248 Ibid.

Chapter 45
A Bird Among Tigers

The world of sports is filled with many fascinating stories of athletes who made history in a very short period of time. One of the reasons the Olympics is so popular is that it is filled with stories of "one event wonders" who defied the odds and won a race or lead a team to victory. Their star shines brightly after the race but often fades into the shadows of history. It is much harder for a baseball player to make a lasting mark in a short career. However, one player defied those odds and had such a short and illustrious career that many believe he helped to save baseball. In this chapter, Bob tells the story of the late Mark "The Bird" Fidrych who I believe, on a per game basis, was the most influential person in baseball history.

During the fall of 1975, Ralph Houk, Detroit's manager, visited the Florida Instructional League. Looking out on a baseball diamond he spotted a tall skinny kid with frizzy hair pitching. The young pitcher was impressive, causing Ralph Houk to think, "He's really something ..."

The Tigers were a bad team; they finished in last place with a record of 57-102 in 1975. It did not take much to impress the Tigers' manager! Detroit's pitching staff owned the second highest ERA in the American League for the 1975 season. His two best pitchers each finished with the second highest amount of losses; one of them also led the league in wild pitches and another was second in the league for hitting batters. So how could anyone blame Houk for getting excited by seeing a kid pitching in the instructional league?

The following spring, he decided to take a chance on the kid, passing over Dave Lemanczyk, Bill Slayback and Fernando Arroyo.

The kid's name was Mark Fidrych, affectionately known as the "Bird," a nickname bestowed upon him by an old teammate at Bristol of the Appalachian League. The teammate noticed that Fidrych bore an uncanny resemblance to Big Bird on Sesame Street.[249]

This young pitcher from Northborough, Massachusetts was known to crouch down and smooth out the opposing pitcher's cleat marks on the mound. This became known as "manicuring the mound." But Mark explained that he was simply filling up the hole so he could make his own, trying not to adjust to someone else's. He added, "That's just my way of concentrating and keeping my head in the game."

Mark was also known to have conversations with the ball, although he explained that it was his way of reminding himself not to repeat what he did wrong with a certain pitch. Sometimes he aimed the ball like a dart. He threw back balls if he felt like they had hits in them. During his first major league game on May 15, 1976, Cleveland's Rico Carty claimed that Fidrych was trying to hypnotize his Cleveland Indian teammates. Judging from the end results of that game, he might not have hypnotized the Indians, but he did psych them out – whether intentionally or unintentionally. During that game, the Bird refused to let the grounds crew fix the mound in the 6th inning. Instead, he helped himself to a handful of dirt from the wheelbarrow and patted it in place. Since he had a no-hitter, Fidrych did not want them to mess up the pitcher's mound.

Fidrych retired the first fourteen Indians' batters in that game. He had a no-hitter going into the seventh inning. The Bird walked Alan Ashby, leading off the top of the fifth inning, realizing that the perfect game was lost, but the no-hitter was still intact. That ended when Buddy Bell led off with a single to left field and Rick Manning moved him to third with another single. The shut out ended when

---

249 "The Bird: The Life and Legacy of Mark Fidrych," by Doug Wilson, Washington Post, March 29, 2013

Rico Carty grounded out to second, bringing home Bell. The pitching phenomenon finished with a two hit, 2-1 victory.

That game was all over the news the next day. Many people claimed that it was the game that rescued baseball. In recent years, the game had lost some of its allure because of fans' dissatisfaction with players and how how they treated it as a business, not like a game. Baseball experienced a brief baseball lockout during the spring of 1976 because an independent arbitrator ruled that players could become free agents when their contracts expired. This ruling angered the owners; following, they briefly locked players out during spring training. Fortunately, no major league games were missed, but this controversy, combined with the economic and political challenges of the country at the time, negatively impacted interest in baseball across the country. One would need to ask, the question, could one game be enough to begin the process of winning back the interest of fans?

Many baseball fans believed that the nationally televised game that Fidrych pitched against the Yankees on June 28th began the turnaround in baseball. The stage was set. It was Monday Night Baseball on the American Broadcasting Company (ABC) television station. This night was the first night that the country got to see the entertaining pitcher responsible for the incredible "hoopla" in the baseball world.[250]

Fiderych's coming out party took place six days before the country celebrated its bicentennial. The Bird reenergized America's pastime. Detroit Stadium was packed with 48,000 fans. Incredibly, more than 18 million viewers watched ABC's "Monday Night Baseball," not to see the first-place New York Yankees, but tuning in to see this entertaining kid called the Bird. This game brought renewed interest in baseball, which had been suffering with lower attendance and the tension between the players and the owners.

The skinny kid with frizzy hair, wearing number 20 for the Detroit Tigers, went out to the mound and was greeted with thunderous

---

250 ABC Monday Night Baseball, June 28, 1976, www.youtube.com/watch?v=sMSDo3BX5Ds

applause! When he began to warm up, the fans cheered; after his catcher, Bruce Kimm, tossed the ball back to him for the start of the game, the Bird got down on his right knee to put the dirt in place with his left hand, which of course was followed by another thunderous ovation. Later on, he talked to the ball, yet another ovation. The fans loved him and thought that he was the "real deal." The young pitcher's magic was what baseball needed at the time.

Rusty Staub supplied all the runs that the Bird needed with a two run homer during the bottom half of the inning. The Bird ended Mickey Rivers' 20 game hitting streak by collaring him on four infield grounders. Mickey's hitting streak was the longest by a Yankee player since 1942. The crowd went nuts over the Bird's performance, but not everyone was a fan of his. Yankee catcher Thurman Munson was not a fan, and called him "bush."

After completing the game, Mark ran off of the mound to disappear in the dugout. The crowd cried out for a curtain call. He came out minus shoes to acknowledge the crowd. Bob Uecker interviewed him for the national television audience. Basking in the glow of the sold out crowd, he admitted to the announcer that: "I didn't bring all these people here."[251]

In the booth, Bob Prince said it (the ovation) was the closest thing he ever saw since Dale Long hit his seventh homer in seven consecutive games.[252] In 1956, Long set a record by hitting 8 home runs in eight consecutive games between May 19 and May 28.

Yes, 1976 was a magical year. I reacquainted myself with the game that I love. It was because of the year "The Bird" would have: 19-9, 2.34 (second in the league), the first rookie pitcher to start an All-Star game. He was voted the Rookie of the Year! Everything was going very well for the Bird in 1977 ... until he tore some cartilage in his knee while fooling around in the outfield during spring training. His first start (May 27th) resulted in a 2-1 loss to the Seattle Mariners.

---

251 Mark Fidrych interview after Yankee game, with Bob Uecker, June 28, 1976, www.youtube.com/watch/vhCdwCRqBGI

252 Ibid.

Some miscues cost him the game, but he defended his teammates. Second baseman Tito Fuentes' error on a hard hit ground ball was one of the reasons the Bird lost the game. Ever the great teammate, the Bird refused to blame his teammate (according to the Saturday, May 28, 1977, "Reading Eagle" paper) "I consider that not an error on Tito because of the bounce it took. You should have seen it bounce. It almost took his head off!" Mark would not win his first game until June 6, an 8-0 shutout over the Angels. His arm went dead, but he was still selected for the All-Star game, yet he declined. Mark finished the year at 6-4, 2.89.

In 1978, he only pitched in 3 games but won two of them. His last major league game was on October 1, 1980. He would retire after 1983.[253] The Bird started 56 games and completed 34. Given the Bird's incredible importance to baseball, it is a shame that he played in so few games. I believe that on a per game basis Mark Fidrych was the most influential player in baseball history.

While the music might have died with the plane crash that took Buddy Holly, Richie Valens and the Big Bopper on February 3, 1959, a part of my baseball memories died for me on April 13, 2009. That is the day that Mark Steven Fidrych also died in an accident. The Reverend Judith E. Wright delivered the eulogy at the funeral, entoning, "He was a humble man, who was loved by all." They sang "Take Me Out to the Ballgame." There was a ceremonial first pitch thrown by Mark's brother-in-law Rich Duda and their nephew Charles Grogan.[254]

His former teammate and friend, Willie Horton added, "He was a trailblazer. Everyone playing in the major leagues owes a debt of gratitude to Mark Fidrych. He brought baseball back to the people. He made it popular again. He helped save the game."[255]

Mark Fidrych proved that if you can't have fun playing the game of baseball, well then what is the use?

---

253 Mark Fidrych's career numbers were 29-19, 3.10.
254 "Family, friends bid farewell to Mark 'The Bird' Fidrych'" by Abby Jordan, Metro Wet Dailey News, April 18, 2009
255 Ibid.

Chapter 46

Nellie King: When
One Door Closes

We all go through difficult times in life. Virtually every adult will lose a job for one reason or another multiple times. Fortunately, for most people when one "door" closes and you lose your job, more often than not another "door" opens and you get a job that is better or leads to a better opportunity. Unfortunately, the time between the closed and open doors is almost always much longer than we want it to be. These open and closed doors significantly influence our lives. If we fall into depression the proverbial door may be closed forever. However, if we are positive, patient and persistent, a job that we really want opens up for us. Nellie King always believed the saying, "When one door closes another one opens." This mantra was the theme of his life. In this chapter, Bob tells the story of his good friend and mentor Nellie King.

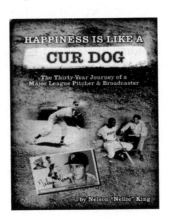

At the end of 2005, I found myself a casualty of a major *"downsizing"* by AT&T. I can remember being quite nervous about being unemployed after working twenty years for the same company. What made the loss of a job even more stressful was because I had a young family to support and had a mortgage to pay. I can still hear my friend Nellie telling me: "Bobby, when one door closes, another one opens." His words had such a calming and memorable effect on me that they helped me through this difficult period in my career.

Nellie King became a mentor in my life. His words and philosophy on life allowed me to handle my unemployment situation. Unbeknownst to him, his advice has helped others that he had never met because I have repeated his words to people I know that became unemployed.

Nellie King was a former major league pitcher and a baseball announcer for the Pittsburgh Pirates. He had been knocked down a couple of times himself during his life's journey, but he never failed to pick himself up. Those words, "When one door closes, another one opens" defined his life. Our friendship grew as I learned more about this man, and how those words defined his life.

Nelson Joseph King was born March 15, 1928, in Weston Place, PA. He was the youngest child of Amelia and Charles King. They lived in a home owned by the company his father worked for called the Locust Mountain Mining Company. Life was tough for the King family – it was rough working in the mines. At the time, the country was in the midst of the Great Depression. Fortunately, Charles King had steady work, which meant maybe working only two or three days a week, but it was enough to put food on his family's table.[256]

Nellie's father died on December 4, 1933. At the time, there were no safety nets for families in King's situation. Unemployment compensation was not available yet. There was no welfare, no medical or retirement benefits, and there was no such thing as Social Security.

---

256 King, Nelson J., Happiness if Like a Cur Dog,(Bloomington, In., Author House, 2009) 12-14

It became painfully obvious that Nellie's mother could not financially hold the family together, not alone, and not with a young son of Nellie's age. She attempted to get him accepted into the Girard College, a home for orphans. Nellie took several physical and intelligence tests which he hoped to fail. Ultimately, he did not get accepted because of a heart murmur. The good news about not being accepted is that it enabled him to enjoy the summer the way an eight-year-old boy should. He did not have to go to an institution so he could play with his friends all summer. Then, at the end of summer vacation, a stranger's visit to the Nelson's home changed his life. Nellie did not know who this woman was but soon learned that she came from the Hershey Industrial School.[257] The school was an orphanage for poor Caucasian boys. Yes, it specified Caucasians in its advertisement. The Civil Rights movement and racial equality were still decades away.

Nellie Joseph King became a student of the Hershey Industrial School on December 4, 1936 ... three years to the day from his father's death. His mother and older brother drove him there. He had no idea what this new environment was going to be like. However, years later he made it clear that he did not have fond memories of the Hershey School.

Milton Hershey had noble intentions when he founded the school. He hoped to instill a healthy work ethic in students. The school accomplished this by assigning the boys to *group* farms, requiring them to do daily chores, such as milking dairy cows. Nellie's farm house was responsible for thirty milking cows that required milking both morning and night. This meant milking sixty cows each day. Unfortunately for the boys, Holstein cows did not celebrate holidays or take off weekends. Not only were there daily chores but each new student was required to build his own bed when he moved in. The school's leaders ran the school based on the adage, "Idleness is the devil's workshop." It was a difficult time in Nellie's life, although it was rescued because he had a chance to play baseball.

---

257 Ibid., 14-19

Nellie points out in his memoir, *Happiness is a Cur Dog: The Thirty-year Journey of a Major League Baseball Pitcher and Broadcaster*, that from the time he graduated high school until today, there were only four years that he did not enjoy at all. These were the two years he spent in the Army and the two years that he attempted to make a living selling mutual funds. He experienced other challenges in life; however, he truly believed that "When one door closes, another one opens." This adage helped Nellie successfully deal with virtually every adversity that he faced in his life.[258]

Baseball became his safety net while he was in school. Nellie and his classmates found time to play baseball after they finished all of their chores. He and his housemates played in a loosely organized league against nearby farms, which meant that most of their opponents were located a mile or two away. Since they did not have access to buses, they had to walk quite a distance to go to their games. The team was not outfitted with fancy uniforms but wore the same overalls and work shoes they wore in the fields. These pick-up games were the extent of Nellie's high school baseball career. The challenging circumstances of these games taught him to truly appreciate whatever he had.

After Nellie graduated from high school he tried out for his first organized baseball program. It was formed by a man named Lefty Hallman, who was the director of the Lebanon, Pa. YMCA. Nellie pitched well enough to be selected to play for one of the six teams in its league. Even though Nellie had no formal training in baseball, his performance in the league was good enough to attract the attention of Charles "Pop" Kelchner, a long time St. Louis Cardinal scout.[259]

Nellie began his professional baseball journey in 1946. The first stop was with the Albany Cardinals of the Class D Georgia-Florida League. He was paid $100 per month. His first uniform had the name "Slaughter" sewn into it.[260] Enos Slaughter was a star for the old St. Louis Cardinals. He was best known for scoring the winning run in the

---

258 Ibid., 1
259 Ibid., 23
260 Ibid., 25

seventh game of the 1946 World Series where the St. Louis Cardinals beat the Boston Red Sox. Nellie was a big Cardinals fan when young Nellie had amassed two giant scrapbooks with their clippings and photos. He thought, "Can it get any better than this?" At eighteen years old, he was living the dream. Unfortunately, he experienced the kind of deep disappointment that many young players experienced when the team surprisingly, cut him loose. Other young men in his situation might have opted for a different profession. Not Nellie; he continued to pursue his dream of playing professional baseball. Later the same year, Nellie was signed by another baseball team, the New Iberia Cardinals of Class D in the Evangeline League. He was paid $125 a month. This time the young pitcher lasted only two weeks, pitching one inning. Nellie had the embarrassing experience of being released by two teams in the same year. This distinction might be deflating to practically anyone, anyone except Nelson Joseph King.[261]

The following year, Roy Dissinger, a former scout for the Cardinals and Red Sox, started his own farm system and invited Nellie to spring training. He got another chance to play baseball when he was signed by the Geneva Red Birds of the Alabama League, another D classification team. The Red Birds finished in last place, 41 ½ games behind. Nellie posted an 8-11 record. A defining moment in the season came when the team's second baseman, Cotton Bosarge advised him how to hold his fastball. He recommended that Nellie begin to hold it with the seams, causing it to sink. This advice helped Nellie have an exceptional year in New Iberia. He threw 284 innings and had a record of 20-13. The Pittsburgh Pirates bought Dissinger's minor league operation. Little did Nellie realize, but he was on the road to Pittsburgh, and the place he would call home for the rest of his life.

His pitching performance at Geneva earned him a promotion to the York White Roses of the Class B Interstate League. York did not have a very successful season; they finished in sixth place at 66-72.

---

261 "Nellie King," by Bob Hurte, SABR Bio Project

But the Interstate league was a good league; Nellie had a respectable record of 16-15 and an ERA of 2.25.

The next year (1950) he moved up another rung on the ladder. This time he was sent to play at Charleston, South Carolina to pitch for Rip Sewell, a former Pirates pitcher, in the Class A South Atlantic League (SALLY), Class A. Nellie posted a 9-10, 3.41 record for the Charleston Rebels.[262]

Just as King's professional baseball career was moving toward his dream, Uncle Sam called. Between 1951 and 1952, he served in the Army during the Korean War. He was unable to play baseball during that time, amounting to another derailment in his baseball career..

He did not enjoy being at Fort Dix. However, it was there that he met the brother of his future wife, Bernadette Earl. This new friend set the two of them up to go on a blind date.[263] This date led to a wonderful relationship. When Nellie completed his service with the Army, he was 25. Other men his age might have given up on the dream of playing major league baseball, but not Nellie. The lessons instilled in him long ago while at the Hershey School, were the reason he never stopped working toward his goal!

In 1953, Nellie played for the Denver Bears of the Class "A" Western League. Up to that season, he was used primarily as a starter. But in Denver Nellie was groomed to be a closer. His pitching record was 15-3, 17 saves and an ERA of 2.09. Nellie walked only 22 batters, 4 intentionally. He also had a streak of 13 wins to start the season.

After the season, he married Bernadette Earl. The morning after their wedding day he picked up a copy of the "New York Times," only to learn that the Pittsburgh Pirates bought his contract. King only stayed with the Pirates for a month, pitching seven innings in four games before being sent down to play for Danny Murtaugh's New Orleans Pelicans. Under Murtaugh's tutelage, he went 16-5, with a 2.25 ERA, being used primarily as a starter.

---

262 Ibid.
263 Ibid., King, 79

Nellie returned to Pittsburgh, which lasted three months before suffering with "dead arm." He came back for the 1955 season to establish himself as a major league pitcher. His record was 1-3 in seventeen games with an ERA of 2.98. Nellie felt that the turning point occurred when he pitched seven innings of relief for Vernon Law to earn a save; then three days later he shut out the Dodgers for his first major league victory. Still, the Pirates' front office decided to farm him out. This did not make sense to King, plus it cost him a chance to qualify for a Major League pension. Nellie rehabbed with the Hollywood Stars of the Pacific Coast League. Bobby Bragan was the team's manager and showed great confidence in Nellie.[264] He produced a 2-3 record with an ERA of 3.70. Bragan decided to use him in the California State Championship.

That winter, the Pirates asked him to play winter ball in Mazatlan, Mexico. Unfortunately, Nellie had to leave with dysentery after a month. He lost a lot of weight, which was problematic since he did not have a lot of weight he could afford to lose.[265]

Nellie King has described the 1956 season as the most enjoyable of his brief major league career. He stayed with the Pirates for the entire season. Nellie posted a 4-1 record with 7 saves and an ERA of 3.15. His long journey finally led him to the mountaintop, until he suffered an arm injury in June. It occurred during a game against the Cubs. King threw a curve to Gene Baker, but when he pitched to the next batter Dee Fondy, he felt excruciating pain. After that game, Murtaugh used him in only mop-up appearances. Nellie made his final appearance in the majors on September 15, 1957.[266] He threw a hanging curveball to Ken Boyer, who hit it out of the park. A week later Nellie was informed that he was not going to make any more road trips with the Pirates. Essentially, his season and his playing career were over.

---

264 Ibid., 155
265 Ibid, 159-61
266 Ibid., 181-83

He was twenty-nine years old and one of only four hundred players in the major leagues in 1957. Nellie had made it to the top of his profession, earning $9,500 per year; he also became a new parent when his first child Laurie was born. Because of the way his career ended, he fell into a deep depression. Bob Friend, a Pirates teammate got him a job in a sales force for Federated Investors, a fledgling mutual fund firm. Nellie quickly found out that he was not good at this type of sales.

Nellie, therefore, decided to move his young family to Newark, NJ to live with his brother-in-law Walter Earl. He worked at John J. Ryan Inc. selling municipal bonds making $70 a week. He also worked weekends at a liquor store and did some caddying at a nearby country club. Neither was fulfilling. But when one door closes, another one opens....

Nellie received a call in January of 1960. It was from Jack Berger, the PR Director of the Pittsburgh Pirates. Jack told him about a call he received from Joel Rosenblum, the owner of three small radio stations just outside of Pittsburgh. Rosenblum was looking for a former baseball player to broadcast sports at his radio stations. The salary would be $10,000 per year. This was an improvement over the $9,500 he made his last year with the Pirates. After meeting with Rosenblum and discussing the position, Nellie accepted the position. He was on his way back to Pittsburgh.[267]

This type of work became a defining moment in his life. Nellie felt fortunate to be on the radio, especially during the emergence of Arnold Palmer on the professional golf tour. He was also on the radio during the improbable championship season of the hometown Pirates. He learned that he was not the only one that benefitted from, "One door closed and another opened." Before the 1967 season, Don Hoak, a former player on the Pirates' World Series team of 1960 decided to leave the broadcast booth for the baseball sidelines.

---

267 "Nellie King," by Bob Hurte, SABR Bio Project

Hoak took a coaching job with the Philadelphia Phillies under Gene Mauch.[268]

This meant an opening in the Pirates' broadcast booth. Nellie was satisfied with his radio career, so he did not even consider the Pirates job. That was until he read Al Abrams' column in the "Pittsburgh Sports Gazette" and learned that he was among the top candidates for the vacant slot. Nellie figured why not? What did he have to lose?

This time Nellie was the one closing the door, to see if another one would open.

He applied and was given immediate consideration. After a few auditions, Nellie did well enough to be given the final interview at the KDKA-TV studio. He aced the interview and got the job. Nellie joined Bob Prince and Jim Woods in the booth for the 1967 season, making a salary of $13,000, which was less than he was making on the air for WHJB in Greensburg.

King's relationship with KDKA radio was enjoyable during his early years. However, it changed a little following the 1969 season. Jim Woods left the Pirates' broadcast booth to go to St. Louis. Gene Osborne was hired. Unfortunately, Osborne did not fit in. KDKA therefore decided to go with just Prince and King in the booth. It was such a happy and successful period that Bob Prince called the time the "halcyon days." Unfortunately, the relationship between KDKA and Prince began to deteriorate in 1971. Then another door closed during October of 1975. Joe L. Brown called Nellie and wanted to meet with him. Nellie had known Brown for over 20 years but had never been invited to his home. He attempted to guess why Brown wanted to see him. In Nellie's mind, it was probably to sign a new contract that would position him for a secure future.[269]

Brown's wife gave Nellie an Iron City beer before her husband came into the room.

The Pirates' General Manager stunned Nellie by telling him, "You won't be returning to do Pirates' broadcasts next year, nor will

268 Ibid., King 215
269 Ibid., 273-74

Bob Prince." Brown explained that Westinghouse's management (the team's sponsor) was having problems with Prince, and wanted to fire him. Nellie asked how Prince's situation had anything to do with him. Brown replied by saying that, "Sometimes the water splashes over and hits other people."[270]

Brown threw Nellie a bone and offered him a part time job doing PR work. Years later the Pirates admitted that the firings were a big PR mistake. Fans held a huge downtown parade for Prince and King.

As Nellie says in his memoir, *Happiness is a Cur Dog*, the door to Pirates baseball had been closed. He still had hoped that when one door closed in his life, another one opened. In his case, it always turned out to be better than the one that shut.

Two seasons before his firing, Nellie did color commentary on the Duquesne University radio station. During the "Fall months" of 1975, when Nellie was dealing with the challenges of unemployment, Clair Brown, the Sports Information Director at the University, decided to leave and take another position.

"Red" Manning, the Athletic Director, asked Nellie if he could recommend anyone for the position. Nellie suggested a good friend of his, Howard "Huddie" Kaufman, who was a sports writer for the Greensburg "Tribune Review." Nellie thought nothing more about the position until he received a call from Manning offering him the job. The cut in salary would be severe, but he was also given the opportunity to do a daily radio sports talk show plus the color commentary for Carnegie Mellon University football. On top of that, the school offered free college tuition for his three daughters.

Nellie King went on to enjoy an 18 year career as Sports Information Director for Duquesne University. He retired in 1993 but remained the University's golf coach until 2004. Sadly, my good friend and mentor died on August 10, 2010. Tragically, it was from a combination of colon cancer and pneumonia.[271]

---

270 Ibid., 274
271 Ibid., 276-77

I guess the last door has opened for my good friend, except this one remained open for eternity!

**Nellie and Bob after watching
a Pirates game.**

(If you are interested in reading Nellie King's book, you can order it from the following website:
https://www.amazon.com/Happiness-like-Cur-Dog-Thirty-Year/dp/1449025471)

Section VIII

Major League
Baseball Owners
And Executives

Chapter 47

Branch Rickey: Baseball's Renaissance Man

It is fascinating how people have the tendency to celebrate human innovation and achievement by focusing exclusively on the successes of the person without giving much thought to the influencing reasons why they accomplished what they accomplished. Most human beings subconsciously believe that successful people were born that way and accomplished what they did without prior influences. This feeds the belief that some people are naturally superior to others. They were born with exceptional skills, intellect and insight. However, the skills they are born with will not make them exceptional without the right influences. This was definitely the case with Branch Rickey. This average baseball player used his skills and influences to become the architect of one of the most important social experiments in US history. His influence as a mediocre player interacting with talented players gave him a unique ability to identify talent. This, combined with his relationship with the first African American professional football player, influenced him to change the world by bringing Jackie Robinson into Major League Baseball.

Branch Rickey was baseball's Renaissance man. He studied law, quoted scripture and developed some unique philosophies of life. Rickey was a dedicated baseball man who played and coached at both the college and professional levels. He was a baseball player, a manager and an executive during his extraordinary major league career. Both his fans and detractors alike felt that Branch was unmatched in his ability to evaluate a player on the baseball field. He was a tough evaluator of baseball talent. If Branch had to evaluate his own playing ability, he would have given himself a failing grade. During his 120 games playing for the Cincinnati Reds, St. Louis Browns and New York Highlanders, Branch batted .239 with a paltry three home runs. As a catcher, he holds a dubious record that may never be broken. When he was a member of the New York Highlanders, Rickey gave up thirteen stolen bases during one game.

> *"He was best known for being a risk taker who took the biggest risk in baseball history, having the greatest influence on the sport of baseball."*

But as a baseball executive, his ability to appraise talent was unmatched. He had the uncanny foresight to identify the talent necessary to improve a baseball team. However, he was best known for being a risk taker who took the biggest risk in baseball history. Because he took that risk, signing Jackie Robinson, many people believe that no one had a greater influence on the sport of baseball than Branch Rickey.

As a baseball executive, Rickey had stops with the St. Louis Browns and Cardinals, the Brooklyn Dodgers and the Pittsburgh Pirates. He was a talented administrator who positively impacted each of the teams he worked for. When Rickey was with the St. Louis Browns, Branch was able to resuscitate them with his new concepts and innovative ideas. He is the one who convinced Mr. Robert L. Hess, who owned the Browns, that in order to keep his team playing in a big city like St. Louis, they needed to focus on significantly increasing attendance at their games. The Browns did not have the finances to compete with teams like the New York Giants, the New York Yankees, the Chicago Cubs or the Pittsburgh Pirates when obtaining major league ready ball players in the minor leagues, so Rickey decided to create another way to find and keep baseball talent.

While with the St. Louis Browns, he evaluated and tracked players during the winter of 1912 in the Midwest and Southern sections of the United States. Rickey created the team's first scouting department.

The scouts that he hired were trained to spot talent and produced a list of minor leaguers that the Browns could draft. They chose 30 of 105 players that were in the draft. This successfully increased the quality of players on the team. Not everyone liked Rickey's unique ideas. The Browns' owners got tired of Rickey's approach and let him out of his contract so he could move on, and become the president of the Cardinals.[272]

During Branch Rickey's time with the St. Louis Cardinals, he created a farm system in 1919. Rickey felt that the Cardinals were constantly at a distinct disadvantage compared to the stronger teams in the NL. For instance, he might hear of a promising prospect in the lower minor leagues and make an offer to the club the prospect played for. Then the team owner would immediately wire the Giants or the Yankees and tell them that the Cardinals liked his shortstop and had offered them $2,000. Then the wealthier of the two teams would swoop down and pluck the player away for an additional $1,000. This was an early version of professional baseball "insider trading" or collusion. This happened so often that it made Rickey furious after realizing that he was essentially scouting players for his opposition.

Several people consider Rickey's farm system idea a stroke of genius. However, it was actually a selfish creation because it provided a way for him to save a lot of money for the club. Rickey's less expensive way of developing players made the Cardinals a consistent contender; those results were simply a byproduct." Rickey saw the minor league owners as individual "communities" who signed players, trained them and then sold them to another club. He sought to change this approach during his tenure with the Cardinals. Rickey felt that the Cardinals should own their own minor league teams. Rickey's farm system began with the Cardinals owning three minor league teams. These were the class "D" Ft. Smith Twins of the Western Association, the Houston Buffaloes (A) of the Texas League and the Syracuse Stars of the International League (AA). The three teams

272 Lowenfish, Lee, Branch Rickey: Baseball's Ferocious Gentleman (Lincoln, Ne., University of Nebraska Press, 2007) 62-63

cost money to run. The Cardinals' goal was not to make a profit off of the teams. Instead, their goal was to run them to break even. The system gave Rickey's team raw material at a lesser cost and guaranteed an exclusive selection of better players than the Cardinals could get on the open market. Another of Branch's unique strategies was to trade one player and then get three or four in return. This enabled him to stock his farm system with quality players. Rickey also profited from these transactions. He was able to get an average of ten cents on the dollar for every player he sold. Rickey built his network largely in cities that no one else wanted to operate in. Because of this unique approach, the Cardinals knew much more about the potential of the minor league players than did other clubs. The farm system's success justified a larger scouting staff, which meant that more players could be signed and then placed on the proper minor league teams. At one time, Rickey had twenty-seven clubs that were either owned by or had a working agreement with the Cardinals. There was a time that the Cardinals had all six teams in the Arkansas State and Nebraska State Leagues.[273]

Not everyone thought the idea was a good one. John McGraw of the New York Giants did not have a positive opinion of Rickey's system; he felt that "It's the stupidest idea in baseball."[274]

Unhappy players referred to the system as being in "the chain gang." If a player was not called up to the majors, they would probably languish in the minors throughout their careers. The system works. The Cardinals' farm system produced many standout players that made major contributions to their teams over the years. This included seven players who eventually were inducted into the Baseball Hall of Famer. They were: Jim Bottomley, Chick Hafey, Dizzy Dean, Joe Medwick, Enos Slaughter and Stan Musial. Between the years 1919 and 1942, the Cardinals won six pennants, four World Series and remained in the first division for most of that period.

---

273 Ibid., 122-24

274 Ward, Geoffrey C. and Burns, Ken, *Baseball: An Illustrated History* (NY, NY, Alfred A. Knopf, 1994) 179

Branch Rickey felt that the farm system gave the "underdog" a chance. He also felt that it leveled the playing field. However, Kenesaw Mountain Landis, the first Commissioner of Baseball, saw it differently. Rickey had become a big supporter of the Commissioner, especially after the Black Sox scandal, but the two men's relationship quickly soured – especially when Landis ruled against Rickey and his farm system. Branch, therefore, became a frequent visitor into the Commissioner's office, but not socially.

In 1921, Judge Landis was still trying to get comfortable with the newly created office of Baseball Commissioner. His primary responsibility was to enhance the integrity of the game. Early on, he set several precedents that would stand for the remainder of his 23 years in office. In 1920, when Rickey was the President of the St. Louis Cardinals, Landis brought Rickey into his office to discuss the reasons that the Cardinals were hiding the contracts of young ball players. One of the players cited was a young man named Phil Todt. Todt eventually became a regular first baseman for the Red Sox. Rickey spotted Phil on the St. Louis sandlots when he was seventeen years old.[275] Then Rickey released him unconditionally, first to Sherman of the Western Association, then to Houston of the Texas League. But evidence showed that Todt had not signed with either team and Rickey did not advise the minor league secretary John Farrell about the player's release. In the meantime, the Browns signed Todt in the middle of the 1920 season. Judge Landis ruled against Branch and in favor of the Browns' owner Phil Ball when he discovered that Rickey had covered up Todt's contract without disclosing it to either the Sherman and Houston teams. In Landis' opinion, the various transfers allowed Todt to be a free agent, meaning that the Browns, not the Cards, could sign him. Todt never played for the Browns, but instead enjoyed an eight-year career as a journeyman player – mainly with the Red Sox. Judge Landis called Rickey a "sanctimonious so and so." Landis and Rickey fought over one issue or another up until the time of the Commissioner's death.

---

275 Ibid, Lowenfish, 130-31

1942 was Rickey's final year as the General Manager of the Cardinals, when they had their best season in franchise history. They not only won 106 games, they also won the World Series. Rickey had been investing in teams over the years. That same year Rickey was hired, he delivered significant ownership of the Dodgers. He purchased 25% of the Brooklyn Dodgers in 1945. This helped to increase his influence on both the team and on baseball in general.

One of the most important influences in Rickey's life was a man named Charles Folis, who was the first African American professional football player. He was also the first African American catcher to go from college baseball to Negro League Baseball. Rickey played professional football with Folis on the Shelby Blues team in the Ohio Football League in 1902 (which was the direct predecessor of the National Football League). Because of this experience, Rickey was convinced that both African Americans and whites were able to work together in professional sports.

When Judge Landis died, it swung open the door for Branch Rickey to make his most significant contribution to the game of baseball. Branch wanted to break the racial barrier for several years, but he realized that it would be difficult if Landis was in charge. Although Landis always claimed that there was never anything preventing African Americans from playing in the MLB,[276] he never acknowledged the secret agreement among the team owners that they would not allow Negro League players to play major league baseball. When Landis died, support for integration began to grow in the United States. Integration in both the armed forces and labor helped to convince Rickey that the time was right to draft African American players from the Negro Leagues. New York City mayor LaGuardia formed a committee to have his city's baseball clubs investigate the feasibility of integrating.

In 1945, Rickey sent his scouts to search for a player that would prove that African Americans had both the talent and the character to

---

276 Rampersao, Arnold, Jackie Robinson: A Biography (NY, NY, Alfred P. Knopf, 1997) 120-21

play with the white players in major league baseball. His scouts came back with a laundry list of qualified players. The list included Josh Gibson, Roy Campanella, Buck Leonard, Marvin Williams, Jackie Robinson, Piper Davis, Cool Poppa Bell and Sam Jethroe.

Rickey's scouts narrowed the list down to Jackie Robinson. On August 18, 1945, under the pretense of forming another Negro league, Robinson traveled to Brooklyn to meet with Mr. Rickey and talk about playing for the Brooklyn Brown Dodgers. Their face-to-face meeting lasted three hours. It was then that Rickey informed Robinson that he did not want Robinson for the Brown Dodgers but for the Brooklyn Dodgers!

When the movie *42* came out in April 2013, it provided the details of the Jackie Robinson signing. Many were not familiar with the difficulty and significance of this important story. While most people knew that Robinson became the "first" black to play baseball, they did not realize the struggles that he faced.

Rickey recounted the story about Charles Thomas on several occasions. Thomas was an African American player that played for him at Ohio Wesleyan College. They traveled to South Bend, Indiana to play Notre Dame, and when the players entered the lobby, the clerk spotted Thomas, who was the team's only African American player. The desk clerk was clearly disturbed by Thomas' presence and immediately informed Mr. Rickey that Thomas would not be given a room. Rickey turned to the team's student manager and asked him to take the team and go to the local YMCA to get a room – but not just for Thomas, for the entire team! Rickey then asked to speak with the hotel manager. After a long conversation between Rickey and the hotel's manager, the hotel relented by putting a cot for Thomas in Rickey's room. When Rickey entered the room he found the player with tears running down his cheeks while feverishly rubbing his arms, saying that it was the color of his skin.[277] Years later, Rickey repeated this story to Red Barber, the Dodgers' radio announcer, adding that it looked like the young man was trying to rub off his black skin.

---

277 Ibid. Lowenfish, 22-24

Rickey admitted to Barber how seeing that image had always haunted him. He regretted not doing enough. Rickey felt that he now had an opportunity to make it right. He was going to make a difference by integrating Major League Baseball![278]

Rickey told Robinson that story and said, "Whatever mark the incident left on Charles Thomas, it was no more indelible than the impression it made on me."[279]

When Happy Chandler became the new Commissioner and learned that Robinson could really play, he gave his full support to breaking this important racial barrier. So when Jackie Robinson debuted on April 15, 1947, both Robinson and Mr. Rickey changed the game and the United States forever![280]

Integrating baseball was not the only thing Branch Rickey accomplished in 1947. He also created the first spring training complex. Since the Brooklyn Dodgers had more than 700 players under contract, they needed a larger facility to insure uniformed training. So Rickey struck up a deal with the U.S. Navy pilot training base on the west side of Vero Beach, Florida and created the Dodgers' training complex.[281] Many of Rickey's training innovations such as batting tees, sliding pits, a string grid to help pitchers practice their control, etc. were on display. Rickey also used a complex system of colors and numbers to organize the training. The minor league players were sorted, trained, analyzed, graded and eventually assigned to minor league teams according to the Rickey methods.[282] Many of the training methods were ones that Rickey developed when he was with the Cardinals.

In Rickey's initial contract with the Dodgers he received a salary plus a percentage of the proceeds from all player sales. Walter O'Malley, who started out as the lawyer for the ball club, wanted complete

---

278 Barber, Red and Creamer, Robert, *Rhubarb in the Catbird Seat* (NY, NY, Bison Books, 1997) 266-67

279 Ibid., Lowenfish, 355

280 Ibid., Rampersao,169

281 Ibid., Lowenfish, 444

282 Ibid., 464-65

control of the Dodgers, while Rickey also wanted to maintain his control and influence, so the two of them got into a heated fight over control of the team. O'Malley used his position as a lawyer to gain control of the majority ownership of the ball club and wanted to be President of the club. Rickey hated O'Malley and did not want to be part of the team anymore so he forced O'Malley to pay him $1 million to be bought out of his ownership and contract.

When Walter O'Malley forced Rickey out of the Dodgers, Branch went on to the Pittsburgh Pirates. He was hired as their GM in November 1950 when he began to reconstruct the Pirates. He brought his loyal scout, Howie Haak with him and had Howie scour the Latin American Countries looking for talent. Searching for talent in this part of the world would benefit the Pirates for decades!

While also in Pittsburgh, Rickey introduced another innovation – one that would change the game. It did not have the same level of influence as the farm system or breaking the racial barrier. However, it was an innovation that changed the appearance of the sport. Longtime Pirates executive Charlie Muse created the baseball-batting helmet. Mr. Rickey pushed for the creation of a protective helmet during the early 1950s. Before that time, batters only wore their cloth caps. Rickey owned a company called "American Baseball Cap Inc." He chose Muse to run the company and design a batting helmet for the players.[283] At first, the players laughed at them and referred to them as miners' helmets. Ralph Kiner added that players did not like the protective gear because they felt it "unmanly" to wear one.

Rickey's Pirates became the first team to wear batting helmets in 1952.[284] Clem Labine of the Brooklyn Dodgers unintentionally increased the league's adoption of the helmet after hitting Joe Adcock of the Milwaukee Braves in the head on August 1, 1954. Adcock claims that the helmet he wore saved him from severe injury. In 1957,

---

283 "Obituary: Charlie Muse; Created Baseball Batting Helmet," Associated Press, Washington Post, May 17, 2005

284 Kiner, Ralph & Pearey, Danny, *Baseball Forever: Reflections on 60 Years in the Game* (Chicago, Triumph Books, 2007) 42-43

the batting helmet became standard equipment in the big leagues. The minor league adopted their usage, as did the Little League. Rickey's company ended up producing 300,000 helmets a year.

After leaving the Pirates, Branch Rickey did not stay idle for long. He was appointed by New York Lawyer Bill Shea as the President of the newly formed Continental League. The plan was to form a third major league. It never materialized, but the threat of its existence ushered in the sport's first expansion.

The League's creation was announced on July 27, 1959, with a promise to begin playing its first season in 1961. Unlike the Players League and the Federal League, the Continental League sought membership within organized baseball, to become an equal partner for major league baseball. After the Dodgers and Giants left New York City, Mayor Robert Wagner appointed a four-man committee to try and bring National League baseball back to New York. Bill Shea became the mouthpiece for this movement, while Rickey stayed in the background. At one point Rickey attempted to dissuade Shea from the idea of expansion; his argument was that expansion teams would not be able to compete against established teams. The Continental League would disband in 1960 without ever playing a game. The MLB owners sensed that Congress was impatient, feeling they were resisting change. The established teams agreed to expand in the American League in 1961 and National League in 1962.[285] This led to the inclusion of the Washington Senators (now the Texas Rangers), the Los Angeles Angels, the New York Mets and the Houston Colt .45s (now the Houston Astros).

To date, the game of baseball has not seen anyone as influential as Branch Rickey. Many of his innovations were developed to make money. However, his most significant ideas were driven by his love of people and the sport of baseball. He clearly loved the game, and was its biggest fan!

---

285 Ibid., Lowenfish, 553-59

Chapter 48

Bill Veeck, Jr.: Baseball's Biggest Promoter

S ometimes simple advice can be so influential that it changes how a person thinks and behaves. Bill Veeck, Jr. was influenced by his father to develop a love of baseball. However, simple lessons about people and money played an influential role in how he viewed the sport. Seemingly basic advice from his father convinced him that people (regardless of their background or race) are not only very similar, they love spending their money on entertainment. These simple insights influenced Veeck to do things that made him one of the most innovative and entertaining people in the history of baseball. In this chapter, we introduce you to the amazing story of Bill Veeck, Jr.

Bill Veeck, Jr. was born in Chicago, Illinois on February 9, 1914. While many people have shaped the game of baseball over the years, one could arguably be hard pressed to find anyone more influential than Bill Veeck Jr.

His father, William Veeck, was a sports writer for the "Chicago American." When Chicago Cubs' owner, William Wrigley, Jr., decided to hire him as Vice President of the baseball club, many felt that Veeck's criticism of the team for his paper, the "Chicago American," was the reason. When the Cubs won the National League pennant in 1918, Wrigley decided to appoint him as the team's President, a position which he held until his death in 1933. During that span, the Cubs won the pennant in both 1929 and 1932.

Bill Veeck's father or "Daddy" as he affectionately referred to him, began taking him to baseball games when he was ten years old. On one visit with his father to the Chicago Cub's box office, his father showed where the money from tickets was counted. This had a lot to do with what Bill Veeck, Jr. wanted to do with his future. When Bill Jr. saw the money spread all over a table, his father turned, looking at his son as he made an observation; "Bill, it's a very interesting thing. You look at all this money and it all looks the same, doesn't it? You can't tell who put it into your box office. It's all the same color, the same size, and the same shape. You remember that."[286]

"Every fan that passes through the turnstile deserved to have the best experience and value for their dollar"
– Bill Veek

Bill Veeck never forgot his father's words. William Veeck felt that every fan that passes through the turnstile deserved to have the best experience and value for their dollar. It did not matter whether the fan was a doctor or a lawyer, a construction or a sanitation worker. The money that came out of their pockets was all the same in Bill Veeck, Jr.'s eyes. He practiced this belief for his entire involvement in the game of baseball.

Bill not only grew up at the ball park, but he also worked at several positions there. He sold popcorn when he was thirteen years old; then at fifteen, he was responsible for mailing out Lady's Day tickets, which was held every Friday. Another of Bill's contributions was planting ivy on the walls of Wrigley Field.

While William Veeck Sr. was a starched, formal gentleman, the picture of the establishment's dignity, his son Bill was known as "Sport Shirt Bill," never wearing a necktie – instead preferring open neck sports shirts. While his father maintained a conservative, professional haircut, Bill had wild, kinky reddish hair. His father nominated

---

286 Veeck, Bill and Linn, Ed, *Veeck as in Wreck* (Chicago, Chicago University Press, 2001) 24

Kenesaw Mountain Landis as the first baseball commissioner, while his son Bill became a thorn in Landis' side, spending his life fighting with the Commissioner.

Bill Veeck Jr. was a fan, just like those he sought to entertain. Often fans perceived that both owners and players were greedy. As an owner, Veeck was the exception. He was a fan himself, sitting in the stands among them. Bill was one part PT Barnum and one part Sam Walton, a combination of showmanship and customer value.

When Bill Veeck was only twenty-seven, he bought the Milwaukee Brewers in 1941. The Brewers were his first professional baseball team.[287] They were in last place at the time. So, Bill went right to work by cleaning and painting the dilapidated Borchert Field where the Brewers played. Then he let his PT Barnum side take over and he began givingaway a prize almost every night. Bill had a fascination for animals because he gave away lobsters, pigeons, chickens, guinea pigs and even a sway back horse. Most of his promotions were not announced in advance, because he desired the element of surprise. During the Second World War, he scheduled morning games so the overnight workers at the war plants could attend. He served cornflakes to all that were attending.[288]

Bill always felt that a trip to the ballpark should be fun, and winning was also important. In 1942, his second year of ownership, the Brewers nearly won the American Association league championship. Then the team went on to win the league title the following three years.

About the time that Veeck owned the Brewers, Gerry Nugent, the owner of the Phillies found himself in deep financial trouble. It did not help that the Philadelphia Phillies had lost 111 games in 1941. Only 231,000 fans passed through their gates that season. The team's operating expenses were $60,000 combined with the $55,000 they owed to the bank.

---

287 Dickson, Paul, Bill Veeck: Baseball's Greatest Maverick (NY, NY, Walker & Company 2012) 55
288 Ibid., 68-69

Ford Frick, the National League President, called a meeting informing National League owners that the Phillies had no cash. The situation forced the league to reluctantly pay off the team's debts. The league also pushed Nugent to sell his team. At the time, Veeck did not divulge his plans to buy the Phillies. He began to quietly secure funding from various sources, including un-named investors from Chicago and Philadelphia, plus the Philly Cigar Company. Another source was the CIO union, which eventually merged with the AFL to form the AFL-CIO. Unfortunately, their dollars came with a stipulation; they wanted Veeck to promise that nine whites would never play with nine blacks on the field. Bill's curt response was: "...I wouldn't tell the manager how to run his club, and I certainly wasn't going to let them (meaning the AFL/CIO)."[289]

Bill was convinced that he had a deal with Nugent to buy the Phillies. When he traveled to Chicago to make sure the funding was in line, he bumped into John Carmichael, a reporter for the "Chicago Daily News," and he explained: "I'm going to buy the Phillies. And do you know what I'm going to do? I'm putting a whole black team on the field."[290]

Several baseball historians dispute that Veeck had such a plan. Others tend to believe it because he signed Larry Doby as well as his history of supporting the Civil Rights movement. I am not sure what the answer is, but Veeck did have a good relationship with Negro League owners. Plus, Bill and his wife also hosted dinners for the Civil Rights demonstrators when they went to Washington D.C.

Veeck's one mistake was, before he left on the train, he decided to alert Landis of his intentions. Since his idea was in line with the recent Supreme Court ruling that mandated separate but equal facilities, he assumed that his plan would not offend anyone, like Landis. He felt that Landis would not say black players were not welcomed, especially when blacks were fighting overseas in WWII.

---

289 Ibid., 79
290 Ibid., 79

Before reaching Nugent's office, Veeck discovered that the Phillies had been already been taken over by the National League the night before, and a new owner was being sought by the league. Veeck was mistaken to think that his father's relationship with Landis would play in his favor. Bill always felt that Landis leaked his plans to Frick.[291]

Bill dreamed of owning a major league team. He eventually put together a syndicate to buy the Cleveland Indians and he took over the team in 1946. He brought along his menagerie of stunts and giveaways. Bill felt that every day at the ballpark could be like Mardi gras, and the fan should be king.

Before purchasing the Indians, Veeck roamed the city, talking with cabbies, visiting bars and entering social clubs such as the VFW and the Knights of Columbus. He learned that the fans in Cleveland loved their Indians, but there was no love lost for the team's owners.[292] Under the previous ownership, when a ball was hit into the stands, it was considered team property and had to be returned to the usher. The Indians were not broadcast on the radio and fans were not able to reserve a block of tickets. Things would soon change with Veeck in charge. Owning the Cleveland Indians was tailor-made for his promotional skills.

The Cleveland Indians had a lackluster season before Veeck arrived. They finished in fifth place in the American League, but the team's fate was about to get better with the arrival of Veeck, along with Bob Feller's return from the Navy.

When Veeck took over the Cleveland Indians he quickly boosted the Indians' 1946 attendance over the one million mark for the first time in club history. That year the club finished in sixth place with a record of 68-86, but with a new attitude. Veeck's mantra was, "A Championship as quickly as possible." Feller got off to a great start and finished with an astounding record of 26-15, 2.18 ERA, 36 complete games and 348 strikeouts. It was also the debut of promising rookies Bob Lemon and Jim Hegan.

---

291 Ibid., 80
292 Ibid., 109

While chatting with Larry MacPhail during the World Series, he learned that the Yankees were no longer enamored with Joe Gordon. They felt that the second baseman's play was lackadaisical. So Veeck proposed a trade that would send Allie Reynolds to New York in exchange for Gordon. It worked out well for the Yankees in 1947; they came in first, won the World Series and Allie Reynolds became the ace of the Yankees' staff by winning 19 games. They also topped 2 million in attendance, which was the most in the AL. It also proved to be successful for Cleveland, as they moved up to 4th place. Joe Gordon hit 29 homers, 93 RBIs and had a .272 average. They drew over 1 million fans, the second best in the AL.[293]

The trade really paid off for Veeck and the Indians in 1948. They finished in first place after winning a one game play-off with Boston in the AL and then beat the Boston Braves in the World Series. Gordon had 32 homers, 124 RBIs and a .282 average. Their three starters had good seasons, Both Lemon, and Bearden won twenty, and Feller won nineteen. It had been twenty-eight years since the Cleveland Indians appeared in a World Series, and longer since they won one. It was only the second time that this happened in the franchise's history. Years later, "The Sporting News" rated the 1948 Indians as the ninth best team of all time.

Bill Veeck could not own a team without entertaining the fans, so one of the first things he did was hiring Max Patkin as a coach. Patkin was a tall, thin man with a rubber face and large nose. Before working for Veeck, Max was a below average pitcher for a team in Wilkes-Barre, Pennsylvania. The club released him because of a sore arm. Max was a born clown. He had the ability to contort his body in unimaginable ways. Patkin picked up his clown reputation while pitching for the Navy during World War II. He gave up a home run to Joe DiMaggio. It must have gotten to him because he joined the "Yankee Clipper" as he was rounding first base and followed him

---

293 Ibid., 117-118

stride for stride around the bases.[294] Patkin was met at home plate by cheering teammates. He became drunk by the crowd's applause.

When Veeck bought the club, the Indians were scheduled to play an exhibition against Wilkes-Barre, so he brought back Patkin as a first baseball coach while entertaining the crowd. It was sort of an audition. One of the baseball's clown's antics was to pretend to faint over close calls at first base. He must have passed the audition; because Veeck gave him a contract to coach for a $1, and a performance contract that paid him $650 a month. Patkin went on to become the "Clown Prince of Baseball."[295]

Veeck wanted to integrate the Indians, he first considered signing Ray Dandridge, a Negro League star playing in Mexico. He even arranged for a meeting between them at his ranch in Arizona. At the meeting, Ray informed Bill that he enjoyed playing in Mexico and the Pasquel brothers paid him well.[296]

It was evident that Veeck needed to turn his attentions elsewhere. To do so, he hired Louis Jones, a successful black Public Relations man plus being Lena Horne's first husband. Jones helped Veeck find Larry Doby, who played for Effa Manley's Newark Eagles. Scouts for Branch Rickey were also interested in the Eagles' star, but once Rickey learned of Veeck's interest, he backed off.

Unlike Rickey's raids of black talent, Veeck intended to purchase Doby's contract from the Newark baseball club. Being aware of Rickey's past practices, Mrs. Manley made it a point not to let it happen to her. She was a tough negotiator. When Bill called, Effa immediately asked how much he was planning to give her for Doby. When he replied $10,000, Effa replied, "Well I'm not a millionaire, but I'm financially secure, ten thousand dollars sounds like ten cents to me. I'm sure if Doby was a white boy and a free agent you'd give him a hundred thousand. But if you feel that ten thousand is a fair

---

294 Ibid., 113
295 Ibid., 113
296 Ibid., 122-23

offering, then I guess I have to take it." Abe Manley, Effa's husband felt that the offer was way too low, but did not want fans to perceive that he was depriving Doby of his chance. [297]

Bill also promised an additional $5,000 if he kept Doby for at least 30 days. Doby played in 29 games, with 33 plate appearance batting .156 with no homers. Doby had a successful 1948 season and garnered 29 MVP votes. Veeck and Doby became friends; they continued their relationship after Larry's playing days, plus, it helped that they both enjoyed jazz music. Bill even made Larry the manager when he owned the Chicago White Sox.

The Cleveland Indians had some real pitching issues during the 1948 season. Bill Veeck felt that it could be fixed by getting some bullpen help. He decided to enlist the help of Abe Saperstein, the promoter for Negro League baseball teams, and the Harlem Globetrotters. Veeck asked if Saperstein could find him a pitcher that might help the team. Abe responded, 'I know just the pitcher you need. If you sign him, you won't have any bullpen worries." Abe was referring to Negro League pitching legend Satchel Paige, who was now forty-one years old. Bill trusted Abe's judgment, he also appreciated Satch's drawing power, but what he really needed was a pitcher that could help his team. Saperstein assured him that Paige would be that pitcher.

Bill informed his manager Lou Boudreau, the team's general manager Hank Greenberg, that he had a pitcher he wanted them to give a tryout. At the tryout, both men looked in total disbelief when Satchel Paige walked onto the field. Satch warmed up by jogging halfway around the park, and then he took a ball and tossed it underhand twice before declaring himself ready for his tryout.

Before he started, Satch handed a handkerchief and asked Boudreau to place it over the plate. Boudreau stood in the batter's box. Paige went to the pitching rubber and proceeded to throw nine of ten pitches across it. Next Satch asked the Indians' manager to move it to the outside and he threw eight out of ten more pitches

---

297 Ibid., 126

across it. Lou could only manage two weak grounders that didn't reach the mound.[298]

"Now I can believe all of those tall stories about his pitching that I have heard over the years." Boudreau smiled. Greenberg turned to Veeck, "...just don't let him outta here unsigned alive!"[299]

That season, Paige went 6-1 with an ERA of 2.48 in 21 games and was named Rookie of the Year. The Cleveland Indians won the American League pennant and beat the Boston Braves in the World Series four games to two. It did not take long, but Bill Veeck brought a championship to the city of Cleveland, by sprinkling some of his magic.

Bill Veeck's next team was the hapless St. Louis Browns and he attempted to revitalize them in 1951. At first, fans speculated that he would try to relocate them. Instead, Veeck's intentions were to run the Cardinals out of town. Unfortunately, the Browns were a terrible team. On his first night as the team's owner, he served a free beer or soda for everyone in attendance. The St. Louis Browns were the worst franchise in the history of major league baseball. Between 1902 and 1953, they managed only eleven winning seasons. In 1951, Veeck's first year of ownership, pitcher Ned Garver won twenty games for a team that lost one hundred, only the second time that has ever occurred. Because of that, Bill made Garver the highest paid player in the club's history.[300]

After that, it became painfully obvious that the St. Louis Browns were not going to win any championships soon, if ever! Veeck needed to concentrate on promotion and stunts. And he came up with a doozy, one that he would kid about in later years.

In an attempt to address the most common complaint against his team – that it lacked a leadoff batter, Veeck sought a perfectly proportioned midget, whose strike zone would be so small that no pitcher could find it. After interviewing several midgets, he finally

---

298 Ibid., 145
299 Ibid., 145
300 Ibid., 195

found the sixty-five-pound Eddie Gaedel. Gaedel was paid $100 for a one plate appearance. There were two contracts; one for the game, he sent another to the league office, the latter which he had conveniently mailed after the last collection of mail.

Veeck's plan required a heavy level of secrecy, but it also needed publicity.

The night before the infamous game, Veeck was out drinking with Bill Broeg, a St. Louis sports writer. Glancing down at his watch, and seeing that it was too late for Broeg to report the scoop that Veeck was about to give him, he off-handedly mentioned his plan to pinch hit a midget. Broeg was disappointed, replying, "We don't have any photographers working this Sunday."

Of course, one of baseball's most endearing and famous photos is of Gaedel standing at the plate.

On Sunday, August 19, 1951, in between games of a double header against the Detroit Tigers, in front of 18,000 fans at Sportsman Park, the Browns celebrated the fiftieth anniversary of the American League. A large cake was wheeled out onto the field, Veeck made sure everyone had a beer to make a toast, when out popped Gaedel, dressed in a miniature Browns uniform! Gaedel presented Zach Taylor, the St. Louis manager, with a brownie.

When the second game started, the Tigers did not score during their half of the first inning. The Browns' leadoff hitter was to be Frank Saucier, a rookie reserved outfielder, and then the public address system announced, "For the Browns, number one-eighth, Eddie Gaedel, batting for Saucier."

The Tigers protested, but the Browns produced a bona fide contract to umpire Ed Hurely who read it, then shouted "PLAY BALL!"

Gaedel skipped up to the plate, brandishing a toy bat. He crouched so low that his strike zone was almost non-existent. He practiced getting into a crouch the week before, but could not resist taking a practice swing with the bat. Bill saw this and reminded him, "Eddie, I'm going to be up on the roof with a high-powered rifle watching every move you make. "If you look as if you're going to swing. I'm going to shoot you dead." Needless to say, Eddie walked on four pitches....[301]

Another of his famous stunts occurred on August 24, 1951. It was called "Grandstand Manager Night." The game was managed by the fans. Two of them won an essay contest. Although American League president Will Harridge banned the boys from being on the field, they were joined by around 1,115 fans that participated in the stands, including Connie Mack who recently retired. Each was given placards marked "Yes" or "No." They would hold them up to determine what the Browns should do next.

The current Browns' manager Zack Taylor took the field in civilian clothes, including bedroom slippers, smoking a curve stem pipe. He spent the game sitting in a rocking chair that was placed near the dugout where he leisurely read a newspaper.[302]

The St. Louis Browns won 3-2. The initial purpose of the stunt was for entertainment value; the victory was an added bonus. Bill Veeck owned the St. Louis Browns for three seasons, 1951, 52 and 53. In 1952, he almost doubled the attendance. It had jumped from 293,790 to 518,796. Unfortunately, attendance dropped in 1953 after the fans learned that Veeck was trying to move the team to Milwaukee or Baltimore. Veeck was able to broker a deal to move the Browns to Baltimore and was assured by William Hardridge, the AL president, that the other owners would approve, but Veeck's ownership was defeated by two votes.[303]

The team moved, but without Veeck. Bill would eventually return to MLB to own the Chicago White Sox in 1959. The White Sox appeared in the World Series for the first time since 1919. However, Veeck needed to sell the team due to health reasons in 1961. In 1975, Bill returned to the club. It was around this time that he convinced Harry Carey to sing "Take Me Out to the Ballgame." In 1979, he suffered his only promotional failure, Disco Demolition Night. The

---

301 "Eddie Gaedel," by Brian McKenna, SABR Bio project
302 Ibid, Dickson, 189
303 Ibid., 209-11

fans essentially came on the field and rioted, the majority of them under the influence of beer and pot. Worse than that, The White Sox ended up forfeiting to the Detroit Tigers![304]

During his involvement in baseball, Bill Veeck Jr. played the roles of both innovator and gadfly. There should be no question that he was successful at both. Without question, sports Shirt Bill was one of the most influential people in baseball. His track record speaks for itself:

- Aside from signing the first negro player for the AL, he was a Civil Rights Advocate
- He was responsible for putting the players' names on the back of their uniforms
- He started 'Bat Day.'
- He held special days at the ball park, such as: Squirrel Day and Music Day, where he gave out free kazoos. He initiated special Days for "A" students, teachers, bartenders, cabbies, transit workers, etc.
- He even had a "Good Old Joe Early Night." This was inspired by a fan that felt the Indians had a night for everyone but the average Joe.
- Veeck advocated the Designated Hitter
- The playoff system
- Free agency,
- League expansion
- Bill thought that the leagues should be realigned into three divisions with a wildcard team.

One might say that baseball is the Veeck's family business. Bill, his dad, and later his son ran professional teams. Bill maximized the ballpark experience for the fan. He sought racial equality. He sought improvements, by thinking out of the box.

Bill Veeck Jr. died in his birthplace of Chicago, Illinois, in 1986. His baseball Hall of Fame plaque states at the bottom "A Champion for the Little Guy."

---

304 Ibid., 314-17

Chapter 49

Phil Wrigley: The Failure of the College of Coaches

We always hear about the innovative ideas that succeed. Unfortunately, most innovative approaches fail. The most successful innovators in history know that exceptional innovations come from frequent trial and error. There are many different reasons why innovative ideas and approaches don't work. Sometimes they fail because they are simply bad ideas or too far ahead of their time or just won't work in a certain environment. Phil Wrigley's "College of Coaches" innovation did not work because it did not provide the influences baseball players needed to get the most out of their skills and come together as a team. In this chapter, we describe an innovation that did not provide the influence necessary to transform a losing baseball team to a successful one.

During the turn of the twentieth century, the Chicago Cubs were arguably the most dominant team in the National League. This team was so special that Franklin Pierce Adams, a sports writer and Cubs fan, wrote a poem called "Baseball's Sad Lexicon" which became known as "Tinkers to Evers to Chance" in the "New York Evening Mail" on July 10, 1910.

"...Words that are heavy with nothing but trouble; Tinker to Evers to Chance." This prodigious double play trio of Tinker-to-Evers-to-Chance led their team to World Series four times the first ten years in the 1900s. The Chicago Cubs won a record setting 116 games in 1906 but unfortunately lost in the World Series to their cross-town rivals the White Sox. Undaunted, they went on to become the first team to win back-to-back World Series in 1907 & 08. They would go on a short hiatus before returning to the World Series in 1910, only to lose to the Philadelphia Athletics. The three players, Tinker, Evers and Chance entered baseball's Hall of Fame together in 1946.

Phillip Wrigley bought the Cubs in 1932. While the team won pennants in 1932, 35, and 38, it did not return to the Fall Classic until 1945 when they faced the Detroit Tigers. According to Chicago lore, it was after this World Series that the team became cursed. It is referred to as the infamous "Curse of the Billy Goat." The curse was placed on them after the fourth game of the 1945 series. A man by the name of Billy Sianis bought two box tickets for game four, one for himself and the other for his goat. Wrigley demanded that the goat leave due to its unpleasant odor. After being ejected, Sianis, the goat's owner uttered, "The Cubs, they ain't gonna win no more!"

Curse or no curse, between 1947 and 1960 the Cubs only won 44% of their games. They never finished above fifth place during that span. This did not sit well with Wrigley, who was accustomed to success. Outside of his ownership of the Cubs, he was a pioneer in commercial aviation, played a part in the establishment of United Airlines, as well as enjoying success in both the banking and hotel industries. He also chaperoned the success of his family's chewing gum business, using his interest in radio and television to advertise the gum.

Because of his business acumen, Wrigley came up with the innovative managerial idea that he called the College of Coaches. It was Wrigley's idea, but its origin belonged to Elvin Tappe. Tappe was a favorite employee of Mr. Wrigley the consummate organization man. Over the years, he served as a utility catcher and a coach. Elvin suggested using roving coaches to teach fielding, hitting and pitching. He felt they could be rotated around the team's minor league affiliates with the hope of providing instruction for the developing players. He never intended for his idea to be used at the major league level.

Wrigley liked the concept with a slight twist, and he reminded Tappe that he was the owner and had the final say.[305]

Thus, the birth of the "College of Coaches," Wrigley felt it was, "Business efficiency applied to baseball." The Cubs would no longer have a manager; instead, they would have a head coach with an eight man coaching staff that took turns rotating through the team's minor league system and one by one, they would take turns managing the Cubs. Wrigley considered managers expendable; his College of Coaches would act like relief pitchers. The Cubs rotated their managers and coaches throughout the year. Each coach was considered an equal. The initial lineup of coaches was: Bobby Adams, Rip Collins, Harry Craft, Velvie Himsl, Charlie Grimm, Goldie Holt, and Fred Martin – and of course, Elvin Tappe.[306]

During the 1961 season, only four men ended up managing the Cubs, starting off with Velvie Himsl, followed by Harry Craft, El Tappe and Lou Klein. Together they posted a record of 64-90. None of the managers posted a winning record, although they did win four more games than in 1960, which was not considered much of a success among the Cubs players.

The most vocal critic after that first season was team captain Don Zimmer. In an interview after the last game of the 1961 season, he was asked what he thought about the College of Coaches.

"A joke that it was doomed to failure the moment it was created."[307]

Zimmer was soon left unprotected and ended up being an original member of the New York Mets.

In his memoir, *Kiss it Goodbye*, Frank Thomas expressed a similar opinion.

"They would each manage the team for a short period before rotating to the next guy. It sounded like a terrible idea right from

305 "The Chicago Cub's College of Coaches, A Management Innovation that Failed," by Richard J. Puerzer (The National Pastime, 2006) 5
306 Ibid., 7
307 Ibid., 11

the start, too many cooks in the kitchen ..." Because of the way the College of Coaches worked, Frank eventually became a player without a position, a forgotten player. The Cubs traded him to the Milwaukee Braves on May 9, 1961.[308]

When Ford Frick, the President of the National League, was asked what he thought he replied, "My only concern is that Wrigley has nine men on the field."[309]

In 1962, the team rotated only three managers through the system. They were El Tappe, Lou Klein and Charlie Metro. Metro began the season as the third base coach, eventually becoming the last to manage the team. When he informed Wrigley that he would not rotate, the Cubs' owner decided to end the innovative managerial idea and to let Charley manage the final 112 games of the 1962 season. They ended up with 103 losses. Fortunately, for them, the Mets set a baseball record for futility with 120 losses.[310]

While Wrigley tried thinking out of the box with hopes of returning the franchise to its winning ways, his idea failed miserably. It is puzzling that someone could believe that more than one ego could exist equally together, especially in baseball. Wrigley miscalculated a manager's influence. There is a need for stability at the top. While the experiment was a great failure it did shed light on the idea of the roving instructors, which was how Elvin Tappe intended his idea.

After letting Metro go, Wrigley hired Bob Kennedy. Ironically, the Cubs finished over .500 for was the first time since 1946. The success might have been due to the abandonment of the "College of Coaches," but more likely it was due to the maturity of younger players such as future Hall of Fame members Ron Santo and Billy Williams. Kennedy's style was the opposite of Metro's. His players

---

308 Thomas, Frank, *"Kiss it Goodbye": The Frank Thomas Story* (Dunkirk, MD, Pepperpot Productions, 2005) 322

309 Boudreau, Lou, and Schneider, Russell, *Lou Boudreau: Covering all the bases* (Sport Publishing LLC, 1993) 185

310 Ibid., Puerzer,12

liked him and they played hard for him. However, the Cubs were not ready to compete, finishing eighth twice and tenth during his tenure.

Philip Wrigley died in 1977. Aside from the College of Coaches, he created the "All-American Girls Baseball League" and maintained Wrigley Field as one of the showplaces in sports. When he died, ownership passed over to his son William, who had little interest in the team and sold the team to the "Chicago Tribune" in 1981.

The Chicago Cubs went 108 years without winning a World Series. That finally ended when they defeated the Cleveland Indians in 2016.

Chapter 50

Lady Bee: The First Female Owner

*I*t is amazing how many influence based stereotypes guide our thinking. One of my favorite riddles is the one that states, "A parent and a child are in a horrible car crash on the way to school and they are rushed to the hospital; just as the young girl is about to go under the knife the surgeon says, "I can't operate – that girl is my daughter." "What relationship does the surgeon have to the girl?" Most people answer that the surgeon is her Dad. However, in this story, the surgeon is her Mom. We are subconsciously influenced to think of most surgeons as men in the same way that we think of most Major League Baseball owners as men. That is why knowing the stories of people who break through stereotypes are so important to society. Helene Robeson Britton, the first female owner of a Major League Baseball team, is one of those important stereotype breakers. In this chapter, we tell her amazing story.*

During the nineteen sixties I grew up in the New York City metropolitan area. So the idea of a woman owner was not so unusual. Joan Whitney Payson was the owner of the New York Mets when I was growing up. She owned the Mets from 1962 until her death in 1974. Miss Payson saw both the highs and lows with her franchise. Her beloved Mets have the distinction of having the worst record in the history of baseball in 1962 with a 40-120 record but have also appeared in two World Series since then, winning in 1969, and losing in 1973. During her tenure, there have been three other women that have owned baseball teams, Joan Kroc, Marge Schott, and Jean Yawkey – although each of them were thrust into this role because of the death of their husbands. Except Ms. Payson; she invested in the New York Mets. Before her Mets ownership, Joan Payson was a minority owner of the New York Giants.

While there were women owners before Joan Payson, only one could be the first. That distinction belonged to Helene Robison Britton, who was the first woman to own a major league baseball team. She owned the St. Louis Cardinals between 1911 and 1918.

Helene was a product of the Progressive Era in the United States between 1890 and 1920. It was a time of both widespread social activism and political reform. While the movement's main objective was to eliminate corruption in government, it was also the formation of the National American Woman Suffrage Association (NAWSA). The movement's signature accomplishment would be the 19th Amendment (1920), which gave women the right to vote. It was also a time when the status of women in society began to change. Women began to enter the workforce and to graduate from college.

As the St. Louis Cardinals were preparing to start spring training for the 1911 season, Stanley Robison, the owner of the Cardinals died. He bequeathed his controlling interest of his baseball team to his niece Helene Robison Britton, making her the first female to own a major sports team in the United States.[311]

The year 1911 was also a time when the Women's Suffrage movement was opening doors; it had become a popular topic in newspapers, although baseball did not seem ready for a woman to run a professional baseball team. The thought of a woman running a major league baseball team was unthinkable to the "old boys club"; but they had not met Lady Bee, the new owner of the St. Louis Cardinals! Helene Robison Britton was a young wife and mother of two small children. She was considered a strikingly good looking woman, a real beauty, with plenty of style and a sparkling personality. On top of that, she absolutely loved the game.

At the beginning of Ms. Britton's reign, newspaper reporters lavished a great deal of grief on the idea of a female owner. For

---

311 Thomas, Joan, *Baseball's First Lady* (St. Luis, reedy Press, 2010) 51-52

example, a cartoon lampooned her in the St. Louis papers, jokingly suggesting that the players' uniforms might soon include bloomers.[312] Newspapers described her as soft-spoken, intelligent and strong willed, but not a militant suffragette.

Helene Hathaway Robison was born in 1879. She grew up living in a mansion that overlooked Lake Erie. Her father and uncle owned a street car business in Cleveland, along with the city's major league baseball team, the Spiders.[313] Her family always encouraged her to become familiar with sports. So, Helene played billiards and she became good enough to challenge her uncle to matches. She attended all of the Spiders' home games and taught herself how to keep score.[314]

Helene would become Ms. Britton in 1901 by marrying Schuyler Britton, a Cleveland attorney employed in a printing business. In 1913, the Brittons moved into a mansion on Lindell Blvd, in St. Louis. Also that year, Mr. Britton was elected as the club's president. At first, the other baseball executives thought that he ran things, but he was just a figurehead; his wife, Helene Robison Britton was actually running the show.[315]

During her first season of her ownership, the team moved up to fifth place. She found this overwhelming; Lady Bee quickly expressed admiration for the team's hardnosed player/ manager Roger Bresnahan. Bresnahan was an inventor, creating shin guards, and the catcher's helmet; it was his idea to put padding into the catching mask.[316] He learned about managing under the tutelage of scrappy John McGraw and he managed the Cards in 1911. Helene Britton felt that he did a good job and rewarded him with a five year contract worth $10,000 per year, plus 10% of the club's profit.[317]

312 Ibid., Thomas, 58
313 "Cleveland Spiders," https://www.baseball-reference.com/teams/CLV/
314 "Helene Britton," by Joan M. Thomas, SABR Bio Project
315 Ibid., Thomas, 56-58
316 "Roger Bresnahan," by Joan M. Thomas, SABR Bio Project
317 Ibid., Thomas, Baseball's First Lady, 63

Unfortunately, the team did not play well the following season and their honeymoon became short lived. A report surfaced that Roger Bresnahan went into a tirade at the Brittons' home to defend himself from rumors that he was throwing games. Then after a loss to the Chicago Cubs, Lady Bee offered her opinion on how he could have better managed the game. Bresnahan blew a gasket, yanking his hat over his ears and screaming, "No woman is going to tell me how to play a ball game."[318]

True, she might have been out of line to make suggestions on how Bresnahan should manage a baseball game, but she did own the team. Lady Bee never stopped being innovative, always trying things to bring fans into the park. Since she was a suffragette, she wanted to encourage females to attend baseball games. So Helene instituted changes to attract more women through the gates to St. Louis Cardinals' games.

She began by promoting Ladies' Days. The idea was not new, but it was uncommon. Women traditionally did not attend baseball games, so owners did not try to attract their attendance. So when Helene introduced Ladies' Days for the Cardinals; the stipulation was that every female accompanied by a male escort got free admission to the grandstand. She charmed her feminine audience by hiring a crooner to sing in between innings.

Lady Bee faced a number of financial difficulties; she lacked the funds to renovate the Cardinals' ballpark. The Cards also fell into last place in 1913. Then the Cardinals faced the pressure of competition, first with the St. Louis Browns of the American League, and then they were joined by a third team, the St. Louis Terriers of the newly formed Federal League in 1913.

The 1916 season started with the owners from each league having a peace conference in January, to figure out a way to dispose of the Federal League. Helene Robison Britton was inundated by offers to sell the Cards. Although Lady Bee was in need of money, she held her ground. Several publications stated that she had a price in mind, which

---

318 Ibid, 70

she denied. While Helene battled business difficulties with the team, she also encountered domestic issues. Helene and Schuyler Britton separated on several occasions. At first, she fired him as club president before filing for divorce the following year. She charged that Schuyler was a violent drunk, prone to frequent absences from the family. Her husband had also incurred large bills, which she was forced to pay. The pressure became too much and she finally sold the team and its ballpark in 1918 to a local consortium headed by Sam Breadon.[319] The Cardinals ended up under the tutelage of Branch Ricky, who turned things around and the team become quite successful. Unfortunately, we will never know what would have happened if Lady Bee remained at the helm. Maybe she was unlucky. Years later, she admitted she regretted selling the team. She loved baseball and the Cardinals.

In August 1920, the 19th Amendment was passed, which gave women the right to vote. Helen Robison Britton was proud of the part she played as the first woman owner of a major league baseball team. Helene is unfortunately a footnote in baseball history. Helene Robison Bigsby, *Lady Bee*, died at the age of seventy on January 8, 1950.

---

319 Ibid., 58

Chapter 51

Marvin Miller: A Game Changer

Far too often the most influential people in sports are often overlooked by the public. Fans of a sport are focused on the well-known superstars and the statistics of their favorite teams and players. They love hearing the stories about the best known players and administrators of the game. However, very few people know about the people who behind the scenes changed a sport forever. In tennis, a woman named Alice Marble changed the sport by writing a letter to the leaders of the sport suggesting that Black players like Althea Gibson be allowed to play in world championships. Her brave stand changed the sport forever by influencing administrators to let Black players enter the major tournaments. Marvin Miller was one of the most influential people in Major League Baseball. Fans know who Marvin Miller is. Many blame him for free agency. Some even feel he was as influential as Jackie Robinson. In this chapter, we tell the story of how Marvin Miller, a fearless advocate for the rights of baseball players, changed the sport of baseball forever.

In 1992, Red Barber, who was arguably one the best broadcasters that the game of baseball has ever seen or heard, stated that Marvin Miller was one of the most important figures in the history of baseball, right there alongside of Babe Ruth, and Jackie Robinson.

Marvin Miller was literally a game changer. Like FDR, he brought a New Deal to the game of baseball. When he took over baseball's union, it was at a time when baseball players were considered the most exploited workers in America. Every major league baseball player after 1975 owes him their gratitude for leveling the playing field. Much like every player of color after 1947 should be thankful for Jackie Robinson!

Marvin Julian Miller was born on April 14, 1917, in the Bronx, NY.[320] His parents moved to Brooklyn shortly after his birth. He quickly became a Dodger fan. Miller became unionized early in life. As a youngster, he walked picket lines with both his father and mother. His dad was a clothing salesman, and his mom a NYC school teacher.[321]

Before taking over the MLBPA, Marvin Miller worked for the National War Labor Board, the International Machinist Union, the UAW and the USW. The United Steel Workers had a bitter presidential election in 1965 which ousted his mentor, David McDonald. That event led him to seek other employment. Miller explored opportunities with the Carnegie Endowment for International Peace, a faculty position at Harvard, before being interviewed for the Executive Directorship of the MLBPA. Miller was not the first choice of the MLBPA, by neither the owners or the search committee.[322]

The union's search committee consisted of Robin Roberts, Jim Bunning, Harvey Kuenn and Bob Friend. Judge Cannon was a favorite; he was a good friend of Bob Friend, who was the front runner, followed by Tom Costello and Bob Feller. Despite Miller's excellent credentials, the committee recommended Cannon.

At first, Judge Cannon campaigned for the position, until realizing the amount of money he would lose from his judicial pension. Pittsburgh Pirates' owner John Galbreath offered to reimburse Cannon for his lost pension money, but Cannon had lost interest in the position even before Galbreath's offer.[323]

Miller's pride was hurt at being the second choice. He stipulated that he would not take the position unless the players voted for him

---

320 "Marvin Miller: American Lawyer," by John M. Cunningham, Encyclopedia Britannica
321 "Marvin Miller and the birth of the MLBPA," by Michael Haupert, SABR-Baseball Research Journal, Spring 2017, 16
322 Ibid. 19
323 Ibid., 18-19

– which they did on April 12, 1966, and team owners were not happy. People could not understand how Marvin could turn down a position at Harvard and take a position with a fledging baseball players' union. He responded that academic jobs were likely to come along again, but the chance to build a union was a "Once in a lifetime" opportunity.

The formation of the Major League Baseball Players Association (MLBPA) marked the fifth time that players sought to organize themselves.

The players' first attempt to organize was the Brotherhood of Professional Baseball Players (1885). Next, they would form the Players League in 1890.[324] While some of the games during that season were well attended at some parks, and not in others, the league was drastically underfunded; causing its owners to lose confidence that it would continue beyond its one season.

Between the years of 1900-03, the Protective Association of Professional Baseball Players was formed during the time when the American and National Leagues were feuding.[325] Their dispute was brief, ending when the NL and AL settled their differences. Subsequently, the Protective Association died.

Another attempt to unionize baseball occurred ten years later, on September 6, 1912. This is when a popular professional baseball and football player named David Fultz formed the Fraternity of Players. It did not hurt that he was also a lawyer. The union existed during the rocky Federal League era and started off with about 300 members. At first, Ty Cobb and Christy Mathewson were officers. The fraternity's goal was to get better player contracts, especially in relation to the reserve clause.[326]

The reserve clause had been around since 1879. It bound a player to a single team, essentially making them chattel, like the slaves of the 1800s. For most of baseball history, the reserve clause was held to essentially mean it would remain in force perpetually so that a player had no freedom to change teams unless he is given his "unconditional release."

---

324 Ibid., 16
325 Ibid., 17
326 Ibid., 17

After a hundred years, the reserve clause was still a major stumbling block.

The new fraternity felt that the players were not treated fairly by ownership. By 1914, there were 1,100 members, most of them minor league players, which is especially important since a third major league was about to start. The Fraternity threatened to strike in 1917, but enthusiasm waned because of World War I. The Fraternity eventually disbanded in 1918 and Fultz moved on to become the President of the new International League.

Years later, Robert Murphy organized the short-lived Baseball Guild in 1946. The Guild lasted for only a year, but it brought about some significant changes that were incorporated when the MLBPA was established in 1953.[327]

A representative from each team was elected to the Guild. The group established a minimum wage of $5,000, plus it created a pension. In the old days, the player's pension was funded by the proceeds from the sale of the World Series radio and television rights. Then the All-Star game revenues became the central source for pension funds. Unfortunately, this was not enough to fund the game properly and by 1949 it was nearly insolvent. Players became annoyed by the underfunded pension and they began to question how it was funded. During the winter meetings in December of 1953, the players formed the Major League Players Association (MLBPA),[328] which they chartered in New York. Bob Feller was elected the MLBPA's first president, serving until 1959. When Bob Feller stepped down, the association decided to hire Frank Scott on a part time basis. Scott was put in charge of overseeing the organization's trivial operations. As the part-time director, he developed a strong relationship with many of the players, but he was nothing more than a "go between" for the membership and management.

Maybe the biggest decision that Scott ever made was to hire a legal advisor for the MLBPA. His choice was the Honorable Judge

327 Ibid., 17
328 Ibid., 17-18

Robert C. Cannon. Cannon got the job over an impressive list of candidates like former baseball commissioner Happy Chandler, future owner Edward Bennett Williams, and Richard Moss, a future legal adviser under Marvin Miller.

Cannon seemed to be more interested in leading the owners than representing the players. He obviously coveted the commissionership over being the union director. He positioned himself for the job at every opportunity; he went as far as to describe the outgoing commissioner, Ford Frick as a "good man ... but who did not have the training to be a commissioner."[329]

Cannon felt that his judicial background combined with a love for baseball was necessary to be a successful commissioner. He might as well have been describing himself. When Frick retired in 1965, Cannon, who was the player's legal advisor, thought he was a shoe-in to be the next baseball commissioner, but team owners decided on Air Force general William Eckert.[330] General Eckert was the antithesis of Cannon's qualifications. He wondered whether the owners rejected him because of his relationship with the players. Whatever the reason, his bid to become commissioner was unsuccessful. Since he no longer had a chance to be the next baseball commissioner, he focused on the MLBPA directorship. At one time, he was the popular choice to replace Frank Scott.

Robert C. Cannon possessed an impressive pedigree. His father, Ray Cannon, fought on behalf of the players during the short lived players' union of the 1920s. He also represented "Shoeless" Joe Jackson in a case against White Sox owner Charles Cominsky in 1924.

Aside from the Cannon bloodline, there were no similarities between the father and the son. Ray Cannon was righteous in his support of the baseball players, while Robert was basically considered a conciliator or go-between, not known to fight for his clients. Robert seemed more interested in benefitting the owners than representing the players.

---

329 Ibid., 18
330 Ibid.

The players' union needed a new Executive Director in nineteen sixty-five. Cannon had been considered a favorite for the directorship. He believed that baseball had an important influence on America's youth because players should be a good example both on and off the field. The major chink in Cannon's armor was a lack of knowledge about the pension; this was by far the major concern for the players' union. Over time, Judge Cannon's support slowly evaporated.

Before Marvin Miller became the new Executive Director, the MLB pension fund was accruing approximately $1.6 million per year. This included an annual contribution by players of $344. Teams contributed 95% of their All-Star ticket revenue. (Players participated in that game for free.) The pension only received 40% of the broadcast fees for both the All-Star and World Series games. Robin Roberts and Jim Bunning, two of the most vocal players' representatives suspected that the owners undervalued media revenues in order to reduce their pension fund obligations. Ralph Kiner felt the players were in need of better legal representations. Los Angeles Dodger Al Ferrara was blunt; he felt that the players were getting <u>screwed</u>![331]

As you can see, the seeds of distrust between players and management were planted well before Marvin Miller's arrival.

George Taylor, a Wharton School of Business professor recommended Marvin Miller for the baseball job. At the time, Taylor was helping with the MLBPA's search for a leader. The committee had a laundry list of candidates, like Judge Cannon, Tom Costello (an attorney from Detroit), Bob Feller, Hank Greenberg, and Chub Feeney. Marvin Miller had a strong interest in the position. Miller was not the favorite choice.

"If the players elect me, I'll accept the job." This was after Marvin Miller was considered the MLBPA's other choice. Miller won by a landslide in the election with votes of 472-34. When Miller took over the baseball union, he considered its membership the most exploited and irreplaceable workers in their field. In time, he turned them into arguably the most powerful labor union in American history, because

---

331 Ibid.

of its success in increasing salaries and benefits for its membership, while safeguarding players' rights. Ownership was unable to prevent Miller from being elected, and he became the Executive Director of the MLBPA on April 12, 1966.[332] Marvin's first contract was for five years at $50,000 per year and included $20,000 in expenses.

Miller realized that the pension was the main concern of members of the MLBPA. In April 1967, Miller negotiated a new pension deal that raised the team owners' annual contribution to four million dollars, which is substantially higher than the 1.6 million dollars they had been giving. Obviously, baseball ownership did not welcome Miller with open arms; they did not enjoy giving away their money, especially to the players.

"Ownership has and will continue to take the ball players for granted."

Joe Cronin, the former MLB shortstop, manager, general manager, Hall of Fame member and former President of the American League had this advice for Miller, "Young man ... players come and go, but owners stay forever."[333]

Cronin's attitude signifies the importance of why the *sport* needed a players' union because ownership has and will continue to take the ball players for granted.

Becoming the executive director opened Miller's eyes to MLB owners' lack of empathy toward former players, even some of their biggest stars.

Several examples surfaced, but when he encountered Joe DiMaggio, the arch nemesis of his Brooklyn Dodgers, he was left depressed. It seemed that Joe DiMaggio was hired by his old team as a part time hitting instructor. DiMaggio showed up wearing a worn out pinstripe Yankee uniform because the team refused to buy him a new

---

332 Ibid., 20

333 Powers, Albert Theodore, The Business of Baseball (Jefferson, NC, McFarland Press, 2003) 174

one (author's note: this would not happen if George Steinbrenner was the Yankees owner). The Yankee legend begged Miller to help him secure a new uniform. Marvin assured him that he would try his best.[334] DiMaggio also lamented how he had to come out of retirement to qualify for the new baseball pension. Miller also assisted him on that point.

Another example of helping a retired player occurred when Miller met Negro League legend Satchel Paige when he was working for the Atlanta Braves. Satchel asked the union leader if he could establish his eligibility for the baseball pension.

Because Satchel Paige's age had always been a mystery, it became a major stumbling block for Satch to qualify for the pension. Miller advised the former star that he needed to provide reliable documentation of his age. Miller suggested his baptismal records. Unfortunately, they were lost in a church fire. This caused Marvin Miller to actively seek other means. Finally, Miller was able to dig up some pitching performances which allowed him to make an age projection that satisfied the pension administrators and made Paige eligible.[335]

Miller arrived on the scene as the MLBPA's second Executive Director during turbulent times, for both baseball and for our nation. The Civil Rights movement had reached its apex, and although legislation had been passed to improve race relations, there was still a lack of racial representation and treatment in the game of baseball.

Maury Wills, the star shortstop of the Los Angeles Dodgers, an African American, was more than happy to share the litany of problems facing both black and Latino players to Miller – such as the lack of integrated living accommodations in Florida during spring training. When Marvin Miller became the MLPA's Director, his feet hit the ground running, and his accomplishments began immediately. For instance, in April of 1967, he changed the way that the Players' pension was funded. Next, he increased the minimum salary for

334 Burk, Robert F., Marvin Miller, Baseball Revolutionary (University of Illinois Press, Champaign, IL, 2015)
335 Ibid.

baseball players, which was $1,000 less than the wage of the average American worker. In 1968, Miller negotiated the first Collective Bargaining Agreement (CBA). He succeeded in raising the minimum wage for players up to $10,000 per year. Miller also negotiated a group license with Coca Cola® to put players' images underneath their bottle caps. In order to do this, Coke needed to airbrush the team logos from the players' baseball caps. This deal resulted in an infusion of $60,000. Throughout his career, Marvin negotiated many licensing agreements that produced substantial income for players.[336]

Marvin Miller changed the very structure of the game.

Malcolm Gladwell, then a staff writer for *The New Yorker*, felt that Miller's goal was to convince the membership to learn lessons from the steelworkers. In fact, he insisted on using the term "workers" to describe the union membership.

When Marvin Miller received a call from Curt Flood in November of 1969, the relationship between owners and players changed significantly. Curt was an outfielder for the St. Louis Cardinals from 1958-69. He was outraged about being traded to the Phillies; he had established roots in St. Louis, plus Philadelphia was not known to be a racially friendly city. He also heard about the trade on the radio, not from Cardinals' management. This also angered Curt Flood. He decided to challenge the reserve clause.

At first, Miller was curious why the ball player was willing to throw away his career or enter into a lawsuit that he had little chance of winning. He learned quickly that Flood was a principled man. This was evident by Flood's reasoning through the letter that was sent to baseball commissioner Bowie Kuhn.

> "Dear, Mr. Kuhn,
> After twelve years in the Major Leagues, I do not feel that
> I am a piece of property to be bought and sold irrespective
> of my wishes ..."[337]

---

336 Ibid.
337 Snyder, Brad, *A Well-Paid Slave* (NY,NY, Plume, 2007) 94

Flood's challenge of the reserve clause was the first one in quite some time.

Flood's suit eventually reached the United States Supreme Court, where both he and the players lost. Justice Blackmun refused to listen to Flood's arguments; instead, he reiterated the point that the reserve clause was intended to protect competitive balance, the game's integrity and public confidence. At the time, it is not the player's decision to change jobs, but the teams.[338]

Although Flood's case appeared to be a defeat, it laid the ground work for a major victory, one that went on to change baseball. It was time for the curtain to rise and to usher in the Reserve Clause Showdown!

Marvin Miller's MLBPA would make their biggest impression on baseball, literally setting it on its head. Obviously, Marvin Miller's impressive career was filled with many accomplishments, but the most influential of them will always be the dismissal of the reserve clause in baseball.

When the 1975 season began, Major League baseball had nine unsigned players. By the summer that number dwindled to just two. They were Dave McNally, who was in the twilight of his career, and Andy Messersmith, whose career was just taking off.[339]

Messersmith was from Anaheim and an All-American at Cal-Berkley. He eventually blossomed into a star. Andy had already won twenty games twice in the MLB. He was negotiating a multi-year contract with a trade approval clause. Unfortunately, negotiations with Al Campanis were acrimonious, causing the Dodger pitcher to decide to deal directly with Peter O'Malley, the owner.[340]

On the other hand, Dave McNally was a former four-time twenty game winner with the Baltimore Orioles. He was a successful veteran. After the 1974 season, Dave McNally had a 181-113 record which was the most wins for a Baltimore pitcher. So, the Orioles were

---

338 Ibid., 19-22
339 "Arbitrator Seitz Sets the Players Free," by Roger I. Abrahms, SABR-Research Journal, 2009,94
340 Ibid.79

startled by his request for a trade. The pitcher's reasoning, "I need a change of scenery to see if it will straighten me out."

McNally was traded with Rich Coggins, a minor league player, to the Montreal Expos for Mike Torrez, and Ken Singleton. Dave's stay in Canada was brief, yet historic. John Mchale, the Expos' general manager promised him a two year contract at $115,000 per year if he waived his ten and five rights and allowed the Orioles to trade him. A player was given "ten and five" rights when they accrued ten years of Major League Baseball service and spent the last five years with the same team. But after he was traded to Montreal he was given a one year deal for five thousand dollars less than what they agreed upon. McNally was furious, feeling that the Expos reneged on their agreement. Initially, McNally decided to retire, which would then leave only Messersmith to fight the reserve clause.

Miller understood McNally's fury with McHale. Since he was also a loyal union man, Dave was also a former Orioles' union representative, Miller convinced him to join his battle against the reserve clause. McNally did not need much prodding. Ultimately, he informed Miller, "If you need me, I'm willing to help."

So, Dave McNally and Andy Messersmith played through the entire 1975 season without signed contracts. On June 9, 1975, McNally announced his retirement from baseball. Since he was always a class act, he apologized to the Montreal fans, yet he never signed the official retirement papers, which would prove to be imperative to the union's case.

When Montreal's GM John McHale figured out what McNally and the union were up to, he rushed up to Billings, Montana to offer McNally a two year contract if he renounced his retirement. McNally would not sign anything!

On December 23, 1975, the independent arbitrator Peter Seitz ruled in MLBPA's favor stating that McNally and Messersmith were free agents after playing without a contract in 1975.

As you might expect, baseball's ownership immediately announced Seitz was no longer acceptable for future arbitration proceedings, meaning they essentially fired him.

Commissioner Kuhn, who was never a friend of the MLBPA, took a dim view of the situation. "I am enormously disturbed by this arbitration decision. If this interpretation prevails, baseball's reserve system is eliminated by the stroke of a pen. This would be a great disaster for the great majority of the players under contract. If we stand to lose them every year, the franchise has little value."[341]

Some observers considered Seitz's decision as Miller's biggest victory as a union leader and for the players. Miller insisted that all the ruling did was to put baseball in line with the other team sports.

Because of the 1975 decision and for years after, fans have complained about players' salaries. It is also common for them to place the blame on Marvin Miller. In my opinion, this is unfair. If you are to blame anyone for the salaries of baseball players, the fault should be placed squarely on the shoulders of the team owners. They are the ones paying the high salaries. What? The players should not accept more money? Would anyone in their right mind, do that?

Miller's hope was to get the same type of treatment for his union's members, aligning them with the average American worker. The average worker is going to go where the money is better, right? Actually, simple economics encourages it. So how can you blame major league baseball players for thinking that way? They suffered under the reserve clause for years, is it not time that they are afforded the same freedom? Before the Seitz decision, major league players were essentially "well-paid slaves," the title of Brad Snyder's book about Curt Flood's free agency.

While Marvin could never convince the owners that they would prosper from an upheaval of the baseball economic order, the years after would eventually prove him right.

---

341 "Arbitrator Frees Two Baseball Stars," by Joseph Durso, New York Times, December 24, 1975, 1

"I loved baseball and I loved a good fight, and in my mind, ball players were among the most exploited workers in America."[342]

– Marvin Miller

Arguably, Marvin Miller was one of the three most influential people in baseball; Marvin was eventually elected to the Hall of Fame in 2020. Ultimately, Miller was in fact finally elected into baseball's Hall of Fame in 2020.

Donald Fehr feels that no one has been as important to the game of baseball during the second half of the twentieth century as his predecessor, Marvin Miller.

Ironically, the former commissioner of baseball, Bud Selig felt that Miller belongs in the Hall of Fame. "… no matter how you feel about him, you cannot say Marvin Miller didn't make a contribution."

And I might add, "Or a bigger influence on the game of baseball!"

Marvin Miller died on November 27, 2012, in Manhattan at the age of ninety-five (95). Unfortunately, he will never be able to bask in the glory of the Hall of Fame.

---

342 "Marvin Miller, union chief who revolutionized baseball off the field, dies at 95," by John Thurber, Washington Post, Novemember 27, 2012

Chapter 52

Theo Epstein: Baseball's Exorcist

*I*t is fascinating how superstitions play such an influential role in sports. Many believe that superstitions are prevalent in the world of sports because so many athletes rely on rituals (wearing the same socks before important games, touching their locker a certain number of times, or having family members sit in the same seats) to enhance their performance. When a team has a long losing streak, then fans try to find a supernatural reason for that poor performance. They frequently suggest that a curse is to blame for the team's losing streak. As a lifelong Red Sox fan, I know too well about the superstition that the Red Sox trade of Babe Ruth to the Yankees led to a curse that prevented them from winning a World Series for 86 years. Chicago Cubs Fans are all too familiar with superstitions as well. Many of them blame a curse related to a billy goat or a black cat for the team's 106 year World Series drought. However, what is more amazing than the respective curses is that the same person is responsible for influencing each of these teams to break the curse by winning the World Series. In this chapter, we explain how Theo Epstein provided the influence necessary to defy the odds and bring World Series victories to both the Boston Red Sox and the Chicago Cubs.

An exorcist is a person who is believed to be capable of casting out the devil or other demons. The *Cambridge Dictionary* defines it as "Someone who forces an evil spirit to leave a person or a place by using prayers or magic."

Two major league baseball cities, Boston and Chicago were believed to be cursed, and it took the same baseball executive to exorcise them both; his name is Theo Nathaniel Epstein!

Theo Epstein grew up in Brookline, a suburb of Boston in the shadow of Fenway Park. When he was in high school, he told his friends that someday he would be the Red Sox GM.[343] Little did anyone realize how prophetic he was.

Growing up, Theo was a huge baseball fan, but the Epstein family had a rule about watching baseball; for every minute spent watching baseball games, the Epstein children must match it by reading for the same amount of time. This should not be a surprise when you consider the Epstein family's emphasis on reading – especially when you consider their lineage, Theo's father was an acclaimed novelist, who is currently in charge of the creative writing program at Boston University.[344] Both his grandfather and great uncles were well known screenwriters; in fact, they wrote the screenplay for the movie *Casablanca*.[345]

On the other hand, Theo began his college career as a philosophy major when he began his studies at Yale, but changed his major to American Studies. This proved to be excellent preparation for law school and other professional programs, in addition to a solid foundation for a career in business, teaching and writing.

Epstein attended and graduated from Yale University; he also managed the school's hockey team. In his spare time, he served as the Sports editor of Yale's "Daily News." After his school year, he wrote letters to several MLB teams hoping to become an intern. Finally, one of his letters ended up on the desk of a Vice-President in the Baltimore Orioles organization. Calvin Hill was an Orioles' executive who was also a Yale graduate. Theo interned as a PR assistant in the Orioles organization during the summers of 1992, 93 and 94.

Theo Epstein is an example of both being influenced and being *an* influence. He can count many of the "new school" baseball executives such as Billy Beane, Bill James and J.P. Ricciardi as his

---

343 "For Epstein '95, a dream fulfilled at 28," by Smita Gopisetty, Yale News, December 11, 2002
344 Ibid,
345 Ibid.

theoretical baseball influences. In fact, one of his role models, Billy Beane, recommended him for the Boston GM job.

During his tenure with the Orioles, Epstein's major accomplishment involved hosting the first reunion around major league cities of Negro League players in Baltimore during 1993, a popular idea in major league cities across the nation.[346]

Theo Epstein's first job after graduating from Yale was working as the Director of Baseball Operations for the San Diego Padres. His boss, Kevin Towers, suggested that he go back to school to earn his law degree. The Padres needed someone with a law degree plus knowledge of contract negotiations. He attended San Diego University while ambitiously working at least seventy hours a week in the Padres front office. After earning his law degree, Theo became a bigger part of the team's high level negotiations.[347]

All of his effort and hard work paid off in 2002; by getting the Boston Red Sox job, he became the youngest GM in baseball history. He was younger than all but two members of Boston's starting lineup.[348]

JP Ricciardi felt that Theo's biggest obstacle was the good ol' boy network – which he was not a part of. Sometimes in baseball, there is a feeling that if you didn't play or manage in the bigs, you don't know what being a big leaguer was.

Being a Red Sox fan, Theo Epstein was well aware of the "Curse of the Bambino." Before 2004, the curse had reached eighty-six years. Over the years the Red Sox organization had nipped at the heels of World Series victory, but always came up short each time. Their fans had suffered near misses in 1946, 67, 75 and 86. Theo was actually the team's third choice to be GM, although he was the only candidate who was invested emotionally. Theo Epstein pledged to upgrade the team at first base, the bullpen and improved the outfield's depth. The

346 Golenbock, Peter, Red Sox Nation: An Unexpurgated History of the Boston Red Sox (Chicago, Triumph Books, 2005) 458
347 Ibid., Gopisetty
348 Ibid.Golenbock, 457

"Sporting News" in its December 2002 issue admitted that Epstein was smart and driven enough to succeed as a GM, but questioned his youthful age.[349] One anonymous baseball executive stated that, at some point, Manny (Ramirez) or Pedro (Martinez) will do something, and he questioned whether Epstein could stand up and confront either of them.[350]

Another snide remark heard at the 2002 winter meetings was, "…by God, when he (Epstein) says don't call him during 'Sponge Bob,' he means it!"[351] The Red Sox front office included the unique combination of Bill James, the Godfather of statistical analysis, and Bill Lajoie, the former Tigers GM, an old school evaluator. In Theo's mind, this combination was the front office of the future, statistical analysis with old school instincts.

Theo quickly rid Boston of $33 million in salaries by eliminating those of Ugeth Urbina, Jose Offerman, Tony Clark, Dustin Hermanson and Darren Oliver. His first move as the Red Sox GM was to acquire second baseman Todd Walker from Cincinnati. Walker had a solid season his one year in Boston before leaving for free agency (13 Home Runs, 85 Runs batted in and a .283 Batting Average). Epstein picked up Kevin Millar, a first baseman, who batted .300 with some power. He became a valuable commodity on the 2003 Red Sox squad. The moves were followed by picking up third baseman Bill Muellar and quietly obtaining David Ortiz, who later became popularly known as "Big Papi."[352]

Theo Epstein never subscribed to the theory that "Pitching is 90% of baseball." He also felt that the "Save" is an overrated statistic. He became the first to test Bill James' theory that a closer was unnecessary if a team had a strong bullpen. Theo put together a bullpen consisting of Kim, Timlin, Mendoza, Lyon and Embree.

349 "Inside Dish," The Sporting News, December 2, 2002
350 Ibid.
351 "Bob Hille's Starting 5," The Sporting News, December 9, 2002
352 Ibid., Golenbock, 459-60

While the pen started out rough it ended the season with arguably moderate success, 25-21, 28 Saves and 4.29 ERA. [353]

The Red Sox finished 2003 with a 95-67 record, resulting in second place after succumbing to the New York Yankees in the ALCS. For a great majority of organizations, such results would be celebrated as a great accomplishment. That was unless you had the unquenchable thirst of the Red Sox Nation or the insatiable desire of its young GM. Theo felt that there was a need to change the person at the helm, and guide the Boston vessel. The Red Sox did not exactly fire Grady Little; they just did not pick up the option on his contract. Little responded with class by saying his replacement will be getting a great bunch of players and a solid GM.

One of the several candidates that he interviewed was a little known bench coach for the Angels named Joe Maddon. Instead, Epstein decided on Terry Francona based on his ML experience for the 2004 season,[354] to be the one that ended the "Curse of the Bambino."

As Boston's GM, Epstein went to the post season six times; that included six 95+ seasons and winning the World Series in both 2004 and 07.

When the Red Sox finished in third place with a 90-72 record in 2011, he felt it was time to exit the Red Sox. He became the President of the Chicago Cubs in 2011, yet another team in need of an exorcism.

While most people might have rested on their laurels after ending a drought of 86 years, Theo Epstein accepted the challenge of the suicidal quest of 108 years of suffering by the Chicago Cubs. To put things into perspective, consider that Mark Twain and Chief Geronimo were still living the last time the Cubs won, or Butch Cassidy and the Sundance Kid were not yet a movie but still alive running away from the law. The Chicago Cubs would come close just once over that period, in 1945, when they played against the Tigers again but lost.

---

353 "AL Insider: AL report," The Sporting News, December 16, 2002, 62
354 Ibid., Golenbock, 486

Cubs failures were always easy to explain, because there was always an excuse, like a Billy goat who allegedly cursed them during the 1945 series, followed by the mysterious black cat that looped around Ron Santo while he stood in the on-deck circle in 1969, and then of course in 2003, when the Cubs infamous fan Steve Bartman's glove prevented Moises Alou from catching a critical foul ball… and once again, the Cubbies fell short!

Over the years, I have become friends with several Chicago Cubs fans. What has made many of them unique was how they seemed to embrace or accept failure; they expected bad things to happen – it became a focal point of their tradition as fans of the team.

Theo Epstein understood this attitude, and because of that he was aware of the importance of turning the Cubs' fortunes around. Fans would stop him on the street in Chicago, like this one:

"My dad is 87, and he's been waiting his whole life to see the Cubs win a World Series; what should I tell him?"[355]

Epstein did not make promises but shared an element of realism.

"Tell him to take his vitamins, because it's going to be a few years."[356]

Was Theo Epstein just ambitious or a glutton for punishment?

When Theo resigned as the Red Sox GM to become the President of Cubs baseball operations, one of his first moves was hiring Jed Hoyer from the San Diego Padres as the team's GM. The two men have an interesting relationship. In 2004, while Theo was the Red Sox GM, Hoyer was an intern for the team and was also his roommate. He also hired Joe Maddon, whom he first interviewed while at Boston.[357] Theo was convinced that the job in Chicago could not be accomplished alone. Epstein gathered his team's coaches and managers in an Arizona hotel that first spring training to discuss the team's batting, defense and pitching. He was convinced that it would

---

355 "Cubs' Theo Epstein is Making Lightning Strike Twice," by Bill Pennington, New York Times, September 29, 2016
356 Ibid.
357 Ibid.

take more than just him to turn the franchise around.[358] Theo felt that having talented personnel did not necessarily equate to success. Most people can handle winning, but it was more important to know how a person dealt with adversity and/ or defeat. Epstein had his scouts interview a potential player's teacher, coaches, friends, girlfriends and even ex-girlfriends. He figured that it was a way to know for sure how a player handled both personal and professional setbacks.

"Failure is inherent to the game. So, if you don't respond well to adversity, you're not going to have a long career."[359]

Similar to the advice Epstein gave Cubs fan on the street, "… Take his vitamins, because it is going to take a few years," Theo did not have a magic wand to wave; instead, his task was assembling building blocks. Theo and the brain trust focused on gathering the right pieces of the puzzle. That was a process for the first three years of his tenure.

Epstein announced that "It was clear we had to start new."

When Theo took over as the Boston Red Sox as GM in 2002, the team was on the doorstep of winning the World Series, but when he took over the reins for the Chicago Cubs, the team suffered a season of 91 losses. The challenge would require a longer plan, and after five years, on November 3, 2016, Theo Epstein succeeded with his second and maybe his greatest exorcism.

Of course, it did not come easy. The series was tied three games apiece; the Cubs had fought back from being down three games to one and were up by three runs after seven innings of the deciding game. Their 6-3 lead vanished at the bottom of the eighth. The Indians were able to scratch out a run, making it 6-4. Then with two outs, two strikes, Rajai Davis nailed a two run homer off of Aroldis Chapman! After nine innings of play, there was a short rain delay. When play continued, the Cubs pushed across two runs to go up by two runs at

358 "The Rainmaker: How Cubs boss Theo Epstein ended second epic title drought," by Tom Verducci, Sports Illustrated, December 14, 2016
359 "Chicago Cubs President Theo Epstein shares how he reinvented the team," by Marguerite War, CNBC: Make It, January 24, 2017

the top of the tenth inning. The tenacious Indians were able to get a run scoring single by Davis, making it a one run game.

Then, with Mike Montgomery on the mound, Michael Martinez hit a slow roller to Kris Bryant, who scooped it up and threw it over to first base for the third out. With the tortured memories of the collapses of 1969, 1984, and 2003, in addition to the alleged curses of black cats and Billy goats, Steve Bartman had finally been exorcised.

A Chicago fan held up a sign, "Now I can die in Peace!"

The next day, a long overdue parade began at Wrigley Field and down Michigan Ave to Grant Park. After 108 years, there is no longer any waiting on Chicago's north side, thanks to the baseball exorcist!

Section IX

Chapter 53

The Home Run's Influence on Baseball

*I*n every major sport, there are players who transcend the game. Legends like *Pele in soccer, Muhammed Ali in boxing, Michael Jordan in basketball, Tiger Woods in golf, Roger Federer in tennis, Wayne Gretzky in hockey and Babe Ruth in baseball. These players were not only the best in their sport, they were celebrities with interesting private lives. Babe Ruth stands out among this list of legends because he not only changed baseball, he saved the sport. Ruth's ability to hit home runs combined with his dynamic personality saved baseball at a time when it had been tarnished because of the White Sox scandal. He almost singlehandedly transformed the sport from a strategic defensive game to one of exciting offense. In this chapter, we describe the extraordinary influence that Ruth had on the sport and how, long after he died, the home run saved baseball once again.*

Baseball suffered a black eye in 1919. Eight members of the Chicago White Sox were accused of committing baseball's cardinal sin; they lost the 1919 World Series on purpose to the Cincinnati Reds! Eliot Asinof wrote a book about it called *Eight Men Out*, and John Sayles made a movie by the same name. The newspapers referred to the Chicago team as the Black Sox.

Apparently, the team was originally given that nickname before the World Series fix. It seems that Charles Comiskey, the club owner, refused to pay for the players' laundry bill, insisting instead that the players themselves pay for it. So the players allowed their uniforms to remain soiled and grim in spite of Comiskey. The team's owner eventually relented and he ended up having the uniforms laundered, but he deducted the cost from each player's salary. Whatever the reason, considering the World Series outcome, the moniker seemed appropriate. Eddie Cicotte, the ace of the pitching staff, had a bigger gripe with Comiskey; because Cicotte was not used the last two weeks of the season and he ended the season with only 29 wins, this denied him of a bonus he was promised for winning thirty games.

Over the years the accuracy of Asinof's books has been questioned. Yet no one could argue that because of the scandal, fans stayed away from the game in droves. Fans began to grow suspicious about corruption after the series. This was the major purpose for Judge Kennesaw Landis becoming baseball's first commissioner.

The timing was ironically coincidental, especially when you consider the emergence of George Herman Ruth. The "Babe" became the savior of the game of baseball. In 1920, Ruth hit 54 homeruns that season. His home runs that year were more than all but two American League teams. Many feel that Babe Ruth put baseball back in the national spotlight. Miller Huggins, one of Ruth's managers, during his career asserted what the American fan likes to see the "… The fellow who carries the wallop!"

Before Ruth ushered in the home run's popularity, the period before was known as the "Dead Ball" era. Games during this time featured low scores with a few or no home runs. The game of baseball was strategy driven. The style was also known as "small ball or inside ball." Teams relied on stolen bases and hit-and-run plays instead of the homer. Little Willie Keeler's mantra of "Hit them where they ain't" defined scientific baseball.

In 1921, the popular *Baseball Magazine* published an article entitled "The Home Run Epidemic."[360] The magazine publicized the magnitude of Babe Ruth's accomplishments; it noted that Babe Ruth not only smashed all existing records, but he destroyed the long-accepted way of hitting a baseball and instead promoted brute force. Newspapers referred to Ruth's accomplishments as

---

360 "The Babe Ruth Epidemic' in baseball, 1921," by John Thorn, Our Game, June 19, 2017

'Bunyanesque,' making Babe Ruth a folk hero, or an icon. Like other traditional folk heroes, he possessed a rebellious nature that did not die down while showing little respect for authority. Fans did not see him as a rascal or a criminal. Instead, they saw him in the same light as a troublemaking kid like Huck Finn, always up to no good but still forgivable.

One person that failed to see him in such a light was Judge Kenesaw Mountain Landis, who was his accidental partner in saving the game of baseball. They were not friends by any means. Landis would suspend the Yankees' slugger for thirty days in 1922 because the Babe ignored Landis' rule about barnstorming between seasons.[361]

Ruth did not only become a hero because he saved baseball, but for what he represented, an American success story. His life read like a Horatio Alger novel. The Babe rose from a Baltimore reform school to become one of baseball's all-time greats. He also starred in the movies, like a short movie entitled *Headin' Home*, where Ruth played a country bumpkin who makes good in big league ball.[362] Movie critics noted that if the Babe did not star in that film, no one would have gone to watch it.

Babe Ruth was one of the most famous people in the world. People traveled for miles just to get a glimpse of him. On top of that, his personality made him extremely approachable, especially by children. When they asked for his autograph, Ruth happily obliged.

Babe frequented childrens' hospitals and orphanages; he always helped out with charitable organizations that benefited children. He loved baseball so much that he liked to expose all children to the joys of the game. The Babe felt, "I won't be happy until we have every boy in America between the ages of six and sixteen wearing a glove and swinging a bat."

Although Babe Ruth popularized the home run as an exciting offensive weapon in 1920, he really changed the face of baseball by

---

361 Stewart, Wayne, *Babe Ruth: A biography* (Greenwood Publishers, West Port, Ct, 2006) 58

362 "Headin' Home," Kessel & Baumann, B&W, silent movie, 1920

hitting 60 of them in 1927. With his typical robust response, the Babe challenged, "Count 'em, 60! Let's see some other son of a bitch match that!"[363]

In a way, I am happy that the Babe was not around to see his record broken four times after he died: Roger Maris with 61 (1961), Mark McGwire with 70 and Sammy Sosa with 66 (1998), and Barry Bonds with 73 (2001).

During his career, George Herman Ruth led the league in runs scored eight times, home runs twelve and runs batted for five. He was the MVP in 1923 and an All-Star twice (1933, 1934). Of course, the All-Star game only started in 1933. For thirty-nine years, his 714 was the most career homeruns hit by anyone. Babe's career stats over twenty-two years were 714 HRs, 2,214 RBIs, .342 BA and a slugging percentage of .690. He hit his final three home runs in Pittsburgh as a member of the Boston Braves. The third one disappeared over the right field fence, the longest ever hit at Forbes Field.

The Smithsonian stated, "Babe Ruth is, without question, the single greatest presence in the history of American baseball, the one player who will always define "the slugger.""

Most importantly, Babe Ruth was a major influence on the game and on American society. His name is synonymous with home run.

The 1961 baseball season was the first year of expansion in the American League. The Washington Senators relocated to Minnesota, along with the Los Angeles Angels. Roger Maris broke the Babe's single season record with his 61st on October 1, 1961, in the final game of the regular season. The Babe held the record for thirty-four years.

Evidently, Babe Ruth and the home run saved baseball in 1920; the home run also saved baseball for me. When the players went on strike in 1994 and the World Series was cancelled, I experienced both anger and sadness. First off, I had doubts for the game's health. Baseball was one of the first things I ever loved. Before that, it was

363 Milliken, Mark, *Jimmy Foxx: The Pride of Sudlersville* (Lanhan, Md., Scarecrow Press,1998) 136

the little blonde haired girl in my third grade class. But my real love affair began with the 1964 World Series between the New York Yankees and the St. Louis Cardinals. I can remember being impressed by Mickey Mantle's three home runs.

When major league baseball went on strike in 1994, minor league baseball became popular. I can remember telling my brother how lucky he was to have a minor league team being formed in his town, Ken, who was never a sports fan, just shrugged it off as a fad … later, I learned that he became a season ticket holder for that team for over twenty years.

The Somerset Patriots have become one of the most successful franchises in the Atlantic League (as of 2021, they became AA team of the New York Yankees).

Living in North West New Jersey, I have several choices for watching minor league baseball in places like Scranton, Reading, Trenton, and Somerset. Although watching Jeff Manto, Rick Shu, or Greg Legg, is not the same compared to Jeter, Ortiz, or Sandberg, but it was an acceptable substitute – especially when major league baseball was not available. *(Editor's note: The Somerset Patriots and the Patriots Stadium were founded by Steve Kalafer, owner of a chain of auto dealerships in New Jersey. Talk about two-way influence: how much the game meant to Steve, and how many people he touched by providing this venue for the sport they love.)*

This was about the time that I read a story about an old time player named Joe "Unser Choe" Hauser. He played on the Philadelphia Athletics with Ty Cobb and played against Babe Ruth. The article mentioned that Mr. Hauser always read his fan mail, and he would write you a personal letter and send a picture of him from his Philadelphia Athletic days, which he also personally autographed to the fan. I wrote him and received a hand written letter, and a picture.

At the time in 1994, Mr. Hauser was the only person to hit over 60 home runs twice in his professional career. He hit 63 in 1930 for Baltimore of the International League, and 69 for Minneapolis in 1933. The most that he ever hit in the majors was 27 at Philadelphia in 1928. Unfortunately, Hauser's MLB career was cut short by a blown knee.[364] Reading about players like Hauser served as a Band-Aid on the void created by the 1994 baseball strike. The after effect was the MLB's popularity.

Then, in 1998, two players fueled my interest in the game of baseball; it was their pursuit following Roger Maris's season record for home runs. The two players were Mark McGwire and Sammy Sosa. It started originally with a homerun battle between Mark McGwire and Ken Griffey, Jr., but by the end of May, McGwire's 27 home runs pulled ahead of Griffey's 19. Then, after May, the home run race's participants changed. This is when a Dominican named Sammy Sosa of the Chicago Cubs replaced Griffey; McGwire and Sosa's home runs captivated the baseball nation with a seesaw battle for the home run lead.[365]

At the end of the season, McGwire slugged 70 homeruns; Sammy Sosa finished with 66. The average gate attendance for baseball and television viewership had increased greatly as they chased Maris's season record. Years later, baseball fans could arguably point to the 1998 season as both the rise and fall of our National Pastime.

Sometime late in the season, a writer for the Associated Press named Steve Wilstern was interviewing McGuire when he noticed a bottle of Androstenedione pills in the player's locker. The pill was normally taken in conjunction with other steroids and could help athletes increase muscle mass significantly; hence, the beginning of the steroid controversy.[366]

Barry Bonds would hit 73 home runs a season a couple of years later. Then accusations by Jose' Canseco, and the following U.S Senate hearings made several sluggers look bad, as well as drug testing provided the media with material and debate. A black cloud grew over

364 "Joe Hauser," by Stew Thornley, SABR Bio Project
365 Vecsey, George (Fwd), *Baseball's Greatest Home Run Story* (London, Carlton Books, 1998) 119
366 "Fifteen Years ago today, Steve Wilstein first shed light on the steroid era," by Cliff Corcoran, Sports Illustrated, August 22, 2013.

the legitimacy of the National Pastime. It would take a while for the game to escape the dark cloud of steroids.

To this day, the home run hitters from that era have been shunned from entering the Hall of Fame. Many baseball fans and writers refer to them as cheaters, not deserving of being placed alongside of Ruth, Foxx or Aaron. It took a while but baseball seems to have made its way back. Thanks to young, apparently non-tainted home run hitting players like Mike Trout, Bryce Harper and Giancarlo Stanton. Think about it; the Chicago Cubs finally won a World Series in 2016!

Chapter 54

America's Influence on the Japanese

Many sports fans do not know the history of Japanese baseball. They understand that Japan has produced some amazing Little League teams and that many Japanese players have done well in Major League Baseball. However, they do not know that Babe Ruth and Lou Gehrig helped to increase the popularity of Japanese baseball. In addition, they are not aware that, because of the influence of Americans, baseball was played as early as 1873 in Japan and the country established its first professional baseball league in 1920. In this chapter, we describe the influences that helped to make baseball one of the most popular sports in Japan.

When my father served in the Korean War, he normally went on leave in Tokyo, Japan. I can still hear him mention how he saw hundreds of Japanese kids playing baseball. He remarked how the children played the game on any vacant piece of land available. So, my dad was never surprised by the Japanese success at the Little League World Series.

The earliest documentation of baseball being played in the "Land of the Rising Sun" was in 1873. A twenty-eight-year-old teacher at *Daigaku Nanko* (South Academy) named Horace E. Wilson is considered the pioneer instructor of baseball in Japan. Wilson was both a devotee of baseball and an American Civil War vet. Baseball is commonly thought to be created during the Civil War.[367]

---

367 Fitts, Robert K., *Remembering Japanese Baseball: A Oral History of the Game* (Carbondale, Il, The Southern Illinois Press, 2000) xix

Here in America, baseball is known as the *National Pastime*, if not for Sumo wrestling, baseball would also be known as that in Japan. In the beginning, the games were not organized. Their games were played only on the sandlot. Eventually, the Japanese developed amateur, collegiate and high school baseball. In 1878, their University team took on the University of Wisconsin varsity baseball team. While the Badgers won the first three toughly contested games they dropped the fourth by the score of 8-0. Japanese baseball history was born.[368]

The Japanese fascination with baseball can be linked to several visits by touring American All-Star teams. The very first to visit the island was in 1908-09 by the *Reach All-American baseball team*. The people at Reach were promoting the trips in hopes of developing an Oriental market for the company's sporting goods. The team featured some of the most outstanding players of the day, including Jim Delahanty, Bill Burns, Pat Flaherty, Jack Bliss, Bill Heitmillar, Babe Danzig and Nick Williams. The Americans played nineteen games and won all of them. The by-product of this tour was the founding of Japan's first professional league in 1920. However, because of financial reasons, the league would soon fold in 1920.[369]

The American All-Star tour of 1934 probably made the most difference in Japanese baseball. The tour was the brainchild of *Matsutaro Shoriki*, the President of the "Yomuiri Shimbun," Japan's most powerful newspaper. On November 2, 1934, half a million fans lined the streets of Tokyo to welcome Babe Ruth and the American All-Stars to Japan. Rows of Japanese fans vied for a glimpse of the American baseball players as their motorcade paraded through Ginza. They waved Japanese and American flags and cheered wildly. The American All-Star team featured such luminaries as Babe Ruth, Lou Gehrig, Connie Mack, Jimmie Fox, Charlie Gehringer, Earl Averill, Lefty Gomez and Lefty O'Doul among others. The Japanese adored

---

368 "Baseball is the National Game in Japan," by Robert Oborjski, SABR- Research Journals Archive, research.sabr.org/journals/baseball-is-the-national-game-in-japan

369 Ibid., Oborjski

Babe Ruth. When he appeared in public, they called out "Bonsai!" Bonsai literally means ten thousand years of life. It is a popular Japanese cheer to express enthusiasm, celebration of victory or just plain "hurrah."[370]

Ruth and his teammates enjoyed the country's hospitality so much that they stayed in Japan for a whole month. The All-Americans played sixteen games with the All-Nippon stars and the Americans won every game. The score of most games were lopsided.[371]

The Japanese played "small ball," which was popularized during the "dead-ball" era in American baseball. Although Japanese fans packed the stadium to watch Ruth take batting practice and watch him hit the ball out of the ballpark. Ruth realized this, and to their satisfaction, launched enormous blasts over the fences. During the 1934 tour, Ruth had 31 hits, 13 of them being home runs. He hit a home run every six at bats. At first, Ruth was not interested in joining the tour; it took his wife Clair to convince him to go. Ruth's participation improved the *Babe Ruth* brand, so, the baseball icon gave in and was grateful that he did.

When the 1934 tour ended, a Japanese team was formed which became the Tokyo Giants. America's baseball ambassador Lefty O'Doul gave them that name.[372] The team traveled to the United States in 1935 and played against various American minor league teams. This experience inspired the Japanese to form another professional league in 1936. Understandably, the league was suspended during WWII, but it was reorganized in 1950, just five short years after the war ended – a testament to the influence of the American sport on the Japanese. As we mentioned earlier, if not for Sumo wrestling, baseball would have become the country's "National Pastime." It was popular due to the

---

370 Fitts, Robert K., *Banzai Babe Ruth, Espionage and Assassination* (Lincoln, Ne, University of Nebraska, 2012) 28-29

371 Ibid., Oborjski

372 Ritter, Lawrence, *The Glory of Their Times* (NY, NY, Harper Perennal, 1957) 276

influence of the Americans before the war, so it was logical to start back up since the two countries were no longer enemies.

Lefty O'Doul contributed to Japanese baseball by making many trips to the island. O'Doul trained countless Japanese baseball players on baseball skills, both before and after WWII. Lefty has been called one of the founders of Nippon Professional Baseball.

O'Doul played eleven years in the MLB, which began as a pitcher in 1919 at the age of twenty-two. His pitching career ended after hurting his arm during a baseball skills contest. After several successful years as a minor league outfielder, he returned to the MLB in 1928 at the age of thirty-one and went on to win two batting titles. In 1929, he had 254 hits and batted .398. Lefty was a starter in the MLB for only six years, where he put up brilliant numbers, but did not play enough years to be seriously considered for MLB's Hall of Fame.

He also proved to be an excellent manager. O'Doul won over 2000 games in the minors. In 1950, he brought the O'Doul's All Stars which included Yogi Berra and Joe DiMaggio to Japan. In 2002, he was elected into the Japanese Hall of Fame.[373]

In 1936, the *Japanese Professional League* consisted of seven teams; the teams were based in Tokyo, Osaka and Nagoya. Four of the original seven still remain in existence, including the famous Tokyo Giants. The Second World War did not affect the Japanese interest in baseball. In fact, professional baseball became more popular than ever in Japan after WWII. It became so successful that it formed two leagues just like in America, and they played a World Series. They were known as the Central and Pacific Leagues. Their World Series was played each autumn since 1950. Two foreigners were permitted on each team's roster, and most of them, except for the Tokyo Giants, filled their quota. The Giants stayed with native players until signing Davey Johnson in 1975. Over the past twenty-five years, a hundred or more players have either coached or played in Japan.[374]

373 "Lefty O'Doul," by Brian McKenna, SABR Bio Project
374 Ibid., Oborjski

While Wally Yonamine, who was born in Hawaii, may not be known by many baseball fans, he was an Asian-American who broke down the ethnic barriers by overcoming stereotypes in both America and Japan. He was the first Asian to play professional football in the United States and the first American to play professional baseball in occupied Japan.

Wally played for the San Francisco 49ers football team in 1947. An injury ended his football career, so he turned to baseball. He played one season at Salt Lake City before signing with the Tokyo Yomiuri Giants in 1951.

Yonamine not only played in Japan, he won three batting titles, including the MVP award in 1957, before going on to coach and manage. Wally Yonamine was a fixture of Japanese baseball for thirty-seven years. In 1994, he was elected to the Japanese baseball Hall of Fame.[375]

The best indications of how far the Japanese came in baseball occurred on September 1, 1964. That was the day that Masanori "Mashi" Murakami joined the San Francisco Giants and debuted against the Mets at Shea Stadium. He became the FIRST Japanese player to play in the MLB.[376] Mashi was a late inning reliever during a game that the Giants lost 4-1. The home crowd of 40,524 gave him a standing ovation when he stepped on the pitching mound at Shea Stadium. The Mets were winning 4-1; he struck out Charlie Smith, the first batter he faced. Murakami appeared in eight more games in 1964.[377] He posted a record of 1-0, 1.80.

Murakami was essentially baseball's exchange student. Japan hoped that their talent would go to America to play baseball but then return to improve the game back home. As John Thorn, the official

375 Ibid., Fitts, Robert K., *Remembering Japanese Baseball: A Oral History of the Game*,21

376 Fitts, Robert K.,Mashi: The unfulfilled Baseball Dreams of Masonori Murakami, the first Japanese Major Leaguer,(Lincoln, Ne, University of Nebraska Press, 2015) 88

377 Ibid., Fitts, Robert K.,Mashi: The unfulfilled Baseball Dreams of Masonori Murakami, the first Japanese Major Leaguer,91-92

historian of the MLB felt, the Japanese did not want to become a source of raw talent for American baseball.

Japanese baseball historian Robert Fitts defined the importance of Mashie's debut by saying; "In baseball, not all pioneers are created equal. Some, like Jackie Robinson, are recognized immediately as formative figures whose impact reverberates forever, in the game and throughout society. Others, though need some time, and distance for their contributions to resonate." Fitts felt that for the longest time, Murakami was just a footnote in baseball history; instead, he should be considered a hero.[378]

John Thorn commented on Murakami's impact: "Until he appeared at the major league level, the general belief among fans and baseball professionals was the Japanese professional league was the equivalent of double "A" minor league baseball."[379]

Mashi went to the United States after graduating high school; where he played single "A" at Fresno, California before making his debut with San Francisco at the age of twenty. After his first season in 1964, the Giants refused to send him back to Japan.

Yushi Uchimura, the Japanese baseball commissioner, compromised by allowing Murakami to return to Japan after he played the 1965 season with the Giants. In 1965, at the age of twenty-one, he posted a 4-1, 3.75 record in forty-five games and struck out more than one batter per inning. Because of a misunderstanding between the American and Japanese baseball organizations, the young pitcher returned to his native land, but never returned to play in the MLB again. Masanori Murakami posted career totals for his fifty-four games with a 5-1 record, 3.43, 100 strikeouts, and nine saves.[380]

It would be thirty years before another Japanese player played in America. Since 1995, there have been 87 Asian players in the

---

378 "Masanori, Murakami: baseball's forgotten Pioneer," Ciampaglia, Dante A., Time Magazine, July 14, 2015

379 Ibid., Ciampaglia

380 "The First of Many: Masanori: the First Japanese Player in the Big Leagues," by Chris Blake and Russell Wolinsky, National Baseball Hall of Fame website

MLB. They represent Japan, Korea, Taiwan, China, Viet Nam and the Philippines. Asian nations have slowly become a source of talent for American baseball, and because of the sport's popularity in those countries, it should undoubtedly grow.

While my father was not surprised, I have always been amazed by the success of the Japanese Little League teams. They have been a part of the tournament since 1962, and as of 2017, have participated twenty-four times, while winning it eleven times.

Much of their success is due to how they approach the sport; they do it with a karate mentality. The Japanese refer to it as 'Konjo,' which basically means grit and tenacity. Repetition is important. Their teams normally practice eight to ten hours every Saturday and Sunday. Each morning is devoted to fielding; players' field bunts and turn double plays one after the other.

Since American players were physically bigger, and Japan had no star players, they relied on a learned discipline of making flawless plays that finally enabled the Japanese players to compete and ultimately win.

While contractual obligations prevented Masanori Murakami from a long career in America, thirty years later another Japanese pitcher was able to open the floodgates for the Asian integration of the MLB. Hideo Nomo, one of Japan's best pitchers was freed from playing in Japan by retiring in Japan on May 2, 1995. Hideo promptly ended his Japanese career and then signed with the Los Angeles Dodgers.[381]

When Murakami was asked about it, he stated, "I was very happy to see another Japanese player finally make it to the major leagues after all of these years, Nomo's performance brought back lots of fond memories for me. My heart was pumping for him."[382] More than forty players since Nomo have jumped to the MLB from Japan. Baseball stars like Ichiro Suzuki, Hideki Matsui, and Yu Darvish.

There are many examples of America's influence on Japanese baseball, but not many match Ichiro Suzuki's visit to George Sisler's

381 Ibid., Ciampaglia
382 Ibid.

gravesite during the 2009 All-Star game in St. Louis. Ichiro wanted to pay homage to the man whose record he broke in 2004 for the most hits (257) in a season.[383]

While the Asian countries are proving to be a talent source for Major League Baseball, it will take some catching up with the Latin countries, especially the Dominican Republic Since 1950, 702 players have come from the D.R., with notable names like Juan Marichal, Pedro Martinez and Vladimer Guerro who is currently enshrined in the National Baseball Hall of Fame, along with other notables such as Sammy Sosa, Felipe Alou, and Albert Pujols.

As of 2021, there are 21 countries represented in Major League Baseball. The sport has become virtually a United Nations.

---

383 "Ichiro Visits Sisler's Grave," ESPN.com, July 15, 2009

Chapter 55

The Influence of Steroids

The 1994 baseball strike was one of the worst things to ever happen to the sport. The disappointment of fans with the owners and players led to 20 million fewer people attending baseball games once the strike was over. As we have described in previous chapters, the home run has proven time and time again that it is a powerful draw for baseball fans. Over the years it has increased attendance for many different teams and made players global celebrities. The home run saved the sport once again after the baseball strike. However, this time the increase in home runs was tainted by a steroid scandal. In this chapter, we discuss the influence of steroids on baseball.

Unfortunately, there was a period of time in baseball when steroids influenced the game at many levels. Yet everyone from management, to the players and yes, even the fans ignored its presence. Then, when everyone began to care, such as the U.S. Senate, it was a little too late. Baseball is a sport that places its records on a pedestal, and when they became tainted, it creates a huge dilemma.

After baseball went on strike in 1994, it was steroids that helped make the game popular again. It was disguised as the home run. In 1993, the year before the strike, attendance finished at 70,257,938 for the season. Attendance during the strike shortened 1994 season was 50,010,016. Eventually, it worked its way back up to 70,601,147 in 1998. Much of the success was due to all of the home runs being hit.

The famous homerun race between Mark McGwire of the St. Louis Cardinals and Sammy Sosa of the Chicago Cubs went back and forth for an entire summer, captivating the American public. Babe Ruth's home runs were credited with saving baseball after the Black Sox scandal. Well, Seventy-five years later, the "long ball" could again be credited with saving the game.

It was during the fourth inning of the game played between the Chicago Cubs and St. Louis Cardinals, on September 8, 1998, Mark McGwire hit a screaming line drive over the left field for his 62nd homer of a Steve Traschel fastball. It was the moment that baseball had waited for all season. Mark McGwire had broken Roger Maris's home run record, which had stood for thirty-seven years.

Ever since the end of the 'Dead ball era,' baseball fans have had a fascination with seeing balls flying over fences. In 1919, Babe Ruth set the home run record with 29, which were more than ten other teams in major league baseball.

Baseball suffered what seemed to be un-repairable damage after the 1994 strike. The strike ended the season; it cancelled the World Series, essentially killed the Montreal Expos possible World Series chances and it prevented Tony Gwynn's opportunity for immortality. Once again, it took the HOME RUN to save the game.

In 1999, the sneaker giant Nike® Inc., released a commercial that basically explained everyone's fascination. It was a spot that featured Tom Glavine, and Greg Maddux, two of the best pitchers in the majors at the time. They were taking batting practice with hopes of catching the eye of Heather Locklear, the star of television's 'Melrose Place,' only to be ignored for Mark McGwire. The reason, as Glavine and Maddux said in the commercial, 'Chicks dig the home run!'

The 1998 season became something special. Mark McGwire and Sammy Sosa were embroiled in a home run race that would eventually shatter the sixty-one home runs that baseball had been chasing for over three decades. It was like a see-saw bout between the two heavy weights. When McGwire hit his sixty-second in September, the question became how many would the new record would be? Sosa tied him on September 13th. McGwire pulled ahead, and then hit number 70, his final for the year on September 27th. Sosa ended up with 66.

Shortly after, the public would hear whispers that the accomplishment might have been tainted ...

The usage of performance enhancing drugs (PEDs) was hardly new to baseball. In 1889, Jim "Pud" Galvin became the first baseball player widely known for using a *Performance Enhancing Drug* known as Elixir of brown Sequard. It was distilled from monkey testicles and was added to his drinks.[384] For those who do not know who Galvin is, let's just say that he held most of Cy Young's records before Cy Young. This is a player enshrined in the Baseball Hall of Fame, who pitched for 15 years, a career ERA of 2.85, averaged over 400 innings per year, won 365 games, 57 of them being shutouts, two coming as no-hitters.

So historically, baseball players have been utilizing performance enhancing drugs since the game has been played in America. It seems ironic that only recently there has been an outcry or a recent concern of such drug's usage. Especially each year when potential candidates are to be voted into baseball's National Hall of Fame. Back when Pud Galvin was using, and I add, it was not a secret, no one seemed to mind performance enhancers; in fact, the "Washington Post" all but pushed the drug in an 1889 article.

More recently, Tom House, a former major league pitcher and a pitching "guru," admitted to using steroids. He described his use in an interview with the "San Francisco Chronicle," as a failed experiment. He went from weighing 190 pounds up to 220. The result did not enhance his substandard fastball and he attributes his usage to his seven knee operations. House stated that during the nineteen seventies, six or seven pitchers on each major league team 'fiddled' with HGH. Back then, players had a willingness to experiment with PEDs.[385]

Performance Enhancement Drugs (PEDs) have been known to be used for years by European athletes, and players in the

---

384 "Pud Galvin," by Charles Hausberg, SABR Bio Project

385 "Retired pitcher, House admits using steroids," by Ron Croichick, San Francisco Chronicle, May, 4, 2005

National Football League (NFL). It was not spoken about in major league baseball, at least not in public. That was until a bottle of *Androstenedione*[386] was seen in Mark McGwire's locker. While this substance was not a banned substance, and at the time was classified as a dietary supplement, it raised a red flag!

McGwire used it as a dietary supplement. Dr. Charles Yesalis, an expert in the study of Steroids has stated that he has never met a Steroid user who didn't use supplements first.

Dr. Yesalis started his experience in the study of Steroids when he became a volunteer strength coach with the University of Iowa.[387] Then in 1980, he chaired a panel of scientists that debated the problem of doping in sports. At the time the panel concluded that steroids were primarily an ethical problem, rather than a public health problem. The biggest issue was using them was against the law, and against the rules of the sport. Players that have been known to use steroids focus their words on how it improves their durability and increases their energy level. Dr. Yesalis puts its usage in perspective, "If everything is equal like hand/ eye coordination, a good big man will hit a ball farther than a good little man. It isn't rocket science."

By the end of the nineteen nineties, steroids would be linked to liver, kidney, and heart disease. Although in 2001, they were still legal in Major League Baseball. Those around the sport were recognizing that they were jeopardizing player's health. Mark Grace, a former player, was quoted saying that usage among players was 'prevalent.' Then a team's GM who wished to remain anonymous called the usage, 'rampant.' Robert Manford, the game's future commissioner stated that the sport would implement 'testing,' although his counterpart in the union, Gene Orza, questioned whether steroids really enhanced performance. Orza must not have noticed how players were hitting over 60 home runs a season with regularity. Or how Brandy Anderson could hit 50 one year.

---

386 https://www.sciencedirect.com/topics/agricultural-and-biological-sciences/androstenone

387 "Playing with Steriods," by Chris DiEugenio, T Nation, November 12, 2007

Halfway through the second decade of the 2000s, many of the players associated with PEDs began to realize the subjective penalty for their usage. The writers that voted for those to be inducted into Baseball's National Hall of Fame in Cooperstown, NY, had shut the doors to them. Such as Barry Bonds, who holds both the record for most homeruns in a season, and most lifetime, and Roger Clemons with 350+ wins, 4,672 strikeouts, 6 Cy Young awards, 1 MVP, and the only man to strike out 20 batters in a game twice.

Eventually, this might change, especially after Bud Selig was elected to the Hall of Fame. He presided as the commissioner during the steroids era.

Chapter 56

Baseball is Life
(Its Influence on Society)

*I*t *can be argued that baseball is the most influential sport in United States history. It is referred to as the "National Pastime" and is considered a symbol of America like apple pie. Baseball terms are used to describe common activities. When someone says that you hit a "home run" it usually means that you did something special. High school students often describe their success on a date by telling their friends whether they made it to "first, second or third base."*

If you try something and fail then it is often said that you "struck out." Baseball played a lead role in racial integration with the groundbreaking play of Jackie Robinson as well as including players from Latin America and Asia.

The legendary people and stories of the game are such an important part of American culture that they are passed down from generation to generation. In this book, we have mentioned many of these amazing stories. This includes: the controversy over the true founder of baseball, Babe Ruth's legendary dominance, Lou Gehrig's courage, the "Black Sox" scandal, breaking the color line, Carl Mays' pitch that killed Ray Chapman, the baseball strike, Negro Leagues and the steroids controversy. The sport was so influential that it helped to make radio and television popular. In this chapter, to conclude the book, we describe the incredible influence of the sport of Baseball.

I can remember flying back from Arkansas with my wife, and the movie on the plane was Kevin Costner's *Field of Dreams*. To this day I can still hear James Earl Jones' voice. I hear it at the start of each baseball season. His monologue defines the game's influence on our society.

"… the one constant through all the years, Ray, has been baseball. America has rolled by like an army of steamrollers. It's been erased like a blackboard, rebuilt and erased again. But baseball has marked the time. This field, this game is a part of our past. Ray, it reminds us of all that once was good, and that could be again, Ray. People will most definitely come…"

The game has survived. It has taught us several hard lessons – like the Black Sox scandal of 1919, where players "threw" the World Series, to having someone killed during a game like Ray Chapin's death at the hand of Carl Mays the following year in 1920, or to have Lou Gehrig's unshakeable courage after learning he had ALS. Baseball has also played a leading role in the Civil Rights movement, by seeing the integration of players from both Latin and Asian countries. More than fifty baseball movies have graced the silver screen from *The Pride of the Yankees* to *Field of Dreams*.

Baseball on Radio

For years, the only way to follow baseball was either attending the games, or reading the newspapers. Radio became a product of the mass market. Manufacturers faced an overwhelming demand for this product. Customers stood in line to buy them. Radio's broadcasting began in 1920 with KDKA-AM in Pittsburgh.

Between 1923 and 1930, sixty percent of American families owned radios. Production did everything it could to meet the great demand. This new form of media featured the programing of popular music, classical music, sporting events, lectures, fictional stories, news of the day, weather reports – and it became a new venue for advertising and marketing! Radio broadcasts featured shows such as "Amos n Andy," "The Grand Ole Opry," "The Hit Parade," etc.!

Baseball was a great help in ushering in this new technology, starting with the first baseball radio broadcast; it featured the Pittsburgh Pirates and the Philadelphia Phillies on August 5, 1921, on

KDKA. This radio station was the first one licensed for commercial broadcast in the United States. Harold Arlin was the first major league baseball announcer. The game caught the ear of the public, the radio craze began!

During radio's heyday, listeners were treated by stellar performances from Red Barber in the "catbird seat," and treated to signature phrases like" Hurry up Aunt Minnie, raise the window!" by Rosey Roswell, Then, in 1951, listeners heard "The GIANTS win the pennant, the GIANTS win the pennant!" by Russ Hodges who went wild after Bobby Thomson's shot was heard around the world.

"Larry MacPhail was an absolute genius in the art of public relations; there was no question about it. He knew how to use the radio." (Red Barber, *Rhubarb in the Catbird Seat*). The old redhead felt that radio was well suited for the game.

Baseball on Television

That was until Red Barber broadcast the first baseball game on television, the Reds vs. the Brooklyn Dodgers at Brooklyn's Ebbetts Field in 1939. The Reds won 5-2. Once again, baseball played a major role in another new medium. Televised games had its share of skeptics, like Branch Rickey. He felt that television could hurt attendance at baseball games, and the following statistics backed up his claim. By 1956, three out of four American households owned at least one television set. Eventually, the baseball owners realized that there was money to be made with broadcasts on television. Of course nowadays, the advanced technology enables multiple ways to watch your team play. No longer do you need to be sitting in the comfort of your home, or even at the game. You can watch them on your computer, iPad or telephone. There is now a network dedicated solely to the MLB. Major league teams no longer rely on attendance to survive; most of their money comes from television contracts, sponsorships and merchandising. The game has evolved into a money making business, not just a sport.

At one time, baseball was considered a simple game; in many cases it still is. All and all, baseball is woven into the fabric of our nation's society. Undoubtedly, the game has invaded our language and at various times has marked our history, whether it is the Civil Rights movement of the sixties or on battlefields over the years. The game had Jackie Robinson and Branch Rickey breaking down racial barriers or stars like Ted Williams and Bob Feller fighting for freedom in foreign lands.

Both radio and television influenced baseball by helping to increase the game's fan base. Also, baseball was influential in putting radios and television sets into American homes. The influence went in both directions.

Influencing Debate

The beauty of baseball has always been its ability to inspire debate. What other American sport is constantly filled with questions? Better yet, arguments? For example, the popular question is, are today's players better than those from the past? What is more fun than defending the enshrinement of a particular player in the Hall of Fame? Or what hallowed sports record can, or will be broken? Should Pete Rose be re-instated and have his plaque on the wall, how about Shoeless Joe? Food for thought, if it is truly a lifetime ban, well; he's been dead for over sixty years. Will the superstars of the steroid era ever be inducted? The debate goes on and on …

Influence of Consistency

There is a tee shirt for sale with the following words emblazoned on its front, "Baseball is Life, and everything else is an interruption."

Consistency has something to do with the game's longevity.

What better place to look for consistency in the sport than the ball used to play the game? As a piece of equipment, the baseball has remained basically the same over the lifetime of the game. Sure it has been made with different materials, inside and out, but its size is essentially the same. It has always been around nine inches in circumference, weighing approximately five ounces, consisting of cork, and wound with yarn, covered with two pieces of cowhide, and stitched by hand about two hundred and sixteen times.

Jim Bouton had a great quote about the game and the ball, "You see, you spend a good piece of your life gripping a baseball, and in the end, it turns out that it was the other way around all of the time."

In my case, the game of baseball gripped me over fifty years ago.

I believe this happened when I got off my school bus one October afternoon in 1964. The minute my sneakers hit the ground, I sprinted home to catch the World Series between the New York Yankees and St. Louis Cardinals. This was the first time that I watched a baseball game; to be honest, I was clueless. What I did know, was all the older boys talked about the World Series at the back of the bus! I was only seven years old at the time, and I wanted badly to be cool like the older boys.

Thus, the moment the game of baseball entered my life. Baseball was life!

Jim Bouton became one of my first MLB influences. Not because of his ability on field, but for his book, a diary that he wrote called *Ball Four*. This book proved to be a best seller and both a famous and infamous all time baseball book. Many readers and players hated it because he wrote about the habits and vices of major league baseball players; he knocked several idols off of their pedestal, such as Mickey Mantle. Bouton became known as both a humorous insider, and a social leper. It depended on your point of view. This groundbreaking book caused fans to look at the game of baseball in an entirely new way. It revolutionized baseball journalism and literature.

> **"Well, it's our game; that's the chief fact in connection with it: America's game; it was the snap, go, fling of the American atmosphere, it belongs as much to our institutions fits into them as significantly as our Constitution's laws; is just as important in the sum total of our historic life."**
>
> **– Walt Whitman**

What it did for me, and other boys my age was to get us to READ! I read a book that I was not told to read, so what if it was about a game. So, I am thankful to Jim Bouton, not only for his pitching ability, but inspiring me to read.

The game of baseball has always played a major role in our country's history and my life.

Baseball's Numbers

Unlike other American sports, baseball has always been about numbers. So, you would think that with my obvious love for the game I would have been better at math! Instead, I spent most of my summers from third to eighth grade at summer school for mathematics. Actually, I needed to go to summer school in ninth grade to pass Algebra, which I passed, barely.

What sets this game aside from football is the importance of numbers! When I was in elementary school, I could tell you why the number 714 was important. That was the amount of career home runs hit by Babe Ruth. This was before Hank Aaron and Barry Bonds passed it. Or 511, the number of career victories by Cy Young. The number 56 represented the number of consecutive games of Joe DiMaggio's hitting streak. Which some have approached, but a streak that is unlikely to be matched or passed. It is doubtful that Lou Gehrig and then Cal Ripken's continuous playing streak will ever be approached. Getting thirty wins in one season was magical; it hasn't been matched since Denny McLain did it in 1968. A 20 win season is now special. A .400 average is remarkable; which has not been accomplished since Ted Williams back in 1941,

Baseball taught me how to do math. I learned how to figure out the earned run average of pitchers, or batting averages. Because of it, division made sense, it had a purpose. If Miss Hankins, my fourth grade teacher would have taught me how to figure out batting averages, instead of wasting my time with long division, I might have never gone to summer school.

Growing up, the most important number in the world was the one on the back of your uniform. I still remember my excitement when I made my junior high team and Coach Halsted gave out our numbers. Since I lived in the New York Metropolitan area, everyone wanted the number seven!

Seven was Mickey Mantle's number. When you were a kid in the New York area, you wanted to be Mickey Mantle. Kids did not expect to play as well as Mantle; they could at least wear his uniform number. It was the next best thing.

Nowadays the number to wear is number two, Derek Jeter's number.

Since my father was from Pittsburgh, I was "brainwashed" to root for the Pirates. I wanted to wear number twenty-one just like the great Roberto Clemente, unfortunately, the uniform numbers for the teams I played for, only went up to twenty. So, my second choice was number eight, which was Willie Stargell's. I wore that number for the next four years of high school. My son Sam also wore number eight throughout youth sports and high school. Not because it was my number, it was the first number he wore when he played T-ball. The first team I coached was the Orioles. So I gave Sam number eight, Cal Ripken's number. The following year we were the Pirates and he still wanted number eight, but not because it was Stargell's like me. He went on to wear number eight for all four years in high school.

The purpose of uniform numbers was to easily identify each player on the field. While this might have been their original purpose, many players choose their number based on a mixture of superstition, emotions and honor. But not always, I think of Roberto Walker Clemente. Roberto wore the number "21." He chose that number by adding all of the letters in his birth name. In Clemente's case, superstition was not involved, or emotional attachment, or honor. It was simply a case of addition

Putting numbers on baseball uniforms began one hundred years ago. The Reading Red Roses of the Atlantic League were probably the first to attach numbers on player's uniforms in 1907. The first major league team to add numbers was the Cleveland Indians in 1916. Branch Rickey's St. Louis Cardinals had numbers on their sleeves. The Yankees added numbers in 1929. The Yankees number signified a player's place in the batting order.

The Father of the Game

Uniform numbers are one way we identify with baseball and baseball with us. BUT, the game has never lacked controversy. Baseball history is chock full of both myths and legends. The game is never at loss for topics to discuss. One of the bigger arguments is "who discovered the game, and who ought to be referred to as the "Father" of baseball." We cannot debate without mentioning the myth or myths. There was a time, when former Civil War General, Abner Doubleday was thought to have created the game of baseball, the general was from Cooperstown, NY, in 1839. This was the result of the Mills Commission formed by A.G. Spalding in 1905. Its purpose was to prove whether the sport originated in the United States, or was it a variation of the English game of rounders.

In 1908, the Commission's findings claimed that Doubleday was the game's creator. This claim eventually received criticism and most, if not all of the modern baseball historians do not support it. Abner Doubleday was not a part of the controversy because he never claimed to have invented the game. The myth grew after his death in 1893.

Nevertheless, the National Baseball Hall of Fame and Museum was built and is nestled in the small hamlet of Cooperstown, New York, the birth place of the game according to the Mills Commission. The Hall opened its doors on June 12, 1939, exactly one hundred years after the game was supposedly played in the same town.

But wait a minute! There is actually another person called the "Father of Baseball" residing behind the doors of the Hall of Fame. In fact, he actually has a bronze plaque, none other than Alexander Cartwright. The plaque calls him the "Father of Modern Baseball" and why not? He is credited with setting the bases ninety feet apart and deciding on nine inning games with nine players to each side. Unfortunately, there is no documentation verifying this. That is … unless you count the amount of letters that Bruce Cartwright's grandson wrote to the Hall of Fame, another "Father of Baseball" myth?

Now think about it, we have a baseball Hall of Fame residing in a town where it was not invented, and a plaque commemorating someone as the Father of Baseball who was not!

Then as if this was not confusing enough, a cricket journalist named Henry Chadwick spotted a fascinating game of baseball during the autumn of 1856. The experience influenced him to begin writing about baseball. His baseball reporting eventually earned him a place on the rules committee. History would then credit him with creating the game's box scores. Chadwick went on to become the editor of A.G. *Spalding's Official Baseball Guide.* He also was referred to as the "Father of Baseball" due to his early reporting and development of the game.

Chadwick believed that baseball was derived from the English game of rounders, to which A. G. Spalding vehemently denied. Doc Adams is another person who has been called by many as the Father of Baseball. John Thorn, the official historian of the major leagues felt that way, "He's the true father of baseball, and you've never heard of him."

As of 2019, he is still not in baseball's Hall of Fame. One thing is for sure, Adams created the short-stop position; his "Laws of Baseball" are considered the Magna Carta of the game. He established nine to a side, nine inning games, and ninety feet between bases, that a ball must be caught on a fly, rather than a bounce.

Baseball Vernacular

Even our English vernacular is not safe from baseball idioms. Many baseball phrases are commonly used on a daily basis in our language, such as "In the ballpark." This literally means a tract of land where ball games, especially baseball are played. It might be used when a homeowner tells a contractor after getting an estimate for their work, "Your estimate is not even in the ballpark," meaning that the contractor's price is not near any of the other people who looked at the job.

How often have you heard someone use "Out of left field," which is American slang for unexpected, odd, or strange? Literally, it refers to the area covered by the left fielder that has the furthest throw to first. For instance, "A fierce storm came out of left field" meaning the unexpected.

"Keep your eye on the ball," is one that you might hear when at a little league field. It basically means that a batter should not pull his head away and not follow the ball. Dictionaries define this phrase as "To watch or follow the ball carefully, especially when one is playing a ball game, to follow the details of a ball game very carefully, to remain alert." Directors and managers may utter it in board rooms and at group meetings. It is about remaining focused on what the ultimate goal is.

The phrase, "Right off the bat," is often used. Its origin is also firmly rooted in baseball. From a baseball perspective, it simply describes that the ball has been hit after a successful swing. When used as in conversation, it is something done immediately, or done in a hurry and without delay.

American conversation is filled with many baseball expressions.

So far, I have shared how baseball has played a role when I was a boy growing up, the importance of its numbers and mathematics, inventions, our language, and on top of all of that, it has even made us laugh!

On the Silver Screen

On a recent visit to the National Baseball Hall of Fame, I spent some time on the third floor where the famous skit "Who's On First" by Abbott and Costello is located. Sixty years ago this Abbott and Costello routine was heard on the Kate Smith radio show in 1938. The film clip was donated to the Hall of Fame.

The definitive filmed version of the skit appeared in the film The *Naughty Nineties*. In it, Costello strolls on stage selling popcorn and peanuts, interrupting the baseball talk by Bud Abbott's character.

Bud begins the routine by saying, "You know, strange as it may seem, they give ball players very peculiar names ... Now, the Cooperstown team we have Who's on first, What's on second, I Don't know who is on third."

Lou asks, "You know the fellows' names?"

Bud, "Who."

Lou, "Well then, who's playing first?"

Bud, "Who."

It was only the beginning of a "back and forth" bantering between the two comedians.

The routine has been performed at the White House. *Time* magazine named it one of the best comedy routines; the Library of Congress has the radio version for the National Recording Registry. It has also been included on the American Film Institute's list as a top hundred most memorable movie quotes. This routine is embedded into the fabric of baseball and American society.

It has witnessed nineteen presidencies, from William McKinley to Donald Trump.

Baseball on the Battlefield

America has been involved in nine military actions, from World War I to Iraq/Afghanistan. The first military action of the Twentieth Century occurred in 1914. The Archduke of Ferdinand and his wife Sophia were assassinated on June 28, 1914. Kaiser Wilhelm II pledged Germany's support for Austria a week later. Then Germany declared war against Russia and France during the first week of August. Britain declared war on Germany. But July 28, 1914, a month after the assassination is considered the beginning of the "War to end all wars" or World War I.

American President Woodrow Wilson appeared in front of Congress to request a declaration of war. The House voted 373-50 in favor of the war, and the Senate ratified it with a vote of 82-6. The United States tried to stay neutral, which is hard considering its ties with Britain, and other propaganda. It did not help when German U-boats sank various ships. America entered the fray on April 6, 1917. The Selective Service Act was passed the following month. The war effort was also financed with "war bonds" or Liberty bonds. When the United States entered the war, most of the minor leagues had to close up shop. They lost a lot of their players due to the draft.

Still, the MLB played its full 1917 schedule, the 1918 season was scaled back to 140 games instead of the scheduled 154. Baseball was supportive of the war effort; most team owners donated both money and baseball equipment.

Over 700 professional players served in the World War One effort, including 28 members of baseball's Hall of Fame. Arguably the most notable were Grover Cleveland Alexander, Ty Cobb, Christy Mathewson, Tris Speaker, and Harry Heilman.

Eleven professional players died During World War I; eight in the majors and three from the Negro Leagues. The first Major League player to die in action was "Harvard Eddie" Grant. Eddie was killed by an exploding shell at Meuse-Argonne in France.

A six hour bombing began the Meuse- Argonne offensive on September 25, 1918. General Pershing then called it off on September 30th but continued it four days later. Before the war, Eddie Grant played both baseball and basketball at Harvard University. Eddie played one year of minor league ball, and then in 1907, he played for the Phillies. There is a story how he found a domino with seven spots on it before a double header against the Giants. That day he went 5-5 against Christy Mathewson, and hit safely his first two times against Rube Marquad, presumably due to the spots on the domino. He went on to play in 990 games with the Phillies, Reds and Giants. He even appeared in two games with the Giants in the 1913 series.

Grant was the first MLB player to enlist, although he was not an active player at the time. He served as a Captain in the 307th Infantry of the 77th Division. Captain Grant died on October 5, 1918, at the Battle of the Argonne Forrest.

The general armistice was announced on November 11, 1918. The popular thought was that it was the end of wars; unfortunately, there was World War II and that did not end all wars of the future...

At 4:45 AM on September 1, 1939, the German army tore into Poland and continued to torment that country for the next six years. World War II was born, lasting between the years of 1939 and 1945. When WWII was over, more than one hundred million people from thirty different countries were involved.

The United States eventually entered the fray after the bombing of Pearl Harbor. The next day, the American population heard a familiar voice on their radios. President Franklin D. Roosevelt started his fireside chat with, "Yesterday, December 7, 1941, a date which will go down in infamy."

Fifty years later, up in Cooperstown, New York at a little baseball card store, I can remember getting dressed down by a sailor who enlisted the day after the bombing. I asked him if he was drafted; he obstinately informed me that he had enlisted. The U.S. Alabama sailor was none other than Bobby Feller, the great pitcher of the Cleveland Indians. Feller was enshrined into baseball's Hall of Fame in 1962. He was 262-162, 3.25 Era, with 2,581 strikeouts when his career ended. Feller was a true American patriot because he arguably lost three prime years to his service in the U.S. Navy. Before he enlisted at the end of 1941, his won and lost record was 107-54.

The day that I met Mr. Feller, we were able to talk "one on one" for about thirty minutes. He informed me that there are hundreds of American League balls at the bottom of the Pacific Ocean because many of his fellow sailors wanted to try and catch his fastball. I have an American League ball that he autographed that day. He had a fantastic sense of humor.

When the country entered the Second World War, so did its "National Pastime." More than 500 MLB players including 37 future members of the Hall of fame joined the war effort; stars like Ted Williams, Stan Musial and Joe DiMaggio. When President Franklin Roosevelt deemed a draft necessary, Hugh Mulcahy was the first one drafted. Mulcahy earned the nickname of "Losing Pitcher of Record" since he was on the losing side of most of the games that he pitched for the Phillies and the Pirates. He lost twenty games twice during his career.

Mulcahy quipped after being drafted, "My losing streak is over ... I'm on a winning team now!"

The first MLB player to die in World War II was Elmer Gedeon. He was from Cleveland, Ohio, and became a three sport star at Michigan University. Elmer was training hard for the 1940 Olympics, but the games were cancelled because of the war. So Elmer went on to sign as an outfielder for the Washington Senators. In 1939, he had 17 plate appearances with three singles, a run scored, while driving in another.

The following year, Elmer Gedeon returned to the minors to play 130 games with the Charlotte Hornets of the class B Piedmont League. He batted .271, with 9 triples and 11 home runs. The following year would prove to be his final year in professional baseball because he was drafted into the Army Air Corps during January 1941. Gedeon went on to earn his pilot's wings.

On April 20, 1944, he was shot down on the B-26B Marauder as it attempted to leave the United Kingdom to bomb a German target in Bois d' Esquerdes, France. Elmer was just twenty-two years old.

Through the past two World Wars, the game of baseball has always stood by its nation. The game provided several of its players and helped raise money for the war effort. On June 12, 1944, President Franklin Roosevelt opened the country's fifth bond drive to help fund the war effort.

A unique baseball game was played at the Polo Grounds in New York City on June 26, 1944. It was called the "Tri-cornered Baseball" game. It was the only one that was ever played. This exhibition's purpose was to help sell war bonds. There were over fifty thousand fans in attendance that day and the game raised $5.5 million dollars. It was a nine inning contest that involved all three NYC teams, with each team playing six innings.

Arthur Daley, a New York City baseball columnist remarked; "All in all, it was a wonderful affair."

There were many current and former baseball greats in attendance, such as: Zack Wheat, Herb Pennock, Bill Dickey, Paul Waner, Leo Durocher, Ducky Medwick and Mel Ott. The game lasted three hours and four minutes; the final score was Dodgers 5, Yankees 1 and Giants 0.

Less than two years later, the United States dropped Atomic Bombs on Hiroshima and Nagasaki in August of 1945, essentially causing the Japanese to surrender on September 2, 1945, and the second Great War was brought to an end!

Racial Barriers

The next battle was not fought in Europe or in the Pacific Ocean, but on the fertile land of the United States. It was one that was waged against segregation, before Civil Rights. As in other cases, baseball took the lead. When Judge Landis, considered by many a racist, died on November 25, 1944, and Happy Chandler replaced him six months later, the over fifty year plus secret – a gentleman's handshake agreement preventing Negroes to play in the MLB, began to be torn down.

There was a leaflet distributed around that time that proclaimed, "Good enough to die for his country, but not good enough for organized baseball." It was accompanied by the photos of two blacks, a dead soldier and a baseball player.

This was followed shortly after by New York City mayor Fiorillo LaGuardia's establishment of a committee to investigate the hiring practices in baseball. It was called, "End Jim Crow in Baseball." It was a four man commission to investigate the possibilities of racial integration. The commission consisted of Larry MacPhail, Branch Rickey, Sam Lacy and Joseph Rainey. The committee did not work out well, mainly because of MacPhail's disinterest. So Rickey grew impatient with him and decided to let nature take its course.

You will recall we recounted how Branch Rickey had been secretively scouting minorities during the early 1940s, but when he announced that his Brooklyn organization was sponsoring the Brooklyn Brown Dodgers in a new six team Negro League, he felt that it gave him carte blanche to openly scout black talent. We detailed in an earlier chapter how he invited Robinson to his office in Brooklyn. Jackie thought it was to play for the Brown Dodgers. Branch had something else in mind. The next year, on April 15, 1947, Jack Roosevelt Robinson became the first black to play major league baseball since Weldy Walker.

The subject of racial equality probably began when President Truman began examining the issue of segregation by appointing a committee on Civil Rights in 1947. So on July 26, 1948, he released Executive Order #9981. The order stated, "It is hereby declared to be the policy of the President that there shall be equality of treatment and opportunity for all persons in the Armed Forces. There was resistance initially within the military, and full integration did not occur until the Korean War.

Years later in 1962, Martin Luther King Jr. informed Don Newcombe, "You'll never know how easy you, Jackie, and Doby made my job by what you did on the baseball field."

The Civil Rights Act was passed in 1964, followed by the Voting Rights Act of 1965.

Baseball and our country survived two World Wars, the Great Depression, inflation, recession, and the breaking down of racial barriers. Our nation and its pastime have always displayed an unwavering resolve.

Through it all, baseball has been able to grow, influence, and inspire. This goes to show, that it is Life, and everything else is just an interruption.

Bibliography

Part One
A Father's Baseball Influences

Books

- Hirsch, James S., *Willie Mays: the Life, the Legend*, Scribner, 2010.
- Eskenagi, Gerald, *The Lip: A Biography of the Leo Durocher*, William Morrow & Company, 1993.
- Leavy, Jane, *The Last Boy: Mickey Mantle and the Endo of America's Childhood*, Harper Perennial, 2011
- Ripken, Cal Jr., and Phillip, Donald T., *Get in the Game: 8 Elements of Perseverance that make the Difference*, Gotham, 2007.
- Ripken, Cal Jr., *The Only Way I Know*, Vintage Books, 1997.
- Griffey, Ken and Pepe, Phil, *Big Red: Baseball, Fatherhood, and My life in the Big Red Machine*, Triumph, 2014

Articles

- "Willie Mays, at 78 Decides to tell his story," Bruce Weber, "The New York Times," January 30, 2010.
- "Cal Ripken Sr. Bio," Jimmy Keenan, Society of American Baseball Research- BioProject,
- "Cal Ripken Sr., 63, Veteran Baseball Coach," Litsky, Frank,"The New York Times," March 26, 1999
- "Kid Gloves: This Season, When it comes to shortstops, it's New York," Klapisch, Bob, "The Sporting News," April 29, 1996.

- "It's a Golden Age at Short," Marantz, Steve, "The Sporting News," August 17, 1998.
- "The Future is Now: Long on Talent and Poise, Derek Jeter Solidifies the Yankees at Short,"
- "The Sporting News," October 28, 1996.
- "Priceless," Wojnaroroski, Arian, "The Sporting News," February 7, 2000.
- "S'Long Jeet," Angel, Roger, *The New Yorker*, September 8, 2014.
- "Jeter State of Mind," Reilley, Rick, *ESPN Magazine*, May 28, 2014.
- "Derek Jeter's Path from Kalamazoo to Cooperstown," Baumbush, Jim," Newsday," September 29, 2012.
- "Cal Ripken Sr.," Keenan, Jimmy, Society of American Baseball Research- BioProject
- "Ken Griffey Sr.," Faber, Charles F., Society of American Baseball Research- BioProject
- "Ken Griffey Jr.," Hawks, Emily, Society of American Baseball Research- Bio Project
- "Ken Griffey Jr. learned much from father- just not a Hall of Fame speech," Cotterill, TJ, "The News Tribune," July 22, 2016
- "Ken Griffey Jr.'s HOF speech- transcript," July 24, 2016
- "Mariners at forefront of establishing Jackie Robinson Day," Johns, Greg, MLB.com

Part Two
Our Baseball Influence

Articles
- "Obit: John Zareas," "The Laconia Daily Sun," November 29, 2001
- "Who Invented the t-Ball game," July 1, 2017, gromimolni. com/who=invented-the –t-ball-game/

- "T-ball" www.topendsports.com/sporte/more/t-ball.htm
- "T-ball has an inventor that reluctantly owns up to it," Tom Hoffarth, "LA Daily News" March 7, 200

Part Three
The Influence of Segregation on Baseball

Books

- Peterson, Robert, *Only the Ball was White*, Oxford University Press, 1992.
- Holway, John B., *Blackball Stars: Negro League Pioneers*, Mecklermedia, 1988.
- Bankes, James, *The Pittsburgh Crawfords: the Lives & Times of Black Baseball's Most Exciting Team*, William C Brown Publishers, Dubuque, IA, 1991.
- Riley, James A., *The Biographical Encyclopedia: the Negro Baseball Leagues*, Carroll & Grof Publications, 1994.
- Higbee, Kirby, and Quigley, Martin, *The High Hard One*, University of Nebraska Press, 1967.
- Eig, Jonathan, *Opening Day: The Story of Jackie Robinson's First Season*, Simon & Schuster, 2007.
- Tygiel, Jules, *The Jackie Robinson Reader: Perspective of an American Hero*, Penguin Books, 1997.
- Rampersad, Arnold, *Jackie Robinson: A Biography*, Alfred A. Knoph Publishing, 1997.
- Linn, Ed, *Leo Durocher: Nice Guys Finish Last*, Simon & Schuster, 1975
- Barber, Red, 1947: *When all Hell Broke Loose in Baseball*, Decapo Press, 1984
- Allen, Maury, *Dixie Walker: the People's Choice*, University of Alabama Press, 2010
- Lowenfish, Lee, *Branch Rickey: Baseball's Ferocious Gentleman*, Lincoln, NE, University of Nebraska Press, 2007.

Articles

- "The Decline of the Negro Leagues," Peterson, Robert, www.britanica.com
- In a League of their Own," Izenberg, Jerry, the "Star-Ledger," February 28, 2006.
- Clyde Sukeforth, "The Dodgers' Yankees and Branch Rickey's Main Man," SABR-*Baseball Research Journal*, Spring 2014 Vol. 43, No. 1.
- "Jackie Robinson: The Chosen One," "Philadelphia Daily News," April 9,
- "Up in Harlem," "The Sporting News," May 7, 1947.

Part Four
Team Influence

Books

- Ceresi, Frank and Holway John B., *Baseball's Biggest Miracle: 1914 Boston Braves*, Minever Press, 2012.
- Kaise, Harold, *An Informed History: The Boston Braves*, G P Putnam's Sons, 1948.
- Nowlin, Bill and Conley, Clem, *The Miracle Braves of 1914: Boston's Original Worst to First World Series*, Society of American Baseball Research Publications, 2014.
- Dewey, Donald and Acocella, Nicholas, *The Biographical History of Baseball*, Carroll & Graf Publishers, NY, NY1995
- Simon, Tom (Ed.), *Dead Ball Stars of the National League*, Dulles, Va, Brassey's Inc, 2003
- Marmer, Mel and Nowlin, Bill, *The Year of the Blued Snow*. The 1964 Philadelphia Phillies, SABR Publications, 2013.
- Kuklick, Bruce, *To Everything a Season: Shibe Park, Urban Philadelphia*, Princeton, Princeton University Press, 1991
- Shiffert, John, *Baseball in Philadelphia: A History o the Early Game*, McFarland & Co, Jeffererson, NC, 2006

- Zimmuch, Fran, *Phillies: Where Have You gone?* Sports Publishing LLC, 2004
- Kruklick, Bruce, *To Everything a Season: Shibe Park and Urban Philadelphia*, Princeton University Press, 1991
- Bisher, Furman, *The Phillies reader: The Many Moods of Mauch*, Temple University Press, 2005.
- Golenbock, Peter, *Red Sox Nation: An Unexpurgated History of the Boston Red Sox*, Triumph Books, 2005
- Reynolds, Bill, *Lost Summer: The 67' Red Sox and the Impossible Dream*, Warner Books, 1992
- Yastrzemski, Carl, *Yaz: Baseball, the Wall and Me*, Doubleday Press, 1990
- Cataneo, David, *Tony C.: The Triumph and Tragedy of Tony Conigliaro*, Summer Games Books, 2016.
- Petrocelli, Rico, *Rico Petrocelli: Tales of the Impossible Dream*, Sports Publishing, 2007.
- Nowlin, Bill & Desrocher, Dan, *The 1967 Impossible Dream Red Sox: Pandemonium on the Field*, Rounder Books, 2007.
- Golenbock, Peter, *Amazin'*, St. Martin's Press, 2006.
- Clavin, Tom and Peary, Danny, *Gil Hodges: The Brooklyn Bums, The Miracle Mets, The Extraordinary Life of a Baseball Legend*, The New American Library, NY, NY, 2002
- Allen, Maury, *After the Miracle: the Amazin' Mets Twenty Years Later*, Franklin Watts Publishing, 1989
- Dunne, Thomas, *Praying for Gil Hodges: A Memoir of the 1955 World Series and on Family's Love for the Brooklyn Dodgers.* Martin's Press, 2005.
- Kahn, Roger, *The Boys of Summer*, Harper & Row, 1971
- Hronich, Colleen, *The Whistling Irishman*, Sport Challenge, 2010.
- Blass, Steve and Sherman, Erick, *Steve Blass: A Pirate for Life*,Triumph Books, Chicago, 2012
- Peterson, Richard, *The Pirates Reader*, The University Press, Pittsburgh 2003

- Markusen, Bruce, *Roberto Clemente: The Great One*, Sports Publishing, 2001
- Maraniss, David, *Clemente: The Passion and Grace of Baseball's Last Hero*, NY, NY, Simon & Schuster, 2006
- Stargell, Willie, and Bird, Tom, *Willie Stargell: An Autobiography*, Harper Row Publishers, 1984.
- Markusen, Bruce, *The Team that Changed Baseball: Roberto Clemente and the 1971 Pirates*, Westholme Publishing LLC, 2006.
- Finoli, David, and Rainer, Bill, *The Pittsburgh Pirates Encyclopedia*, Sports Publishing LLC., 2003.
- McCollister, John, *Tales from the 1979 Pittsburgh Pirates Dugout: Remembering the FAM-A-LEE*, Sports Publishing LLC, 2005.

Articles
- "This Great Game," 1914 Miracle Braves, www.thisgreatgame.com/1914-baseball-history.html
- "1914 Braves' Title Run was hardly a Miracle," by Mike Lynch, sabr.org/latest/lynch-1914-braves-tite-run-was-hardly-miracle
- "George Stallings," by Martin Kohout, Society of American Baseball Research
- "The Year of the Blue Snow," Wulf, Steve, *Sports Illustrated*, September 25, 1984.
- "The National Pastime: The 1964 Phillies, Fans, and Media, Miller," Andrew, Society of American Baseball Research, 2013
- "A.J. Reach and Company," Baseball-Reference, www.baseball-reference.com/A.J._Reach_Company
- "Worcester Ruby legs," Baseball-Reference, wwwbaseball-reference.com/teams/WOR/index.shtml
- "Eddie Sawyer," by Ralph Berger, Society of American Baseball Research
- "Hats Off," "The Sporting News," August 5, 1967
- Dick Williams," The Sporting News," April 15, 1967

- Obituary: Dick Williams, Richard Goldstein, the "New York Times," July 7, 2011
- "69' Mets: team finally got serious under Gil Hodges," Hermann, Mark, "Newsday," September 22, 2000.
- "Spring of '62: Revisiting the Dawn," Lipsyte, Robert, "The New York Times," February 19, 2012.
- "30 Years Ago, the first All-black lineup," Markusen, Bruce, Baseball Guru website, 2001.
- "Where Are the All-black nine now?" Markusen, Bruce, September 2, 2011.
- Obituary: Danny Murtaugh, Sarasota Herald-Tribune, December 3, 1976.

Part Five
Players' Influences

(Player Interviews)
- Earl Averill Jr.
- Steve Blass
- Steve Braun
- Gil Caldwell (talking about Ernie Banks)
- Jim Campanis
- Al Ferrara
- Minnie Forbes (Last Living Negro League Owner)
- Bob Friend
- Jim Gosger
- Dave Guisti
- Chris Hammond
- Gary Kroll
- Carolyn King
- Vernon Law
- Paul Mirabella
- Denny McClain
- Frank "the Original" Thomas

- Tom Walker
- Wally Westlake

Part Six
Baseball in Player's Lives

Books
- *Happiness is Like a Cur Dog: The Thirty Year Journey of a Major League Pitcher & Broadcaster*, King, Nelson, Author house, 2009.

Articles
- "Mark Fidrych," by Richard Puerzer, SABR Bio Project
- "The Bird: The Life and Legacy of Mark Fidrych," by Doug Wilson, Washington Post, March 29, 2013
- "Mark Fidrych: The Tale of the Bird," by Dave Marsh, The Rolling Stone, May 5, 1977
- "The Bird that Fell to Earth," by Gary Smith, Sports Illustrated, April 7, 1986

Part Seven
Major League Owners and Executives

Books
- Rickey, Branch and Montelone, John J., *Branch Rickey's Little Blue Book*, McMillian Press, 1995
- Graham, Frank, *The Brooklyn Dodgers: An Informal History*, Putnam's and Sons, 1948
- Ward, Geoffrey C., and Burns, Ken, *Baseball: An Illustrated History*, Alfred A. Knopf Publishers, 1994
- Spink, J., *Judge Landis and My 25 Years in Baseball*, Thomas Y. Crowell Company, 1974

- Lowenfish, Lee, *Branch Rickey: Baseball's Ferocious Gentleman*, University of Nebraska Press, 2007 (Branch Rickey)
- Lieb, G.P., *The St. Louis Cardinals: the History of a Great Baseball Club*, G.P. Putnam's Sons, 1947.
- Mann, Arthur, *Branch Rickey*, the Riverside Press, 1957.
- Kiner, Ralph, and Peary, Danny, *Baseball Forever: Reflections on 60 Years in the Game*, Triumph Books, 2004
- O'Toole, Andrew, *Branch Rickey in Pittsburgh*, McFarland Press, 2000. Thomas, Frank J., *Kiss It Goodbye: The Frank Thomas Story*, Pepperpot Productions, 2005
- Burk, Robert F., *Marvin Miller, Baseball Revolutionary*, University of Illinois Press, 2015.
- Snyder, Brad, *A Well Paid Slave*, Plume, 2007.
- Veeck, Bill and Linn, Ed, *Veeck as in Wreck*, The University of Chicago Press 2001.
- Dickson, Paul, *Bill Veeck: Baseball's Greatest Maverick*, Walker Books, 2013
- Lieb, Frederick G., *The St. Louis Cardinals: the Story of a Great Baseball Club*, Reedy Press, 2010.
- Boxerman, Burton A., *Ebbetts to Veeck to Busch*, Van Rees Press, 1947
- Thomas, Joan M., *Baseball's First Lady: Helene Hathaway Briton and the St. Louis Cardinals*, (St. Louis, Reedy Press, 2010)
- Golenbock, Peter, *Red Sox Nation, Triumph Books*, 2005.
- Lewis, Michael, *Moneyball*, W.W. Norton & Company, 2004.

Articles

- "Batting Helmet Creator Muse Dies," Associated Press, May 16, 2005.
- Obituary: Branch Rickey, The New York Times, December 10, 1965.
- "Bill Veeck," by Warren Corbett, SABR BioProject
- "Larry Doby," by John McMurray, SABR BioProject
- "Eddie Gaedel," by Brian McKenna, SABR BioProject

- "The Veracity of Veeck," by Norman L. Macht, and Robert D. Warrington, *Baseball Research Journal*, Fall 2003
- "The Truth About Bill Veeck and the '43 Phillies," by David Jordan, Larry Gelach, and John Rossi, The National Pastime, No. 18, 1998
- "The Chicago Cubs College of Coaches: A management Innovation that Failed," Puerzer, Richard J., The National Pastime, SABR, Spring 2006.
- "Marvin Miller and the Birth of the MLBPA," Hauper, Michael, SABR-BRJ, Spring 2017.
- Obituary: Marvin Miller, New York Times, November 27, 2012
- "Miller & Kuhn: New Free Agents," "New York Times," January 1, 1983.
- "Two Sides in Player Negotiations," Koppett, Leonard, "The Sporting News," January 6, 1973.
- "Buy Our Shoes, Players Ask at Bargaining Table," "The Sporting News," March 3, 1973.
- "Seitz Decision and Andy Messersmith," "The Sporting News," January 10, 1976.)
- "Marvin Miller's Glaring Omission From the Hall of Fame," *Sports Illustrated*, December 9, 2013
- "Hall of Fame Voter's Inexplicably Snub Marvin Miller Again," Perry, Dayn, www.cbs.com, Dec9, 2013.
- "Baseball's HOF Needs to Explain Miller's Exclusion," Shanklin, Bill, "LA Times," December 9, 2013.
- "Baseball History: Baseball Personalities"- Helene Britton, www.stevesteinberg.net.
- "First Lady, Helene Britton Takes over the Cardinals," www.dazzyvancechronicles.com.
- "Mrs. Bigsby, First Woman to Own a Major club Dies," "The Sporting News," January 18, 1950.
- "The Rainmaker: How Cubs Boss Theo Epstein Ended a Second Epic Title Drought," www.si.com/mlb/2016/12/14/theo-epstein-chicago-cubs-world-series-rainmaker

- "The Babe is 28 year Old Theo Epstein- Youngest G.M. in History," Vault-website, December 23, 2002
- "Cubs Epstein is Making Lighting Strike Twic"e, Pennington, Bill," New York Times," September 29, 2016
- "Cubs End 108 Year Wait for the World Series Title, After a Little More Torment," Witz, Billy, "New York Times," November 3, 2016.

Part Eight
Influential Events

Books

- Fitts, Robert K., *Banzai Babe Ruth: Baseball, Espionage and Assassination*, University of Nebraska, 2012
- Fitts, Robert K., *Mashi: the Unfulfilled Baseball Dreams of Masanori Murakami, the First Japanese Major Leaguer*, University of Nebraska Press, 2015.
- Dawidoff, Nicholas, *The Catcher Was a Spy: The Mysterious Life of Moe Berg*, Pantheon Books, 1994.
- Gurherie-Shimizu, Sayuri, *Transpacific Field of Dreams*, Chapel Hill, 2012
- Ritter, Lawrence, *The Glory of Their Times*, Harper Perinnel, 1957.
- Fitts, Robert K., *Remembering Japanese Baseball: An Oral History of the Game*, The Southern Illinois Press, 2000.
- Bryant, Howard, *Juicing the Game*, Viking, 2005.
- Canseco, Jose, *Juiced: Wild times Rampant Roids, Smash Hits and How Baseball Got Big*, Regan Books, 2005.

Articles

- "A Hero to Save the Game," http://xroads.virginia.edu/~ug02/yeung/baberuth/hero.html.
- "The Babe is Born," www.baberuth.com

- "Masanori Murakami: Baseball's forgotten Pioneer," Ciampaglia, Dante A., *Time* Magazine, July 14, 2015.
- "The First of Many: Masanori Murakami, The First Japanese Player in the Big Leagues," National Hall of Fame website
- "The Secret to Japan's Little League Success: 10- hour practices," Kuhn, Anthony, NPR, August 28, 2015.
- "The Secret History of Baseball's Earliest Days," NPR, June 14, 2014.
- "Ichiro Visits Sisler's Grave," EPSN.com July 15, 2009.
- "A different Kind of Performance Enhancer," Smith Robert NPS, March 31, 2006.
- "Pud Galvin: the Godfather of Juicing," Hoverson, Joe, Bleacher Report, June 15, 2011.
- "Meet Pud Galvin, The Monkey Testicle- Drinking to the Argument that PED Users shouldn't be in the Hall of Fame," Deadspin, January 12, 2013.
- "Our View of the Week: Mac Attack," Powell, Shaun, The Sporting News, September 7, 1998
- "Muscles in a Bottle," "The Sporting News," January 18, 1999.
- "The Dark Side of the Power Surge," Rosenthal, Ken, "The Sporting News," July 30, 2001.
- "Lynch: In Time, Tide Could Turn on Steroid ERA Player and Hall of Fame," Lynch, Dennis, January 6, 2015
- "Hey, While We're at it, Can We Kick Mickey Mantle Out of Cooperstown?," Neyer, Rob, SB *Nation*, July 12, 2012.
- "Baseball's Major Milestones," Haupert, Michael, *Baseball Research Journal*, Spring 2011.

Websites

(invaluable to baseball research)

www.baseballlibrary.com

www.baseball-almanac.com

www.retrosheet.org

www.thebaseballcube.com

www.baseball-reference.com

www.sabr.org/bioproj

Pictures Credits

(Not in actual order)

1. Nellie King, Sam Hurte, and Bob Hurte (2008) after a Pittsburgh Pirates game - Bob Hurte's private collection.
2. Neil Walker and Tom Walker - Tom Walker's private collection.
3. Tom Walker and Neil Walker - Tom Walker's private collection.
4. Harry Zeiser and Frank Thomas - Minor Leagues, Tallahassee.
5. Wally Westlake- after home run, Pittsburgh Pirates - Tim Corr collection.
6. Wally Westlake- Pittsburgh Pirates - Tim Corr collection.
7. Wally Westlake with a fish.
8. Wally Westlke autographed ball to my father, Bob Hurte Sr.
9. Westlake Cleveland Indians.
10. Wally Westlake, fish, Wally Jr.
11. Billy sample and Bob Hurte- Bob Hurte private collection.
12. Nellie King and Bob Hurte - Bob Hurte privated collection.
13. Steve Blass and Bob Hurte - Bob Hurte private collection.
14. Frank Thomas Christmas card.
15. Steve Blass - Sally O'Leary's private collection.
16. Bob Hurte (7 years old) at T-ball All-Star game - Bob Hurte collection.
17. Bob Hurte and *The Year of Blue Snow* (SABR Book) - Bob Hurte private collection.
18. Wall Krohl autographed ball - Bob Hurte private collection.
19. Wally Westlake painted ball.
20. Bob Hurte and Bobby Thomson - Bob Hurte private collection.

21. Letter from Bob Broeg - HOF baseball writer - Courtesy of Bob Hurte.
22. Neil and Tom Walker during travel baseball - Courtesy of Tom Walker.
23. Wally Westlake batting - Collection of Tim Corr.
24. Autographed ball by Wally Westlake - Courtesy of Bob Hurte.
25. Gary Kroll Autographed Ball - Courtesy of Bob Hurte.
26. Jackie Robinson (Stock Picture)-
27. Bob Hurte posing with book: Year of the Blue Snow - Courtesy of Bob Hurte.
28. Picture of Pirate Hat with Steve Blass & Manny Sanguillen bobble head - Courtesy of Bob Hurte.
29. Wally Westlake with large fish - Tim Corr Collection.
30. Frank Thomas Christmas Card - Courtesy of Bob Hurte.
31. Harry Zeiser with Frank Thomas (Minor Leagues- Tallahassee) - Courtesy of Rocky Zeiser.
32. Gil Caldwell Jr., Ralph Abernathy & Dr. Martin Luther King Jr. - Courtesy of Dr. Dale Caldwell.
33. Steve Blass at Three Rivers Stadium, Pittsburgh Pa. - Courtesy of Sally O'Leary.
34. Steve Blass & Bob Hurte at PNC Park, Pittsburgh Pa. - Courtesy of Bob Hurte.
35. Tom Walker in Montreal Expos uniform - Courtesy of Tom Walker.
36. Bob Hurte and Tom Walker at PNC Park, Pittsburgh, Pa. - Courtesy of Bob Hurte.
37. Bob Hurte & Bobby Thompson at Knights of Columbus in NJ - Courtesy of Bob Hurte.
38. Picture of "Happiness is like a Cur Dog" - Nellie King's memoir.
39. Nellie King with Bob Hurte - Courtesy of Bob Hurte.

About The Authors
Dr. Dale G. Caldwell

Like many other baseball fans, I was influenced to love my favorite team because of my birthplace. I was born in Boston and, therefore, have been a Boston Red Sox fan for my entire life. I am also a passionate tennis player and fan who has served on the Board of the United States Tennis Association (USTA) and as president of the USTA Eastern Section. As the CEO of Strategic Influence, I discovered the power of influence and wrote the book *Intelligent Influence: The 4 Steps of Highly Successful Leaders and Organizations*. In this book, I explain how the *Intelligent Influence* process that I created is the foundation of success in business and life. In the book and my presentations, I attempt to open readers' minds to the reality that they *"do what they do, think the way they think and accomplish what they accomplish because of influence."* I have had the blessing of utilizing my *Intelligent*

Influence competency framework to provide strategy, operations and human capital consulting advice to corporations, government agencies, schools and nonprofits around the world.

When Bob and I first met several years ago we quickly came to the conclusion that there is an amazing relationship between influence and the success or failure of professional baseball players and teams. As we researched many of the amazing stories of baseball, we found a fascinating connection between influence and baseball success and failure. This book shares what we have learned from the stories of baseball.

My parents influenced me to value learning and strive to receive the best education possible. I have been fortunate to receive a BA in Economics from Princeton University, an MBA in Finance from the Wharton School of the University of Pennsylvania, and, an Ed.D. from Seton Hall University. I continued my education by completing the Harvard Kennedy School Senior Executives in State and Local Government program and the Rutgers University Leadership Coaching for Organizational Performance.

I love watching sports and remaining active spiritually, mentally and physically. I am the author of six books and a published dissertation. In addition, I have completed three marathons and received national rankings in tennis, triathlon and duathlon. I live in New Jersey with my wonderful daughter Ashley.

Also by Dale G. Caldwell

Intelligent Influence
Breaking the Barriers
Tennis in New York
School To Work To Success
Fruit of the Spirit Hymnal and Calendar
Fruit of the Spirit Hymns and Poems

Robert V. Hurte Jr.

I cannot remember not being passionate about baseball. It has always been a big part of my life. I played organized ball from T-ball to high school, then in the senior leagues until I was nineteen years old. My dad used to buy me baseball cards, the "Baseball Digest" and "The Sporting News" when I was young, which I devoured. In 1993, my wife sent me to Pittsburgh Pirates Dream Week in Bradenton, Florida where I met many of my baseball heroes. I met Frank "the Original" Thomas, who was one of my coaches, and we began a twenty-five year correspondence. Then in 1998, I joined the Society of Baseball Research (SABR). After a few years, I decided to become a member of the Bio Project and wrote my first bio on Frank Thomas, a former Pirate and original Met. It was published online and I have written over twenty players' bio's since.

I have also written several articles on baseball history for Seamheads.com, *NJ Baseball Magazine* and *The Black and Gold*. I have contributed to five baseball books: *Sweet 60* (1960 Pittsburgh Pirates), *The Year of the Blue Snow* (1964 Philadelphia Phillies), and *Pitching to the Pennant* (1954 Cleveland Indians), *75: The Red Sox Team that Saved Baseball* (1975 Red Sox), and *When Pops Led the Family* (1979 Pirates) and *The SABR Book of Umpires and Umpiring*.

I enjoy reading about American history, especially the Civil War, biographies and anything involving baseball. Over the years I have amassed a significant baseball library, and own a substantial collection of bobble heads, and players' autographs. We live in the tiny hamlet of Stewartsville, NJ; my wife Barbara, my children Tegan and Sam, and our cat Brave Heart. On a regular basis, I converse with several retired baseball players, and have had the good fortune of becoming friends wth Wally Westlake, my father's childhood hero, and Gary Kroll, who won the first game I remember going to at Connie Mack Stadium on July 31, 1965. God and baseball are my biggest influences.

CPSIA information can be obtained
at www.ICGtesting.com
Printed in the USA
BVHW041250100222
628586BV00011B/721